✔ KU-365-844

WILLIAM WALSH

THE USE OF IMAGINATION

IMAGINATION

Educational Thought and
the Literary Mind

PENGUIN BOOKS

IN ASSOCIATION WITH
CHATTO AND WINDUS

Penguin Books Ltd, Harmondsworth, Middlesex, England
Penguin Books Australia Ltd, Ringwood, Victoria, Australia

—

First published by Chatto and Windus 1959
Published in Peregrine Books 1966

—

—

Made and printed in Great Britain
by Cox & Wyman Ltd
London, Fakenham and Reading
Set in Linotype Pilgrim

For
T.M.W.
M.E.W.
T.J.W.

. . . the civic use of the imagination – a faculty for the possible fine employment of which in the interests of morality my esteem grows every hour I live.

HENRY JAMES

CONTENTS

ACKNOWLEDGEMENTS

I AM indebted to the editors of the following journals for permission to use matter already published by them: *The Cambridge Journal, The Journal of Education, The British Journal of Educational Studies* and *The Western Humanities Review*. I am also indebted to the Editor and the publishers of the *Pelican Guide to English Literature, Volume V*, for allowing me to draw on my essay on Keats.

I am deeply grateful to the following for allowing me to quote extensively from works protected by copyright: to the literary executors and the Oxford University Press for permission to quote from the works of Gerard Manley Hopkins; to Mrs W. B. Yeats and Messrs Macmillan for permission to quote from the following poems of W. B. Yeats: *Among School Children, The Dancer at Cruachan and Cro-Patrick, Ego Dominus Tuus, Easter 1916, The Coming of Wisdom with Time, An Acre of Grass*; to the literary executors and Messrs Faber and Faber for permission to quote from the works of Walter de la Mare; to the Frieda Lawrence Estate and Messrs Heinemann for permission to quote from *The Letters* of D. H. Lawrence and from *Education of the People*; to T. S. Eliot and Messrs Faber and Faber for permission to quote from *Four Quartets*; and to F. R. Leavis and Messrs Chatto and Windus for permission to quote from *Education and the University*.

PREFACE

THIS book is addressed to two classes of readers, those interested in literature and those interested in education. In particular it is intended for those whose concern is with literature *in* education, not as a part of the curriculum, as a subject to be taught, but as a source of life and ideas. It is with the aim of making literature accessible to education in this way that I have examined the works of several great writers from Coleridge to the present day. I have chosen writers who seem to me especially well qualified to offer educational enlightenment. I hope that I have done at least the beginnings of justice to the variety of these writers. I hope too that I have shown among them a certain unity of intention, a certain community of conception as to the nature, ends and means of education. These writers, I am convinced, compose a single, coherent tradition, both literary and educational.

The method is that initiated by Coleridge in his *Treatise on Method*. There he conducts his argument on the nature of intellectual method by means of an analysis of *Hamlet*. Accordingly I have discussed each of a series of educational themes through an examination of the work of an author, or a small group of authors, which appears peculiarly relevant to it. Frequently the association will be self-explanatory, as in *Wordsworth and the Growth of the Mind*, or *The Literary Critic and the Education of an Elite* or *The Writer and the Child*. Elsewhere the connexion may be less direct; but although I am far from claiming that the theme I have selected to accompany any particular writer is the only pertinent one, I hope that in every case the reader will be able to conclude that my choice is a natural and not an arbitrary one.

I am and have been conscious throughout, that literature is literature and not an illustration of educational ideas. But I believe that there are in the manifold richness of a major literary work – when, and only when, it is enjoyed, intelligently read as literature

– elements, values, meanings, feelings, incomparably strengthening to the educational sense. It is profoundly important, therefore, that all students of education be brought into touch with the vivifying influence of literature. The student of education is concerned only secondarily with extending his knowledge and accumulating information; his first concern is with cultivating personal quality, with deepening his power of discernment, with increasing the nervousness and relevance of his response, with forming a standard which is personally significant and of more than personal validity. And of all studies that of literature is the discipline which most intimately affects the character of a person's self, which most radically and permanently modifies the grain of his being. This is important at all times; it is urgent in our own when other traditions are weakening and dissolving and the tradition of literature is one of the few still active and life-giving. Perhaps the tradition is most important because it embodies with depth and subtlety a vision of humanity, and the teacher must have a rich and complex perception of the humanity it is his task to improve, a vision of its possibilities for triumph and disaster. The one essential professional qualification for a teacher is that he be educated, and no one can be considered educated who has not come under this supremely civilizing influence.

CHAPTER I

COLERIDGE AND THE AGE
OF CHILDHOOD

WE are accustomed to think of the twentieth century as the age in which children have come into their own. We can point to the elaborate studies devoted to children and the degree to which the arrangements of life are accommodated to them. We are apt to contrast our own century, with its extensive knowledge of children and its anxiety to do justice to them, with the nineteenth century when the relation of the adult to child was apparently so formal, rigid and uncomprehending. It is surprising, therefore, that if there is one respect in which many major writers, both British and American, in the nineteenth century notably excel those of our own day, it is in the power with which they perceived and communicated the life of the child. Wordsworth, Coleridge, Dickens (at his best), Mark Twain, Henry James appear to have been endowed with a faculty for divining the experience of childhood and a capacity for realizing it in words against which we can set only a well-intentioned but external sympathy with children and a pertinacity in collecting information about them. It is significant that no major twentieth-century writer (if we think of Henry James as the last great nineteenth-century novelist) has written with power and conviction of the world of childhood, with the exception of Lawrence, who was peculiarly gifted by genius and disposition to undertake such a theme. There is also, on another scale, the minor exception of Walter de la Mare.

The pre-eminence of the nineteenth century in this respect is all the more remarkable when we remember the stricture passed by some modern critics on its educators, that they put into practice the theory of the eighteenth century and treated the child as a miniature adult. And there was undoubtedly in the nineteenth century a habit of mind, a relic of the Enlightenment, for which the young John Stuart Mill was not the tiny intellectual Caliban he seems to us but rather the ideal which ordinary children, in larger or smaller measure, failed to attain. This aridly rationalist ideal was accompanied, not surprisingly, by a corrupted sensibility which in many lesser writers and in so much of Dickens gave us a grossly sentimental and sickeningly unreal tribe of fictional children: that horrid cluster of homunculi that we commonly take to be representative of the nineteenth-century idea of the child. We are not, however, likely to fall into the error of taking the child to be a miniature adult. We are, indeed, disposed to think of him as a totally different kind of being. But however partial the nineteenth-century view of the child, it did assume between child and adult a common human nature which we, in our stress on the autonomy of childhood, are in danger of disregarding. A communion in a shared humanity gave the nineteenth-century imagination at its highest an access to the reality of childhood which for us is blocked by a nervous insistence on the immensity of the difference. But we are separated from the child by a more impassable obstacle. The child accepts the amazing universe. He is astounded by it but never despairs of it. He supposes an answer to exist for every question, and his chief difficulty is to articulate the question. His world is undisturbed by doubt. 'The deep intuition of our oneness' with childhood, which is the condition of an imaginative perception of it, is possible only in an age of firmer certainties and fewer uncertainties than our own. But we live in an alien Cartesian world, under the jurisdiction of doubt, and we neither speak nor understand the language of the child.

Some may feel surprise that the name of Coleridge should appear in the context. It is true that he has no extended work or even the major part of a work devoted to children. But in letters, in poems, in his writings on education, in a profusion of remarks incidental to other themes, in the strangest places, for example in his notes on Jeremy Taylor, he reveals a sense for the exact nuance of childhood, so fine and sure, that it is not surpassed even by Wordsworth, Dickens or Mark Twain. Indeed, this sense is often in Coleridge more delicately precise, more subtly flavoured with particularity than it is in Wordsworth, and the score on which Coleridge chiefly attacked part of the *Ode on the Intimations of Immortality* is just its generality, the transposability of its epithets, its air of large and unconfined significance. Of course, no one had so infallibly deft a touch in the choice of minutely organized particulars as Dickens, but there remained in most of his work a discrepancy between the integrity of the object and the quality of the feeling. The details are always sharply delineated, seen with the clearest eye, but the feeling is all too often clouded with the impurity of unconscious self-pity and illegitimate identification. In those passages in his letters to Poole expressly on his own childhood, a subject in which the trap of sentimentality is always prepared to be sprung, Coleridge, by reason of an ironic self-depreciation, is wholly exempt from Dickens's self-indulgent weakness. To say this is not – or it is not chiefly – to make a moral claim for Coleridge at the expense of Dickens. We all acknowledge Dickens's generous heart, genuine indignation and powerful will, and we know what Eliot had in mind in saying that Coleridge was one who followed the vocation of the ruined man. (We are, of course, entitled to the view that the vocation of the ruined man is sometimes to be preferred to the career of the successful one.) If Coleridge is the superior of Dickens, it is in that other kind of morality which Whitehead called 'the morality of mind'. Coleridge was the possessor of a more civilized mind, a finer style of thought, sensibility and expressions. Dickens is the barbarous, Coleridge the civilized, genius. The civilized mind realizes, responds and evaluates within an order of acceptance and assurance. The uncivilized mind strains under the intolerable burden of creating all without collaboration. And therefore its products are marked by protestation instead of affirmation, violence instead of strength, confusion instead of coherence. Coleridge's vision of childhood is finer because it is more adult; Dickens's, despite its unexampled force and particularity, is cruder because the product of a primitive mind. And the primitive mind betrays itself by an improper intrusion of self, a lack of awareness as to its purposes, and an incapacity to establish its findings within an adult universe. None of these marks of Philistinism disfigures Mark Twain's master-piece. *Huckleberry Finn* is a less messianic undertaking than a Dickens novel, and sounder and more homogeneous in execution. The mind which conceived it and the world it represents were intimately and faithfully related, the one informed by, the other embodying, a genuine civilization of the people. A folk civiliza-tion, 'which savours thoroughly of the local soil', is a very different thing from the civilization, formal, literary, philosophic in the grand manner, which preserved Coleridge from spiritual solecism and crudity of feeling. But it performed the same pur-pose, as efficaciously and with greater economy. The inwardness of experience, the authority of the vision, the grasp of the moral order of childhood exhibited in *Huckleberry Finn* make it (among other things) an important source of educational wisdom. And if in the end one judges Coleridge to be a more important source, this is not because of an inferiority in the civilization portrayed in the novel, but rather because the civilization implicit in Cole-ridge's thought, in spite of some – though surprisingly few – con-temporary and ecclesiastical absurdities like his rhapsody in praise of Bell's monitorial system, is less intimately engaged with one particular context in time and space. Neither is it because one requires a deeper insight into the life of the child than Mark Twain's (is such a thing conceivable ?) but because of Coleridge's genius for the apt, the lucid, the transforming generalization.

What distinguishes Coleridge in so many fields of thoughts is the co-presence of powers usually divorced. He united, as few others have, a poetic power of reconstructing experience in its fullness and uniqueness with a philosophic power of creative speculation. And this, while always relevant to the perception from which it rises, is also a source of new light and an aid to an even more seeing perception. His perception is peculiarly sensitive, tremblingly responsive and able to discriminate between the most filament-like delicacies. But for Coleridge no experience, however vivid, was insulated; it struggled to connect. No experience was complete until it had fulfilled its aspiration towards coherence. Thus his work has the vigour and definition of the concrete, and the flow and movement of that which strives towards order. His concern to give for an experience both the precise shade of its being, and the most relevant and general law of its being, may be seen in his remarkable commentary on the self of the child.

Two things we may learn from little children from three to six years old: 1. That it is a characteristic, an instinct of our human nature to pass out of self – i.e. the image or complex cycle of images . . . which is the perpetual representative of our Individuum, and by all unreflecting minds confounded and identified with it. . . . 2. Not to suffer any one form to pass into me and become a usurping self.[1]

In these words Coleridge describes what is, as he indicates, a general characteristic of mankind, but one seen most clearly in the child. It is on the one hand that restless search for release from the confinement of the single image of one self, and on the other a solicitude to keep inviolable the privacy of another self. To one in touch with children this will come home as a strikingly first-hand and penetrating observation. And by his distinction between the representative and the real self, between the image and the principle of individuality, Coleridge succeeds in easing the tension between the two terms of his paradox and conciliates them in one consistent judgement. It is worth notice that he introduces his account with the phrase 'Two things we may learn'. The point of the lesson could be taken with profit by every adult, and especially by every teacher. For too many maturity means a narrowing into a dull or resigned acceptance of a limited representative self and a disavowal or oblivion of the real self. Similarly, too much teaching offers insufficient opportunity and too feeble a provocation to enrich the image of self by imaginative participation in many modes of being; just as, all too frequently, it is, in face of the helplessness of the child, an unjust invasion of the real self. But the mature adult – and this is what every teacher should be – is one who senses in others, because he has felt it in himself, beneath the image of the representative self the secret movements of a deeper self. For the image he has imaginative liberality, sympathy in feeling and tact in action; for the true self he has reverence. 'Reverence the individuality of your friend. It is the religion of the delicate soul,' said Coleridge.

In speaking of the child's resistance to the intrusion of an alien form, Coleridge invokes a concept which he, in common with most of the best minds of the nineteenth century, accepted as part of the structure of the meaning of childhood, but which has today fallen into disrepute. The concept is that of the innocence of childhood. It is asserted by Coleridge rarely in overt statement, but rather – and with all the more effect – by implication, image, overtone and language expressing a note of delighted awe. In the past this idea was ridiculed by those religious puritans for whom the child was a limb of Satan, and at a later date by those behaviourists for whom the child is an animal, properly to be described as innocent only if the term signifies an inhuman tranquillity of attitude and contentment in action. Coleridge reminded the puritans of his own day that Christ blessed the children not in order to make them innocent but because they already were so. And he would have agreed with the comment of Suttie that the child's mind is less like that of the primitive animal than the adult's. 'It is less like the animal mind since it is adapted to a milieu and a mode of behaving vastly different from that of the free-living, self-supporting animal.'[2] Moreover, and in another idiom, it may be remarked that it is sad but true that many are never so truly human as when they were children, never again so little dominated by appetite, or so imaginatively free.

But it is the influence of Freud which has so thoroughly dyed the modern mind that it finds itself unable without embarrassment even to use the phrase 'the innocence of children'. Freud attempted to give a natural history of sexual guilt, traced back by devious routes to obscure beginnings, and his theory of infantile passion, especially in the callow form so widely prevalent, has shattered the very notion of innocence. In doing so it has destroyed a kind of discernment without which it is impossible to begin to form an adequate understanding of the state of childhood. (It is interesting to recall Coleridge's remark in a letter to Poole on the first three years of his own life. 'Here I shall end, because the remaining years of my life *all* assisted to form *my particular mind*; the first three years had nothing in them that seem to relate to it.' Coleridge was probably wrong in this judgement, but it is to be doubted if it is wrong with the sort of error a

Freudian would discover in it.) For what is meant by the innocence of childhood? Certainly more than a mere absence of sexuality, and its existence is not disproved if such an absence is refuted. It is both positive and complex, and to think of it as necessarily related to sexual feeling is to fail to dismiss something which is fundamentally irrelevant. Innocence belongs to disposition, to judgement and to action; it is both a quality of sensibility and a mode of insight. It includes candour which has not yet come to be acquiescence in the routine corruption of the adult world, single-mindedness untainted by the hypocrisy of conventional valuation, spontaneity undrilled into the stock response, and a virtue of intense, of the fiercest honesty. The honesty of innocence is elucidated by Eliot, appropriately enough in his essay on the poetic character of Blake.

The strangeness . . . is merely a peculiar honesty, which, in a world too frightened to be honest, is peculiarly terrifying. It is an honesty against which the whole world conspires, because it is unpleasant. . . . He was naked and saw man naked, and from the centre of his own crystal. . . . He approached everything with a mind unclouded by current opinions. There was nothing of the superior person about him. This makes him terrifying.[3]

The innocence of children declares itself unmistakably in their play. Children's play, as Riesman said, 'is often filled with terror and morbidity, but at its best it is one of the unequivocally good things of this earth'. To its unequivocal goodness Coleridge gives the respect of the religious man, while he evoked with a poet's force the special quality of joy that informs it; a feeling rapt, utterly faithful to that out of which it arises, unsullied by regard for the extraneous and the conventional. He writes of his own children at play : 'Hartley is a spirit that dances on an aspen self – the air that yonder sallow-faced and yawning tourist is breathing is to my babe a perpetual nitrous oxide.'[4] 'I look at my doted-on Hartley – he moves, he lives, he finds impulses from within and without . . . he looks at the clouds and mountains, the living beings of the earth, and vaults and jubilates.'[5] 'Hartley and little Derwent running in the green where the gusts blow most madly, both with their hair floating and tossing, a miniature of the agitated trees, below which they were playing, inebriate both with pleasure – Hartley whirling round for joy, Derwent eddying, half-willingly, half by force of the gust – driven backward, struggling forward, and shouting his little hymn of joy.'[6] The joy of the child is so complete, so self-delighting, because it is the accompaniment of those primary movements of the imagination by which he discovers and furthers his humanity, and finds and increases his freedom. 'To carry on the feelings of childhood into the powers of manhood . . . this is the character and privilege of genius.'[7] It was a character Coleridge himself possessed. And the *Ode to Dejection* witnesses in its desolation at the demise of the 'shaping spirit of imagination', in its anguished sterility at the absence of joy, to the depth and power with which he had felt its presence.

It is necessary, and perhaps prudent in the light of Coleridge's reputation, to insist that he took no unduly ecstatic view of the nature of childhood. He was not a disciple of Rousseau, and if he was a Wordsworthian it was only in a severely qualified way. The attitude which sees in childhood a deserving object of admiration for certain ineffable or mystical qualities was both incomprehensible and distasteful to him.

In what sense [he asks, criticizing this ungrounded and delirious sort of thinking in the *Ode on the Intimations of Immortality*] is a child of that age a philosopher? In what sense does he read 'the eternal deep'? In what sense is he declared to be 'for ever haunted' by the Superior Being, or so inspired as to deserve the splendid title of a mighty prophet, a blessed seer? by reflection? by knowledge? by conscious intuition? or by any form or modification of consciousness? Those would be tidings indeed; but such as would presuppose an immediate revelation to the inspired communicator, and require miracles to authenticate his inspiration. Children at this age give us no such information on themselves; and at what time were we dipped in the Lethe, which has produced such utter oblivion of a state so God-like? There are many of us that still possess some remembrance more or less distinct, respecting ourselves at six years old; pity that the worthless straws only should float while treasures, compared with which all the mines of Golconda and Mexico were but straws, should be absorbed by some unknown gulf into some unknown abyss.[8]

Coleridge not only recognized the intellectual and moral limitations of childhood, but he also indicated precisely where they lay.

Reflect on the simple fact of the state of a child's mind while with great delight he hears or listens to the story of Jack and the Beanstalk. How could this be if in some sense he did not understand it? Yes, the child does understand each part of it – A, and B, and C; but not ABC=X. He understands it as we all understand our dreams while we are dreaming, each shape and incident or group of shapes and incidents by itself – unconscious of, and therefore unoffended at, the absence of the logical copula or the absurdity of the transitions.[9]

The realism of his observation gives added point to his recommendations on intellectual education. Since immaturity of thought in the child consists in the appreciation of but few and simple relations and the command of few and crude transitions in expression, the education of the intellect, he maintains, should aim at refining the sense of relation and making subtler the power of 'pertinent connectives'. And it should attempt to realize this aim slowly and tactfully, 'for the comparing power, the judgement, is not at that age active, and ought not to be forcibly excited, as is too frequently and mistakenly done in modern systems of education, which can only lead to selfish views, debtor and creditor principles of virtue, and an inflated sense of merit'.[10] As these words suggest, he was, for all his conviction of a child's innocence, equally clear about its moral limitations, something borne out by his account of himself when a child.

I was fretful and immoderately passionate, and as I could not play at anything and was slothful, I was despised and hated by the boys; and because I could read and spell and had, I may truly say, a memory and understanding forced into almost unnatural ripeness, I was flattered and wondered at by all the old women. And so I became very vain, and despised most of the boys that were at all near my own age, and before I was eight years old I was a *character*. Sensibility, imagination, vanity, sloth and feelings of deep and bitter contempt for all who traversed the orbit of my understanding, were even then prominent and manifest.[11]

These remarks ring with a true and uncracked sound. They

convince as a close notation of a genuine self-knowledge. The moral imperfections thus mercilessly exposed were certainly personal to the child Coleridge, but they are as well those to which not only gifted but all children have a positive inclination. The child is self-centred, self-admiring and often arrogantly unjust. Nor should it be supposed that Coleridge is imposing on childhood adult standards quite alien to it. For children the moral categories to which reference is made by Coleridge in his letter lack the clarity, fullness and complexity they have for the developed person. But they are in principle the same. The child's is a moral world. His actions are to be described as conduct rather than behaviour. The moral world of childhood is, in Coleridge's terms, 'a form proceeding' not 'a shape superinduced'. Because moral categories cannot be applied to children by adults without delicacy and tact, and because adults are frequently blundering, arbitrary and incompetent, some modern educationists fall into the worse error of obliterating the moral order for the child and of regarding him as an amoral being. But before the child satisfies the definition of a child he satisfies that of a human being, and as Coleridge says, 'it is still the grand definition of humanity that we have a conscience which no mechanic compost, no chemical combination of mere appetency, memory and understanding can solve'.[12] 'Children,' he insists, 'are much less removed from men and woman than generally imagined: they have less power to express their meaning than men, but their opinion of justice is nearly the same: this we may prove by referring to our own experience.'[13] It is not extravagant to maintain that children suffer more from those who fail to treat them as human beings than from those who fail to treat them as children. 'Never let it be forgotten that every human being bears in himself that indelible something which belongs equally to the whole species as well as that particular modification of it which individualizes him.'[14]

Coleridge's collocation of the terms moral and intellectual is to be attributed neither to custom nor to accident. It is deliberate and significant. For Coleridge one is the source of the other. And in contrast to the more received opinion, which assumes the moral to be the consequence of developed intelligence, Coleridge considered the moral to be the impulse of the intellectual. 'All speculative truths begin with a postulate, even the truths of geometry. They all suppose an act of the will; for in the moral being lies the source of the intellectual.'[15] To know is preceded by to choose, and the moral life consists in decision enlivened by faith. The life of the child exemplifies this truth.

Have you children [asks Coleridge], or have you lived among children, and do you not know that in all things, in food, in medicine, in all their doings and abstainings, they must believe in order to acquire a reason for their belief? . . . To believe and to understand are not diverse things but the same thing in different periods of its growth.[16]

To the belief of the child corresponds the authority of the teacher. Authority is a word likely in current educational discourse, pragmatically resistant to the external and the given, to be met with suspicion and dismissed with contempt. But the word cannot be avoided, for authority enters deeply into the relation of learner to teacher. Educational authority is not, of course, coercive power, nor is it anything that can be conferred like a diploma or assumed like a gown. It is the quality of one who can be consulted with trust; and it is to be attained only by labour, patience and the abdication of self. The authority of the teacher is constituted in part by his pupil's recognition of his sincerity, in part by the worth of the standards he upholds. The first part of this proposition receives some attention today, but the second in a collective and irrelevantly egalitarian age attracts only the minimum of formal notice. The plight of modern civilization is to be menaced more and more closely by the barbarism of literacy uninformed by value, by what Coleridge called 'the plebification of knowledge'. Upon the teacher at all times rests the obligation of speaking for intellectual sanity and spiritual health. In our time his obligation is all the more urgent for he is one of the very few with any power to be heard. If value has not the protection of the teacher's authority, civilization is condemned. Few teachers entertain the amiably simple, progressive reasons of Thelwall, Coleridge's friend, for passivity in the defence of value, but many more, through uncertainty, indifference or scepticism, are equally ineffective, acting as he would have acted and producing results that he would have approved.

> Thelwall thought it very unfair to influence a child's mind by incul-
> cating any opinions before it should have come to years of discretion
> and be able to choose for itself. I showed him my garden and told him
> it was my botanical garden.
> 'How so?' said he, 'it is covered with weeds.'
> 'Oh!' I replied, 'that is only because it has not yet come to the age
> of discretion and choice. The weeds, you see, have taken the liberty to
> grow and I thought it unfair in me to prejudice the soil towards roses
> and strawberries.'[17]

In fostering that 'prejudice towards roses' upon which depends the humanity of the individual and the quality of civilization, the strongest appeal should be to the imagination, the power by which the child prises himself free from the present and loosens the clutch of the immediate. In the imaginative act the child disengages himself from the partial and the broken, 'from the universe as a mass of little parts', and comes to conceive of a larger unity and the more inclusive whole. The now is extended, the here complicated. The pressure of the momentary is relaxed and the actual charged with the possible. Alternative courses of action loom up and define themselves for choice. The source separates from the outcome, and the distance between act and consequence increases. Thus a centre of attribution is established, and the concept of responsibility begins its long and difficult pregnancy. In the *Eleventh Lecture* Coleridge outlines the role of the imagination.

> In the education of children, love is first to be instilled, and out of
> love obedience is to be educed. Then impulse and power should be
> given to the intellect, and the ends of a moral being be exhibited. For
> this object thus much is effected by works of imagination; – that they
> carry the mind out of self, and show the possible of the good and the
> great in the human character. . . . In the imagination of man exist the
> seeds of all moral and scientific improvement; chemistry was first
> alchemy, and out of astrology sprang astronomy. In the childhood of
> those sciences the imagination opened a way, and furnished materials,

on which the ratiocinative powers in a maturer stage operated with success. The imagination is the distinguishing characteristic of man as a progressive being; and I repeat that it ought to be carefully guided and strengthened as the indispensable means and instrument of continued amelioration and refinement.[18]

Imagination, it will be seen, receives an importance as an educative agency greater than the attenuated respect given it by most modern educators. For these to exercise the imagination is to cultivate a sense of the aesthetic. And this, in a civilization which confounds the artist with the aesthete, and confuses the severity and the chastity of the one with the preciousness and frivolity of the other, means a trivial and decorative addition to more seriously important human powers. But imagination is not a garnish of the soul, a mere finish according to a fashionable specific. 'The rules of the imagination are themselves the very powers of growth and production.'[19] The life of the child before school is quick with the propulsive energies of imagination which 'carry the mind out of self'; the duty of the school is to bring before the learner works of imagination of such quality (and science is also a human achievement imaginatively initiated) that 'they show the possible of the good and great in the human character'. The bleakness of so much schooling and the dehumanizing influence of most science teaching come from confining imagination to a cramped parish of aesthetic activity. But imagination is the air in which new knowledge breathes, as it is the salt preserving the savour of the old. 'Knowledge,' it has been said, 'does not keep any better than fish.'

The forces at large in our society making for the depreciation of imaginative activity are strengthened in the sphere of education by the influence of the objective testing movement. The tester, whose assumptions, canons and purposes are now invested with a nearly final educational authority, conceives of childhood as a phase in a process of development from thinking which is arbitrary and imaginative to thinking which is balanced, amenable to evidence and conceptually controlled. He sees childhood as a passage from unreason to rationality. At first glance this may seem such a description as Coleridge himself might have given –

childhood as a movement from a life in sensuous particulars to a life in the idea. The differences reveal themselves when we consider the points of origin and destination between which the transition of childhood proceeds. Rationality, the goal of childhood as the tester apprehends it, is a painfully limited conception. Exposed in the Intelligence Tests, it shows itself, at the lowest, as a drab and down-at-heels common sense, of which the main characteristic is a conformity to an accepted pattern, at the highest, as that mere cleverness which Coleridge defines as 'a genius for instrumentality'. But to Coleridge rationality meant something immensely more complex, deeper reflection, finer judgement, appreciation of ends, principle grasped and applied, a power to compose new and more inclusive orders of intelligibility. Discrepancy between Coleridge and the tester sharpens into more flagrant disagreement when we contrast their notions, not of the nature of the child's early thought, but of the value to be set on it. They are at one in specifying it as chaotic and intuitive and its products as peremptorily absolutist and happily inconsistent. They are at odds in assessing its importance. The tester judges the child's thought to be a relic of a more primitive mentality which must be utterly outgrown. It is a chaos over which reason must achieve a total victory. But for Coleridge it performs an essential preparatory office; it is the necessary antecedent of rational intelligence, as in the history of literature, poetry is of prose. It is a disorder out of which order must evolve, or as he said of the development of language, 'a chaos grinding itself into compatibility'. The profusion and confusion of the child's thought is not a rank growth to be cut away, but the careless prodigality of the beginnings of life. In the following passage Coleridge describes this character and appraises its value:

In the infancy and childhood of individuals (and something analogous may be traced in the history of communities) the first knowledges are acquired promiscuously. – Say rather that the plan is not formed by the selection of the objects presented to the notice of the pupils; but by the impulses and dispositions suited to their age, by the limits of their comprehension, by the volatile and desultory activity of their attention, and by the relative predominance or the earlier

26

development of one or more faculties over the rest. This is the happy delirium, the healthful fever of the physical, moral and intellectual being – nature's kind and providential gift to childhood. In the best good sense of the words, it is the light-headedness and light-heartedness of human life! There is indeed 'method in't', but it is the method of nature which thus stores the mind with all the materials for after use, promiscuously indeed and as it might seem without purpose, while she supplies a gay and motley chaos of facts, and forms, and thousand-fold experiences, the origin of which lies beyond the memory, traceless as life itself, and finally passing into a part of our life more rapidly than would have been compatible with distinct consciousness and with a security beyond the power of choice! . . . Promiscuously, we have said, and seemingly without design: and yet by this seeming confusion alone could nature . . . have effected her wise purpose, without encroachment on the native freedom of the Soul and without either precluding, superseding, or overlaying the inventive, the experimentative, combinatory and judicial powers.[20]

If the opinions of Coleridge and the tester clash on this question, that is not because the nicety of psychological acumen which he commanded in his literary criticism failed him when he turned his eyes upon childhood. On the contrary. Whether 'psychology' is taken to be the intuitive, intimate awareness of the constitution and conflicts of particular human characters displayed by the novelist and the dramatist, or whether it is to be a scientist's observation and classification of the regularities of human conduct, Coleridge has every right to be acknowledged more than competent in each kind. Probably sufficient evidence has been adduced even in the course of this discussion to justify – what any page of Coleridge demonstrates – the soundness of his reputation as an unusually brilliant literary psychologist. But his versatility as psychologist extended also to the scientific mode. Bringing to bear upon others a minutely precise observation and upon himself an unprejudiced and microscopic introspection, and without any of the formidable apparatus of modern psychological study, he yet succeeded in anticipating important conclusions of some of its most elaborate and penetrating inquiries. In these remarks on arithmetic, for example, he forestalls one of the significant findings of Piaget's treatise on the development of the concept of number. 'In the child's mind there is nothing fragmentary; its numeration table is truly Pythagorean. The numbers are each and all units and integers, and slowly and difficultly does it exchange this its first and awakened arithmetic for that of aggregation, opposition, in one word of result.'[21] Again in the *Philosophical Lectures* he has an utterance which is only one of the many where he is, as Kathleen Coburn pointed out, astonishingly prophetic of Freud. 'The first education which we receive, that from our mothers, is given to us by touch; the whole of its process is nothing more than, to express myself boldly, an extended touch by promise. The sense itself, the sense of vision itself, is only acquired by a continued recollection of touch.'[22] A child's sensory activity begins with a direct tactual acquaintance with objects (including himself): it becomes, as sight grows keener and more adept in recognition, more distanced and more detailed, a fuller and more governed kind of awareness. The vision of the forms of objects ousts the feeling for their textures as the dominant mode of experience. But there is in the knowledge derived from sight a deceptive clarity which beguiles the mind away from speculation, and an illusory completeness which betrays it into a rigid and static certainty. In Coleridge's view a main end of education is to rescue the child from 'the despotism of the eye', a result to be achieved by cultivating in the child a greater consciousness in the use of words. Coleridge writes of the child so trained, in a passage that could serve both as model and warning to the genetic psychologist:

He will at least secure himself from the delusive notion, that what is not *imageable* is likewise not *conceivable*. To emancipate the mind from the despotism of the eye is the first step towards its emancipation from the influences and intrusions of the senses, sensations and passions generally. Thus most effectually is the power of abstraction to be called forth, strengthened and familiarized, and it is this power of abstraction that chiefly distinguishes the human understanding from that of the higher animals – and in the different degrees in which this power is developed, the superiority of man over man mainly consists.[23]

More important than the explicit sense of Coleridge's statements is the direction of his thought, which is significantly different from the ruling trend of contemporary opinion. Whereas this is retrogressive and concentrated on the circumstances of origin, Coleridge's is prospective and attentive to the possibilities of attainment. It looks forward rather than backward, to final rather than to efficient causality. The contemporary bias, introduced into educational thought by the influence of the more traditional sciences, has been confirmed by the general assimilation of the study of education to the social sciences. In particular, the infatuation of social scientists with the enumeration of causes has led educators to have a more than due regard for the analysis of motives and a less than sufficient one for the quality of purposes. But the notion of conscious purpose is an essential part of the concept of education. Education, as distinct from training, may be defined as the transformation of necessary, confused and volatile motives into free, deliberate and constant purposes. The assumption – that it is the motives that make the man – on which the social scientists and their educational disciples proceed, is the exact opposite of Coleridge's.

It is not [he writes] the motives that govern the man but the man that makes the motives; and these, indeed, are so various, mutable and chameleon-like that it is often as difficult, as fortunately it is a matter of comparative indifference, to determine what a man's motive is for this or that particular action. A wise man will rather enquire what the person's general objects are – what does he habitually wish.[24]

It is the teacher's business to be at all times making this inquiry of his pupils in the form of an indirect question; it is his aim to provoke them to make it of themselves in the form of a direct question. Until they do, they can come to no adequate conception of their humanity which is to be both conscious and responsible. For the questioning of purposes according to a criterion of value is the condition of the exercise of responsibility. The ordinary difficulty of the educator's work is aggravated in a period when the circumstances of life in a mass society more and more circumscribe the area of individual responsibility, and when the influence of theories devoted to diluting the idea of responsibility has the effect of reducing the human person to an ineffective point at the centre of a narrowing circle. The social scientist excises responsibility from the individual and transfers it to society; the psychoanalyst pushes it down below the lucidity of consciousness to depths 'submarine and profound'. For many contemporary minds responsibility is no more than a pragmatic device, or an operative fiction, or a regulative error. But education is committed to consciousness and to responsibility. It is dedicated to refining consciousness and to realizing responsibility. Its constitutive purpose is the fostering of conscious responsibility. Unless they conceive of their undertaking in this way, educators cannot hope to succeed in achieving what the duties of their office and their obligations to civilized standards require, namely the enhancement in their pupils of the power to withstand the assault of a barbarizing environment. It is not the least of Coleridge's claims to permanent status and contemporary relevance that his work and especially his writings on childhood supply us with a theory, grounded in human nature and endorsed by history, of resistance by the person to the encroachment of the context

CHAPTER 2

WORDSWORTH AND THE GROWTH
OF THE MIND

THE vision of childhood offered by the great writers of the nineteenth century is conspicuous not only for a peculiar intensity
that comes from alert recognition, an unmuffled mind and an
unfilmed eye, but as much for its generous range and liberal
variety. Throughout the century the finest and most diverse
talents applied themselves to enriching and refining our notion of
childhood. The result, so full, subtle and various, a world to be
entered rather than a series of findings to be tabulated, baffles the
analyst with his handful of simple categories: the gleaming
mackerel refuse to be netted. Yet however intricate and intercon-
nected that world may be, there are different parts in it, and
minds with different capacities for exploring one part rather than
another. There is a proportion between Coleridge's exquisite perception and the complex organization of the child's self. There is
a congruity between the powerful, arrested genius of Dickens and
the curious private universe observed by the child's eye. The
visual bias of Dickens's sensibility, its effects of brilliance of foreground, unnatural clarity of detail, of the absence of blur or adult
uncertainty – all this is marvellously suited for presenting that
simple, violent world, full of the immediate and empty of implication, sown with recurrent and fantastic crises, which is the
common meeting-place of children and an alien territory for
adults. There is a correspondence between the mind of Mark
Twain and the part of the child's life rendered by him with incomparable fineness and conviction, the child's role as stranger,
as critic of adult society. There is also a ratio of suitability
between Wordsworth's severe, geological imagination and the
growth of the child's mind. The growth of the mind is a theme
exactly fitted to make Wordsworth's genius work with intense

and characteristic life. It possesses the triple qualification of a Wordsworthian subject. It fixes the poet's eye upon himself, and when his self-scrutiny relaxed or his attention turned elsewhere, Wordsworth was apt to fall into gestures of large and unconfined significance. But even more it fixes his eyes upon himself as a child, and the further he moved from this primary source of his poetry the less necessary, the more fabricated it became: in Wordsworth's own words his poetry ceased to flow from 'an inward impulse' and became celebrally 'proposed and imposed'. Moreover, the growth of the mind is a theme in which the movements of individual life exemplify deeper, cosmic rhythms, and for Wordsworth those experiences were the most richly productive in which through 'familiar shapes' he glimpsed the looming of 'huge and mighty forms'. It is the perfect conformity of its theme to every requirement of Wordsworth's creative power which gives the early books of *The Prelude* a vitality, an actual and present life, which deserves to be called dramatic.

And this in spite of Wordsworth's claim that in the circumstances of the nineteenth century the true voice of the poet was the narrative not the dramatic. In a letter to Coleridge Wordsworth censured Lamb for failing to see that now the dramatist must give way to the narrative poet.

When it is considered what has already been executed in Poetry, strange that a man cannot perceive, particularly when the present tendencies of society, good and bad, are observed, that this is the time when a man of genius may honourably take a station upon different grounds. If he is to be a Dramatist, let him crowd his scene with gross and visible action; but if a narrative Poet, if the Poet is to be predominant over the Dramatist, then let him see if there are no victories in the world of spirit, no changes, no commotions, no revolutions there, no fluxes and refluxes of the thoughts, which may be made interesting....[1]

Wordsworth did not make the claim, which his best poetry would certainly have sanctioned, that a narrative conducted with his fidelity, with his devoted and undistracted attention, ceased to be merely a commemorative record and became a rendering of the events it describes. *The Prelude*, for all its air of meditative sobriety and its undramatic form, becomes by virtue of its unswerving allegiance to a subject inherently dramatic, a dramatic reconstruction of the growth of the human mind. The action of the poem is not dramatic in Wordsworth's sense of being 'gross and visible'; it is, in another phrase of Wordsworth's, 'fine-spun and inobtrusive'. But it has its conflicts – 'the changes and commotions of the mind', its crises – 'the revolutions, fluxes and refluxes of the thoughts', its resolutions – 'victories in the world of spirit'. For Wordsworth the growth of the mind is not a set process proceeding according to inescapable laws; and 'continents of moral sympathy' divide his recreation of it from an analysis based on any such presupposition. As I suggested in asserting that Wordsworth's subject was 'inherently dramatic', mental development is more than organic, and the growth of the mind is inseparable from the refinement of emotion and the maturing of a moral sense. Wordsworth is not dealing merely with the elaboration of a primitive into a sophisticated structure, but with the unfolding of human powers which make moral discernment and decision (and moral disaster) possible; he is concerned with the coming into being of those qualities which transform man from a physical object into a tragic person.

It may be objected that the subtitle of *The Prelude* is 'Growth of a Poet's Mind', not 'Growth of a Human Mind'. But the poet's mind is the most truly representative human mind. He is representative not as the norm of mediocrity, as the statistical average in which every living difference is obliterated, but representative in being genuinely and freely human. The poet is the standard of humanity, not the standard man. He is the standard of man as poetry is the standard of human discourse or – as Wordsworth said – as 'The true standard of poetry is as high as the soul of man has gone, or can go.'[2]

High among the qualities of the responsible man Wordsworth set 'simplicity . . . and insight into the constitution of the human mind'.[3] These were gifts of character and intellect which he himself had in good measure, and their combination gives to Wordsworth's sensibility its special flavour, generosity of understanding towards lives and natures very different from his own together with a manner, strict, controlled and ascetic; a prodigality of

sympathy and an austere idiom. It is certainly true that no one
has excelled the massively adult Wordsworth in the exact regis-
tration of the rhythms of the opening consciousness. Nor has anyone noted with a finer delicacy and acuteness the way in which
the infant's mind is expressed and enlarged by touch.

> From early days,
> Beginning not long after that first time
> In which, a Babe, by intercourse of touch,
> I held mute dialogues with my Mother's heart
> I have endeavour'd to display the means
> Whereby this infant sensibility,
> Great birthright of our Being, was in me
> Augmented and sustain'd.[4]

Like Coleridge, he appreciated that touch was for the infant more
than a momentary contact of the flesh, and the source of more
than sensuous comfort. Touch is for the infant a medium of
expression. It is also an entrance into a life of mutuality. It is the
infant's first language, and like language it is both an agency of
reciprocal influence and a means by which meanings are made
permanent. Through the 'mute dialogues' of his first language, 'by
intercourse of touch', the child gives and receives a flow of feeling
which composes into a unity the detached particulars of his life.

> Such feelings pass into his torpid life
> Like an awakening breeze, and hence his mind
> Even (in the first trial of its powers)
> Is prompt and watchful, eager to combine
> In one appearance, all the elements
> And parts of the same objects, else detach'd
> And loth to coalesce.[5]

Wordsworth – in this like Coleridge too – accepted as the marks
of human experience first that it aspires towards unity, and
secondly that it develops in part by creative, self-constituting
activity.

> there exists
> A virtue which irradiates and exalts
> All objects through all intercourse of sense ...
> For feeling has to him imparted strength,

34

> And powerful in all sentiments of grief,
> Of exultation, fear, and joy, his mind,
> Even as an agent of the one great mind,
> Creates. . . .[6]

Wordsworth's addition to this view was to insist that the life of the youngest child included elements, rudimentary but real, of genuinely human experience. True human experience is inextricably connected with language, and it was Wordsworth's discernment that touch was for the infant – in an imperfect and inchoate way – a kind of language that enabled him to claim for the baby an essential humanity.

Wordsworth's witness to the originating energy which makes the mind a shaper and not just a receptacle of its existence is the more telling because he had in some respects a keener sense than Coleridge of the mind's dependence upon the world outside itself.

> Emphatically such a Being lives,
> An inmate of this *active* universe.[7]

And this 'active universe' meant a more intricate notion than the conventional understanding of Wordsworth would lead us to expect. It meant not only the physical world,

> The gravitation and the filial bond
> Of nature,[8]

and

> Whate'er there is of power in sound
> To breathe an elevated mood,[9]

It meant more than

> familiar shapes
> Of hourly objects, images of trees,
> Of sea or sky.[10]

It included the influence of individuals and of the community, all that part of existence symbolized by the 'one beloved presence', 'the discipline of love', and 'the household of social life'. It included even the world of ideas,

> general truths which are themselves a sort
> Of Elements and agents, Under-Powers
> Subordinate helpers of the living mind.[11]

It included too, though in a more unemphatic way than we should agree was sufficient today, the influence of traditions, historical and literary, 'the generations of illustrious men' and 'that garden of great intellects'.

But all these, nature, home and tradition, are subordinate to 'that first great gift, the vital soul' and its 'plastic power'. To say that the infant is an 'inmate of an active universe' is to recognize the mind's receptivity, its power to be worked upon; at the same time it is to impute to the mind a real if qualified independence. The inmate is distinct from the universe he inhabits, the house-holder is not absorbed into his abode, and in neither case is the first to be explained wholly as a product of the second. Even the frail and all but helpless infant, whose life more than that of any other human being seems composed of acts of accommodation and conformity, whose nature more than any other seems to be pure, unrealized potency, is from the first constructing his own experience and staining its events with an individual dye. Even this seemingly most passive of creatures is from the start labour-ing to organize his own world and learning, with the indispensable help of others, to organize it more effectively. He is studying to frame it in his own image, to persuade it to correspond to his own style. To convey his sense of the infant's formative power, Wordsworth juxtaposes assertions of weakness with images sug-gestive of muscular effort and bodily stress. Statements of weak-ness consort with metaphors of movement and activity.

> blest the Babe,
> Nurs'd in his Mother's arms, the Babe who sleeps
> Upon his Mother's breast, who, when his soul
> Claims manifest kindred with an earthly soul,
> Doth gather passion from his Mother's eye! . . .
>
> Thus, day by day,
> Subjected to the discipline of love,
> His organs and recipient faculties
> Are quicken'd, are more vigorous, his mind spreads,
> Tenacious of the forms which it receives.[12]

The tenacity of the young mind is not the same as the retentive-ness of conscious memory; and the forms it receives are not the bright, summonable images of memory. They are the perspectives from which we see, the dimensions by which we grasp, the frames that stabilize, the categories that define and sort our experience. They are not the ideas, but rather the grounds of the ideas – of identity and otherness, sequence and disjunction, intention and consequence, the singular and the manifold, which are the primordia and roots of thought. Too important to be biddable by consciousness, they are yet the preliminaries and premises of all consciousness. These discoveries, 'the mystery of personal identity, the mystery of the immanence of the past in the present, the mystery of transience', in Whitehead's words 'massively qualify our experience. . . . They are always securely there, barely discriminated, and yet inescapable.'[13]

The mind's first efforts are bent on instituting and reinforcing these primary forms of thought. The grinding of the lenses of relation and proportion which will be henceforth the instruments of all the mind's vision and the later mastering of language are two feats of learning so phenomenal that hardly any mind, whatever it afterwards achieves, equals – much less surpasses – them. Wordsworth did not believe that once this immense leap towards humanity was accomplished, once these forms were incorporated in the mind and employed with ease, relevance and increasing subtlety, the child's experience from then on flowed in a smooth, gliding continuum. He did indeed reject the view, not uncommon now, that one could trace as from effect to cause the state and quality of a mind to some particular event or events.

> But who shall parcel out
> His intellect, by geometric rules,
> Split, like a province, into round and square?
> Who knows the individual hour in which
> His habits were first sown, even as a seed,
> Who that shall point, as with a wand, and say,
> 'This portion of the river of my mind
> Came from yon fountain'?[14]

Nevertheless, he insisted, there were experiences, to every outward appearance merely commonplace, which struck home with extraordinary force and effect. There were, he was sure, experiences which an observer would judge unremarkable that might be deeply disturbing and unpredictably influential. In spite of his condemnation of analysis clumsily inappropriate to the unified life of the mind, he did not take the view that experience was unilinear and not to be discriminated as more or less important. In the eleventh book of *The Prelude*, when meditating on the history of his mind, now brought to laborious completion, he writes:

> There are in our existence spots of time,
> Which with distinct pre-eminence retain
> A vivifying virtue whence . . .
>   our minds
> Are nourished and invisibly repair'd,
> A virtue by which pleasure is enhanced
> That penetrates, enables us to mount
> When high, more high, and lifts us up when fallen.[15]

These pre-eminent spots of time, he notes in the same place, are scattered throughout our lives but are conspicuously concentrated in childhood. They are 'those passages of life' in which 'an efficacious spirit chiefly lurks', moments in which the mind, 'to herself witness and judge', realizes that it is passing from one order of comprehension to another. Light-enfolded they stand out from the general murk and obscurity of human life as phases of critical significance, when the 'hiding-places of . . . power seem open'. These experiences, in which the mind expands and sees that it is expanding, is transformed and knows that it is being transformed, are notable for two seemingly contrary characteristics. The first is shown implicitly in the three great models of such experience which Wordsworth chose to delineate in the first book of *The Prelude*, the famous episodes of snaring, boating and skating. In these passages, it will be remembered, the poet shows himself to possess, to have possessed as a boy, a superlative acuity of the senses. He portrays an unsoiled world meeting a clean and naked sensibility. Nothing here qualifies the eagerness of the eye or the fineness of the ear's discrimination. To 'those hallow'd and pure motions of the sense' physical objects have an unusual brilliance and definition. The heightened senses note how

> The frost and breath of frosty wind had snapp'd
> The last autumnal crocus,[16]

or how the boat moved on

> Leaving behind her still on either side
> Small circles glittering idly in the moon,
> Until they melted all into one track
> Of sparkling light.[17]

And they are even aware of remoter objects inaccessible to ordinary sensibility, like the slow secret movements of the revolving earth.

> then at once
> Have I, reclining back upon my heels,
> Stopp'd short, yet still the solitary Cliffs
> Wheel'd by me, even as if the earth had roll'd
> With visible motion her diurnal round;[18]

The other characteristic of these periods Wordsworth describes in one of those general statements which as used by him are never brisk summaries or formulae of compromise but rather the slow, even the grudged, deposit of years lived with scrupulous integrity and examined with a steadily adverted mind.

> This efficacious spirit chiefly lurks
> Among those passages of life in which
> We have had deepest feeling that the mind
> Is lord and master, and that outward sense
> Is but the obedient servant of her will.[19]

At first glance this claim for the authority of the mind over submissive senses and an amenable world hardly squares with the first books of *The Prelude*, which show, I have suggested, active senses intent on providing an unusually brilliant version of a world seen as more than ordinarily vivid and felt to be firmly and insistently there. But the discrepancy is unreal. In attributing to these experiences such seemingly opposed characters Wordsworth is only affirming what has often been argued by philosophers and psychologists, namely the indivisibility of sensation and perception. But where the philosopher and psychologist emphasize that no sensation is pure but always alloyed with perception, Wordsworth stresses that the mind's most piercing perception is always grounded in sensory particulars; and the more spiritual the one, the more vivid the other. And where the philosopher and psychologist argue a case, supporting it with evidence abstracted from a whole, Wordsworth's aim is to realize the completeness of a deeply felt event of his own life. What in that event corresponds to a philosophical idea or a psychological hypothesis remains wholly engaged in the particular instances in which it was experienced.

To keep the idea shining through the detail, to enclose the general in the particular requires of the poet a rare integrity of intelligence. It asks for subtlety in selecting, and restraint in not exaggerating or over-accumulating, the concrete particulars. It takes percipience to seize, and temperance not to expose unduly or abruptly, the idea. These virtues of intellectual continence and moral sensibility are expressed most fully in *The Prelude*, most intensely in *Tintern Abbey*. They are also the constituents of that 'wise passiveness' which enabled Wordsworth to accept his experience without forcing it and to record it without distorting it. And it is these gifts which helped him to define the nature of the mind's influence on these moments of growth, to specify exactly the quality of that 'auxiliar light' which the mind played upon them. If we scrutinize any of the passages devoted to these experiences in *The Prelude*, we find that they are compounded in a strange way of fear and joy, of panic and serenity.

> 'twas my joy
> To wander half the night among the Cliffs
> And the smooth Hollows, where the woodcocks ran
> Along the open turf.[20]

But the delight – delight of the body, of the eye and spirit – which dances in the movement of these lines was accompanied by an intensifying anxiety.

> On the heights
> Scudding away from snare to snare, I plied
> My anxious visitation, hurrying on,
> Still hurrying, hurrying onward; moon and stars

> Were shining o'er my head; I was alone,
> And seem'd to be a trouble to the peace
> That was among them.[21]

The same note of 'troubled pleasure' sounds throughout the episode of the rowing-boat. There the contrast is between the lively boat, the cadence of the oars, the glittering water – nimbleness and light – and the 'huge Cliff, as if with voluntary power instinct' – an enormous and incomprehensible threat. Even the elation – 'to me it was a time of rapture' – in the great skating passage, a superbly supple expression of bodily rhythm and physical verve, cannot wholly muffle another tone. Wordsworth calls it 'melancholy', but it is not a mellow and acceptable feeling. It is rather the first mutter of uneasiness, a sign of the onset of fear. And the context – 'the leafless trees, the icy crag' – with which Wordsworth surrounds this 'alien sound' mutely emphasizes its grimness.

> with the din,
> Meanwhile, the precipices rang loud,
> The leafless trees, and every icy crag
> Tinkled like iron, while the distant hills
> Into the tumult sent an alien sound
> Of melancholy, not unnoticed, while the stars,
> Eastward, were sparkling clear, and in the west
> The orange sky of evening died away.[22]

In revealing the subtlety of structure of these important childhood experiences, Wordsworth proves himself, like every other great poet, an expert in recognizing and organizing patterns of complex feeling. His mastery of organization, intricate, lucid, complete, is apparent in the great passages in *The Prelude* referred to; the clarity of his recognition is seen in those spare and studied statements which occur throughout *The Prelude* as conclusions distilled from what has gone before or announcements introducing what was to come. The essence of these moments of growth, Wordsworth considered, was to combine 'the characters of danger and desire'. In them the child was at once 'drinking in a pure organic pleasure' and 'under the impressive discipline of fear'. And when at the height of his powers, brooding over his childhood, he gave his deliberate judgement on the influences that were the chief impulses towards his maturity, it was these he chose to name,

> Fair seed-time had my soul, and I grew up
> Foster'd alike by beauty and by fear.[23]

In an age acid with fear it is still hard for us to see fear as anything but a destructive element, impossible to conceive it as a beginning of wisdom. In a universe like ours contracted to the merely natural, fear means a sour collective terror, a promise of moral collapse and physical annihilation. The Wordsworthian fear, on the other hand, is a solitary emotion, the mood of one for whom being alone is a state both positive and intense. It is also a response to something which, though involved in or symbolized by nature, is felt as superior to nature in the hierarchy of being. It is this, incidentally, which makes much discussion of Wordsworth's 'pantheism' irrelevant, nature being for him what 'magic' was for Yeats, a system of symbols and a machinery of realization, with the difference that Wordsworth's natural symbols have the advantage over Yeats's magical ones of the public and constant over the private and arbitrary. Moreover, the effect of Wordsworthian fear is not restrictive or immobilizing but enlarging and provocative of growth; it is, says Wordsworth, to feed 'a sense of possible sublimity'. Thus while Wordsworth hung alone on the perilous ridge of rock,

> With what strange utterance did the loud dry wind
> Blow through my ears! the sky seem'd not a sky
> Of earth, and with what motion mov'd the clouds![24]

And again when he had left the boat and gone secretly home through the meadows

> for many days, my brain
> Worked with a dim and undetermin'd sense
> Of unknown modes of being.[25]

Fear was the agency which released from 'familiar shapes of hourly objects' 'huge and mighty forms that do not live like living man'.

It is worth remarking that the image of 'working' is that under which Wordsworth commonly figures these experiences of fear. As used by Wordsworth 'to work' is a word sufficiently versatile to carry a double meaning, to signify both the effect and the action of fear. These moments

> Impress'd upon all forms the characters
> Of danger or desire, and thus did make
> The surface of the universal earth
> With triumph, and delight, and hope, and fear
> Work like a sea.[26]

The essential mark of this kind of fear is the liquefaction of set limits or the disturbance of accepted amalgams. Boundaries are upset, edges blurred, different orders of being flow in upon one another, and the ordinary conceptual pattern of the universe is shattered. There is an entry in Dorothy Wordsworth's Journal which shows exactly this agitation, and which also proves that these experiences are not to be confined to childhood. 'William went to John's Grove. I went to meet him. Moonlight, but it rained. I met him before I had got as far as John Baty's – he had been surprised and terrified by a sudden rushing of winds, which seemed to bring earth, sky and lake together, as if the whole were going to enclose him in; he was glad he was in a high road.'[27] Here again we find the conjunction of fear and the melting away of conventional rigidities. In the presence of fear the variety of received forms of existence dissolves, their constancy and separation lapse, and the mind 'works' with a sense of the mysterious unity of being. It feels

> the sentiment of Being spread
> O'er all that moves, and all that seemeth still,
> O'er all, that, lost beyond the reach of thought
> And human knowledge, to the human eye
> Invisible, yet liveth to the heart,
> O'er all that leaps and runs, and shouts, and sings,
> Or beats the gladsome air, o'er all that glides
> Beneath the wave, yea, in the wave itself
> And mighty depth of waters.[28]

In poetry itself, Wordsworth observed to Landor, it was only that which exhibited this relaxation of limits, which presented the community of being, that powerfully affected him; and in the same letter he offers an explanation of why it should be so.

This leads to a remark in your last, that you are disgusted with all books that treat of religion! I am afraid that it is a bad sign in me, that I have little relish for any other – even in poetry it is the imaginative only, viz., that which is conversant with, or turns upon infinity, that powerfully affects me, – perhaps I ought to explain: I mean to say that, unless in those passages where things are lost in each other, and limits vanish, and aspirations are raised, I read with something too much like indifference.[29]

'Where things are lost in each other and limits vanish' – these words describe a negative state of release from, an untethering of the tight restrictions, the pre-conditions of rational thought, with which the mind has laboriously bound itself. And if such a negative state does not lead to frenetic anarchy, it is because it is connected in these experiences, both in literature and in life, with a positive state – profound, important and today almost wholly neglected – the state of being conversant with infinity. In Wordsworth's opinion the universe was for the child what literature could be for the adult, a store of 'types and analogies of infinity'. To the images of poetry corresponded what he calls in a letter to Catherine Clarkson 'images of sense . . . holding that relation to immortality and infinity which I have before alluded to'. 'The Bible of the Universe' – a phrase he uses in the same letter – is the child's introduction to 'the great thought by which we live, infinity and God'. If Wordsworth's claim strikes some as fantastically false to the way things now are, the fault is not with the claim but with a mechanistic society which, although through and through naturalistic in belief, yet reduces the natural universe to fractional and peripheral attention, which huddles the organic away behind the fabricated and which drowns out the rhythms of nature with the jerkings of the combustion engine.

Others may want to dismiss Wordsworth's claim that nature may be the source of the idea of the infinite as the characteristic generalization of a poetic pantheist, vague, mystical and unmeaning. As to the pantheism, Wordsworth wrote sharply about a Miss Patty Smith who 'condemns me for not distinguishing between nature as the work of God and God himself. But where does she find this doctrine inculcated? Where does she gather that the author of the Excursion looks upon nature and God as the same? He does not indeed consider the Supreme Being as bearing the same relation to the universe as a watchmaker bears to a watch.'[30] As for the generalization, Wordsworth realized like Henry James 'that the only balm and the only refuge, the real solution of the pressing question of life, are in this frequent, fruitful, intimate battle with the particular idea'.[31] And that he meant his affirmations on the impulse of the idea of the infinite to be taken in a specific, precise and even homely way, can be seen in a record of a conversation he had with his son aged four and a half, which he offers as an example of 'these innumerable types and analogies of infinity'.

'How did God make me? Who is God? How does he speak? He never spoke to *me*.'
I told him that God was a spirit, that he was not like his flesh, which he could touch; but more like his thoughts, in his mind, which he could not touch. The wind was tossing the fir trees and the sky and light were dancing about in their dark branches as seen through the window.
Noting these fluctuations, he exclaimed eagerly, 'There's a bit of him, I see it there.'
This is not meant entirely for Father's prattle.[32]

Others again would agree that *The Prelude* is utterly faithful to Wordsworth's own development, but at the same time they would argue that it is too much to generalize from the life of a genius of the power of Wordsworth to the growth of the ordinary human mind; and altogether wild to think of Wordsworth's remarkable experiences of the numinous in nature as corresponding to anything in the life of the mass of mankind. It was contended above, in anticipation of this objection, that the poet's is closer to the model of the human mind that that of any other category of person. Certainly Wordsworth himself had no doubt but that he was reconstructing the history of the common human mind and not the unprecedented biography of a unique one. He even hoped for a future popularity for his poetry 'because I have endeavoured to dwell with truth upon the points of human nature in which all men resemble each other, rather than on the accidents of manner and character produced by time and circumstance'.[33] And he wrote to Coleridge, 'One of the principal aims in *The Excursion* has been to put the commonplace truths, of the human affections especially, in an interesting point of view; and rather to remind men of their knowledge as it lurks unoperative and unvalued in their own minds than to convey recondite and refined truths!'[34] Nor should we suppose that in claiming for all children the possibility of experiences of the sort Wordsworth describes, we are imputing to them a richer awareness than they could possibly have. For as Henry James says: 'Small children have many more perceptions than they have terms to translate them; their vision is at any moment richer, their apprehension even constantly stronger than their prompt, their at all producible vocabulary.'[35]

If at this point we pause to draw the argument together we see that, according to Wordsworth, the growth of the mind begins with an effort directed to establishing the forms which make thought possible and the categories under which experience is organized. The effort could not be made except by a mind endowed with a primary constructive power; it could not succeed without the sustained collaboration of others, first through the language of touch and then through the immeasurably subtler language of words. These forms once established and brought to easier and more fluent use, the mind becomes, in certain moods of heightened sensitivity, marked both by elation and by fear, peculiarly responsive to the emblematic character of natural objects and processes. The boundaries that ordinarily separate one sort of existence from another relax, and the mind is persuaded that it is, or can be, 'conversant with infinity'.

> and now
> Rush'd in as if on wings, the time in which
> The pulse of Being everywhere was felt,

> When all the several frames of things, like stars
> Through every magnitude distinguishable,
> Were half confounded in each other's blaze . . .[36]

If the first phase is to set up the conditions for thought, the second is to enable the mind momentarily to transcend them; if the first is to learn to hear with accuracy and to interpret with relevance, the second is to become aware of an order of sound beyond normal hearing.

> One song they sang, and it was audible,
> Most audible then when the fleshly ear,
> O'ercome by grosser prelude of that strain,
> Forgot its functions, and slept undisturb'd.[37]

Wordsworth puts a heavy emphasis on these imaginative and numinous experiences, an emphasis to be explained both by the distinctive pattern of his own genius and by the excessively intellectualist tradition he was rejecting, and to be justified not by their frequency but by their importance. But we should not be gaining a just idea of Wordsworth's conception of the growth of the mind if we supposed that he paid no heed to what we customarily understand by the term, namely the refining of intelligence. He gives it a place, if not the most prominent one according to his order of priorities. It is indeed, in his view, the main business of the third phase of the mind's growth. He sees it, in essence, as an activity of analysing and sorting, first, the discovery of 'manifold distinctions' and then 'the observation of affinities', both together making for a surer and finer discrimination into stricter and more relevant categories. The danger of analysis is the temptation to halt at the stage of discovering manifold distinctions. Then it ceases to be an intellectual instrument designed to strengthen and enrich a sense of the concrete and the whole, and becomes

> that false secondary power, by which,
> In weakness, we create distinctions, then
> Deem that our puny boundaries are things
> Which we perceive, and not which we have made.[38]

But we should be in error if we deduced from this salutary warning that Wordsworth was an opponent of analytic intelligence or that he stood exclusively for the imaginative and intuitive. He had too strong an eighteenth-century bent, was too much given to its admiration for solid good sense, although he is seldom credited with either. His dismissal of Locke's fundamental premise – the passivity of the mind – did not entail a wholesale rejection of eighteenth-century psychology, at least not that part, a big one, depending on close empirical scrutiny. Wordsworth, for all his devotion to the 'visionary power', was like Locke a firm believer in bringing 'all I have said to a rigorous after test of good sense, as far as I was able to determine what good sense was'. Although he threw over the eighteenth-century watchmaker's view of the universe, he retained an eighteenth-century feeling for logical order and rational harmony.

> I had an eye
> Which in my strongest workings, evermore
> Was looking for the shades of difference
> As they lie hid in all exterior forms,
> Near or remote, minute or vast . . .
> Which spake perpetual logic to my soul,
> And by an unrelenting agency
> Did bind my feelings, even as in a chain.[39]

One who thought so highly as Wordsworth of the place of analytic intelligence – 'the logical faculty' – in the composition of poetry itself was unlikely to decry its importance in the development of the mind. 'The logical faculty has infinitely more to do with poetry than the young and the inexperienced, whether writer or critic, ever dreams of. Indeed, as the materials upon which that faculty is exercised in poetry are so subtle, so plastic, so complex, the application of it requires an adroitness which can proceed from nothing but practice.'[40]

One would not claim either special originality or remarkable perception for Wordsworth's account of the analytic aspect of intelligence. More suggestive is his understanding of matters – to speak his own idiom – collateral to the sharpening of intellect. To begin with, he realized that the cultivation of intelligence is not to be separated from the progress of the affections. Between the learner and the learned, the mind and the object, there must be not only a cognitive but also an affective relationship. In our low-toned, neutral language we call it a bond of interest; for Wordsworth it was 'this most watchful power of love'. The word 'watchful' is an important one: the quality of the mind's atten-tion to its object depends not just on intellectual advertence but as much on an intensity of feeling which braces and sharpens that advertence. The strongest and subtlest learning is the issue of

> that more exact
> And intimate communion which our hearts
> Maintain with the minuter properties
> Of objects which already are belov'd,
> And of those only.[41]

Above all, the permanence of learning depends on discernment charged with the energy of feeling.

> And every season to my notice brought
> A store of transitory qualities
> Which but for this most watchful power of love
> Had been neglected, left a register
> Of permanent relations, else unknown.[42]

But if intellectual advance is connected with the presence of feeling, the converse is also true. Intensity of feeling becomes fineness of sensibility through being submitted to the play of intel-ligence. Sensibility might almost be defined as feeling becoming intelligible. And the means by which this transformation is effected is language. Through language feeling is clarified by thought, and through language thought is energized by feeling. In some advice which he sent to Hamilton for his sister, Words-worth speaks of this very matter, 'She will probably write less in proportion as she subjects her feelings to logical forms, but the range of her sensibilities, so far from being narrowed, will extend as she improves in the habit of looking at things through the steady light of words; and to speak a little metaphysically, words are not a mere vehicle, but they are powers either to kill or to animate.'[43]

Intelligence then is intimate with feeling, feeling with sensibility, and sensibility with language. There is also another 'collateral' inextricably involved with these. It is the moral element. No conception of the growth of intelligence which omits it can be adequate, no discussion of the mind which neglects it can be sufficient. Ultimately it is because *The Prelude* is throughout the expression of a moral sensibility that it is so inwardly, minutely faithful to the growth of the mind. Values are implicit in the intention of a poet who would undertake such a theme. 'It is not enough for me as a Poet, to delineate merely such feelings as all men do sympathize with; but it is also highly desirable to add to these others, such as all men *may* sympathize with, and such as there is reason to believe they would be better and more moral beings if they did sympathize with. . . .'[44] They are also part of the object which the poet would describe. It is acting without a real recognition of this truth which corrupts the commentaries of so many critics of the mind and its education.

Of those who seem to me to be in error two parties are especially prominent; they, the most conspicuous head of whom is Mr Brougham, who think that sharpening of intellect and attainment of knowledge are things good in themselves, without reference to the circumstances under which the intellect *is* sharpened, or to the quality of the knowledge acquired. 'Knowledge,' says Lord Bacon, 'is power', but surely not less for evil than for good. Lord Bacon spoke like a philosopher; but they who have that maxim in their mouths the oftenest have the least understanding of it. . . .[45]

Henry James defined the lesson of a work of art as 'the idea that deeply lurks in any vision prompted by life'. On this understanding it is permissible to ask, what is the lesson of *The Prelude*? The answer, it seems to me, is that *The Prelude* is an invitation to make suppler and more inclusive our idea of reason. The standing it is permissible to ask, what is the lesson of *The Prelude*? so tonic a corrective for the eighteenth century, when reason came to stand for an attenuated and depthless good sense, fits it to be a remedy for our own even more impoverished conception. The current concept of reason turns it into a curiously disembodied faculty, ghostly and diagrammatic, hardly more than a capacity to follow logical rules or to arrive at a set of statistical results. It is a power – if that is not too vigorous a word – thought of as separated from feeling, sensibility and value, and so delicate that it is likely to be muddied by the impurities of the living language. But in *The Prelude* reason means intellect enlivened by feeling, made nervous by sensibility, dignified by a concern for value, and intimately connected with words.[46] Above all it means intellect kindled by imagination, for at the highest stage Wordsworth will allow no division between these. The most advanced intellectual life cannot exist without imagination which is only another name for

> – clearest insight, amplitude of mind,
> And reason in her most exalted mood.[47]

Comprehensiveness is one character of the developed mind and one standard by which we should judge it. This was implied in Wordsworth's comment on Lamb, 'Lamb has not a reasoning mind, therefore cannot have a comprehensive mind, and, least of all, has he an imaginative one.'[48] The other character and the other standard is unity, or rather the mind's bent towards unity, its instinct to achieve coherence among its experiences and cooperation among its powers.

> The mind of man is fram'd even like the breath
> And harmony of music. There is a dark
> Invisible workmanship that reconciles
> Discordant elements, and makes them move
> In one society.[49]

'A dark invisible workmanship' – the phrase is distinctively Wordsworthian, combining suggestions of depth and mystery with suggestions of sobriety and discipline. Less explicitly but as surely, it communicates an attitude of respect for the living mind and its possibilities. This attitude, expressed in the lines quoted, in terms appropriate at this point in the poem, derives from a disposition manifest throughout *The Prelude*. It is a disposition which makes Wordsworth so magnificently an influence for good, so redemptive a poet. It is a spirit of reverence for life and a feeling for the miraculousness of its common operations, a continuing sense, strong and sane, intensely felt and temperately expressed, of the marvels of existence.

CHAPTER 3

COLERIDGE AND THE EDUCATION
OF TEACHERS

IF Coleridge was a seminal mind – and I believe the term is peculiarly appropriate to him – he was seminal in a way very different from, say, T. H. Huxley. Coleridge established no movements – Pantisocracy was only a dream – founded no institutions, sat on no committees (the picture of Coleridge the committee-man is an alarming one), he altered no machinery and negotiated no agreements. He had not a portion of that flood of intellectual and administrative energy which Huxley employed so devotedly and effectively for what we must recognize were good if limited ends. Coleridge produced nothing in the way of observable results; even his literary works were fragmentary and incomplete. And yet who can doubt that it is Huxley whose importance is purely local, Huxley whose reputation is creaky and antique, and that it is Coleridge who is unconfined by time and Coleridge who is increasingly relevant to us in the twentieth century? We have assimilated Huxley, taken some minor nutriment from him, and finished with him; we haven't even caught up with Coleridge.

But it is a crude gauge of educational importance which attempts to correlate a man's significance with a number of specifiable results in which his hand can be seen. Coleridge's influence worked at a more profound level, at the roots of action, where the quality of practice is determined. Coleridge's influence was seminal in that it operated in depth among motives and purposes, assumptions and values. It made a difference not just to men's judgements, but it altered the kind of mind, the structure of beliefs they brought to bear in making these judgements. If we ask why Coleridge should have been able to exercise so intimate an influence on the modern mind, the answer must be, I think, that Coleridge himself represented – and in representing constituted – the first truly modern consciousness. There is a sense in which Chaucer and Pope belong to one world, a world of God and order and defined and accepted categories. This is a world which is utterly vanished for us. Ours is a world of the nervous individual consciousness, of fluid categories and disintegrating order. Coleridge was the first to speak the language of this world, to address himself to its particular problems, and the first to feel himself obliged to offer answers to questions which had never even been formulated before. Coleridge's works, themselves so shockingly disorganized, so disturbed and unsatisfactory as works of art, are in their very imperfections – their lack of finality and completeness – analogues of the modern mind. They also compose a kind of *Summa* of suggestiveness for contemporary civilization, a *Summa* which is not dogmatic, articulated and certain of itself, but fluid, tentative and unorganized. And they are this both negatively and positively. What Coleridge rejected the modern world has rejected, namely the eighteenth-century world of order and common sense. What Coleridge positively offers is what the best and most serious of modern minds – due allowance being made for differences of time, stress and formulation – have come to approve and strive for.

In this chapter I want to inquire into Coleridge's idea of education, and to show its relevance and importance for those engaged in the study of education and the training of teachers.

When Santayana spoke of pragmatism as 'the philosophy of the dominance of the foreground', he described incidentally a weakness to which formal education is always susceptible, and to which much modern education has succumbed. Education is conspicuously under the dominance of the foreground, the sustained and peremptory dominance of subject-matter.

It is possible to explain if not to justify this state of affairs. What the teacher conceives of as an obligation to society and to the child, the extravagant claims made for various studies, the impossibility of teaching or learning in a vacuum, and, it must be admitted, the readiness to be convinced that the work is done when so many items of information are imparted – all these tempt the teacher to allow subject-matter (in a limited sense to be defined) to engage the largest share of his attention. But if we judge by the standard of permanence, subject-matter discloses itself as of much slighter importance. Some simple learning and skill aside, few of us, unless professionally required to do so, could or would wish to recover from the discard into which our minds have thrust it much of the truck on which we and our teachers spend effort, energy and patience at school.

Subject-matter – in the same limited sense – exercises a similar dominance and a similar transient influence in the training of the teacher. However earnest the student, however retentive his memory, it is to be doubted whether he preserves more than some dislocated fragments of all that theory, psychology, history and method, or whether if he could, he would find it, as customarily taught, particularly appropriate or helpful. And – more importantly – it is to be doubted how much has been forgotten because it has so modified his mind and made subtler his perception that it is no longer an object of thought but a means of insight. For it is not the permanence of memory but the permanence of being and power which is the criterion most relevant here. And what lasts, what enters into our being as a result of school and college, is a blend of value, attitude and assumption, a certain moral tone, a special quality of imagination, a particular flavour of sensibility – the things that constituted the soul of our education.

A good education persists not as a collection of information, an arrangement of intellectual bric-à-brac, but as a certain unity of self, more or less coherent, more or less rich, and a certain method of thinking and feeling, more or less complex, more or less sensitive. Unity and method are, in Coleridge's view, the qualities of the educated mind.

What is that [writes Coleridge] which first strikes us, and strikes us at once in a man of education, and which among educated men, so notably distinguishes the man of a superior mind? . . . Not the weight or novelty of his remarks, not any unusual interest of facts communicated by him. . . . It is the unpremeditated and evidently habitual arrangement of his words, grounded on the habit of foreseeing in each integral part, or (more plainly in each sentence) the whole that he intends to communicate. However irregular and desultory his talk, there is method in the fragments.[1]

He develops the point further in *Biographia Literaria*:

. . . the intercourse of uneducated men is distinguished from the diction of their superiors in knowledge and power by the greater *disjunction* and *separation* in the component parts of that, whatever it be, which they wish to communicate. There is a want of that prospectiveness of mind, that *surview*, which enables a man to foresee the whole of what he is to convey, appertaining to one point; and by this means so to subordinate and arrange the different parts according to their relative importance, as to convey it at once, and as an organized whole.[2]

The training to which our teachers are submitted is certainly calculated to be one in which a multitude of facts is amassed and conveyed, but hardly one which encourages this kind of unity of self or this kind of method in communication. Just as in the teaching of children, so in the training of teachers, we have been too much concerned with 'specific information that can be conveyed from without, storing the passive mind with the various sorts of knowledge most in request, using the human soul as a mere repository',[3] and we have been too little concerned with exciting 'the germinal power that craves no knowledge but what it can take up into itself, what it can appropriate and reproduce as fruit of its own'. At the end of a course of training, the mind of the young teacher is too frequently 'an aggregate without unity', too rarely informed with a principle of 'vitality which grows and evolves itself from within'.[4] Thus the ordinary professional course prepares not a full but a 'pollarded man, with every faculty except reason':[5] reason, that is, in Coleridge's meaning, as the source and organ of self-consciousness and 'the power by which we become possessed of principles'.[6]

No one can educate another who is not himself educated, and to be educated is to have a principled, not a cluttered, mind, one which sees what it knows, not one which merely knows what it likes. It is often assumed that there is some necessary relation between the educated mind and a wide range of scholarship, a notion to which university teachers are especially prone. But this seems to be a dubious assumption. It is founded on the habit of thinking of subject-matter in a grossly materialistic way as an area to be covered, or as a volume to be exhausted or a bulk to be chipped at. It is confirmed by the other habit of taking subject-matter as a single instead of a double concept. But the term subject-matter disguises an equivocation. It conflates two related but distinct meanings. On the one hand any subject-matter is a system of clues, concerned with human existence, organized about some initiating and defining concept, expressed in language and argued by men. On the other hand subject-matter is that world of meaning, order of nature, physical process, pattern of events, organization of feelings which the former kind of subject-matter enables us to conceive. It is that labyrinth of reality through which and towards the understanding of which any particular discourse is a directing and guiding thread.

Unless subject-matter in the first sense contributes to our power of comprehending subject-matter in the second sense, it fails to serve its purpose as a means and arrogates to itself the status of an end. This is what all too much contemporary teaching does. And this is what is meant by referring to the dominance of the foreground in education. What is in the foreground, what is instrumental is disconnected from that which gives it point and significance, and treated and taught as though it were self-sufficient and autonomous.

Subject-matter in the common, unexamined sense of what is expected to be readily accessible, examinable information, both for child in school and teacher in training, has distended to monstrous proportions, monstrous in its immensity, shapelessness and horrid incoherence. It has become, as Coleridge said of the botany of his own day, 'a mass enlarging by endless appositions'.[7] Nevertheless, it contrives to exclude the one knowledge which Coleridge[8] thought it every man's duty and interest to acquire, self-knowledge, together with the one art by which it may be attained, the art of reflection. The phrase, the art of reflection, should make it plain that Coleridge's requirements would not be met by an even more elaborate study of the science of psychology.

Psychology as a science attempts to order a series of observations into a system of uniformities. It is general and abstract and aspires towards law. Reflection as an art begins, continues and concludes in precision and particularity. It is individual and concrete, a mode of personal experience. Reflection must be distinguished also from introspection, understood in the technical psychological sense as a means for investigating the mind, because of the relation of subject to object. Introspection in this sense is a form of what Coleridge called 'abstract knowledge' in which 'the understanding distinguishes the affirmed from the affirming', in which 'we think of ourselves as separated beings, and place nature in antithesis to mind, object to subject, thing to thought. . . .' But reflection is 'the contemplation of reason, namely, that intuition of things which arises when we possess ourselves as one with the whole. . . . Here there is neither singly that which affirms, nor that which is affirmed; but the identity and living copula of both.'[9] In introspection the subject struggles to hold himself aloof from the object, even when that object is his own mind. In reflection there is a 'coincidence of an object and subject . . . the objective and subjective are so instantly united that we cannot determine to which of the two the priority belongs. There is here no first and no second; both are co-instantaneous and one.'[10]

The sense of 'fine and luminous distinction'[11] that Coleridge praised in Wordsworth he himself possessed in an eminent degree. His own work is, indeed, an extended commentary on an array of fundamental distinctions, a commentary informed with the three powers he specifies as 'wit, which discovers practical likeness hidden in general diversity; subtlety, which discovers the diversity concealed in general apparent sameness; and profundity, which discovers an essential unity under all the semblance of difference'.[12] His various distinctions between fancy and imagination, understanding and reason, the outer and the inner sense, civilization and cultivation, arise and flow harmoniously from one profound 'realizing intuition', the distinction between an aggregate of parts and a vital whole, between the discrete many and a living unity.[13] The error of education is to ignore or neglect the latter in concentrated pursuit of the former. In the practice of education the error expresses itself in a determination 'to shape convictions and deduce knowledge from without by an exclusive observation of outward and sensible things as the only realities', as well as in an obstinate inattention 'to the simple truth that as the forms in all organized existence, so must all true and living knowledge proceed from within'.[14] Such an intellectual policy may produce Coleridge's 'civilization' or technocracy (for which his symbol is 'trade'), the efficient management of practical affairs, but not 'cultivation' or wisdom (for which his symbol is 'literature'), the reverent appreciation of excellence. Such an education may produce a competent technician; certainly it will not produce a good teacher.

If in accord with the spirit of Coleridge's distinctions we contrast as ends the man who has been taught and the man who has been educated, the knowledgeable man and the wise man, we may also oppose as means corresponding to them the two modes of learning he named observation and reflection. No inconsiderable part of Coleridge's criticism both in literature and education derives from his concern to discriminate between these two, to exhibit their proper relation and to stress how seriously in contemporary society this had been disturbed. For him, to observe is to attend to evidence furnished by 'the notices of the senses' with the aim of enlarging knowledge of the world outside the borders of self; to reflect is to turn the mind's regard inwards in order 'to refine consciousness of self'. Reflection is not, it must be remarked, to be confused with reverie, a lackadaisical, bemused sauntering in the company of a mere sequence of notions and images. It is difficult, an athletic and ascetic exercise calling on the full energy of thought. 'It requires', says Coleridge, 'no ordinary skill and address to fix the attention of men on the world within them, to induce them to study the processes and superintend the works which they are themselves carrying on in their own minds.'[15]

Ideally the relation between reflection and observation should be one of mutual enrichment, observation clarified by reflection, reflection strengthened by observation, in a rhythmic interchange of prompting and response. And in fact there never is a complete disjunction between reflection and observation in learning.

But the natural difficulty of reflection, severe enough in itself, is aggravated in a period when scientific knowledge is taken as the paradigm of all knowledge and where the value of knowledge is judged by the measure in which it satisfies the canons of scientific knowledge, namely, that it be definite, 'objective', publicly verifiable, and apt to widen control of the physical universe.

Teachers in every sphere, at school, training college and university, play their part in confirming this contemporary trend towards illiberality. And a candid person would have to admit that those engaged in the training of teachers contribute as vigorously as others towards the growth of narrowness. They do so not by expulsion from the curriculum of studies which, if they are to be worth anything at all, must work through reflection towards the deepening of reflective power, but rather by an expectation that all studies should approximate, as closely as may be, to the mode and purpose of scientific studies, through observation to the sharpening of observation. Literary and historical studies thus pursued suffer such confinement that only the more than usually gifted and the more than usually indifferent to examination success are open to their influence. But the philosophic study of education is cramped to the point of lifelessness; and this study which should be the most vivifying, the most transforming, manifests itself to teachers in after life as of all their preparatory studies the most vapid, the most diffuse, and the most pointless.

The study of the theory of education could become relevant, vigorous and lifegiving only if the practice and purpose of its teachers suffered an extreme change; if a questioning replaced an assertory tone, if reflection were given the primacy over observation, and if the aim of the study were to be the revelation of principle instead of the retailing of doctrine. As it is, it is no more than 'the translation of the living word into a dead language for the purpose of memory, arrangement and general communication'.[16] Uninformed by speculation, it is a frivolous and trifling scholarship, tacitly acknowledged by the teacher as a shamed gesture towards 'culture', at once recognized by the student as without even a tenuous connexion with the present or any influence on the future. Begun in confusion, conducted without conviction, it provokes at the worst disgust, at the best indifference. It is an indictment of those charged with preparing students to be teachers that this should be so of that part of their preparation which should be a vivid experience, disturbing and tenaciously influential. If education is to become what Coleridge thought it ought to be, 'that most weighty and concerning of all sciences',[17] it must do so by an utter conversion here at its centre. It must become an inquiry, active and intimately personal, devoted to the interrogation of self, to all that is grounded in the self, and to that transformation of self hoped for in learning. In this inquiry only those questions should be posed which are pointed, revealing and important. And these will be found to be those which have excited and been framed by the best minds in any age. In no other way can Coleridge's hope be realized, 'that men may be made better, not only in consequence, but by the mode and in the process of instruction'.[18]

To ask that the study of the theory of education should aim at self-knowledge by the method of reflection is to require it to be, what it is not at present, a mode of liberal education. For as Coleridge wrote to James Gillman in 1827, 'all knowledge, not merely mechanical and like a carpenter's rule, having its whole value in the immediate outward use to which it is applied . . . all knowledge . . . that enlightens and liberalizes, is a form and means of self-knowledge, whether it be grammar or geometry, logical or classical'. Educational theory collapses into an invertebrate huddle precisely because it lacks the leading idea that Coleridge named 'the self-unravelling clue'.[19] Thus it is impossible for it not to be lax without principle and blundering without purpose. Only that is informed by principle, and therefore imbued with purpose, which progressively realizes the intelligible, which lucidly elaborates an ordering concept.

Throughout his writings Coleridge insists that an essential means of reflective self-knowledge – and an unsurpassed educative agency – is an active analysis of language, and especially an interrogation of the texts of great writers.

Reflect on your thoughts, actions, circumstances and – which will be of especial aid to you in forming a *habit* of reflection – accustom yourself to reflect on the words you use, hear or read, their truth, derivation and history. For if words are not things, they are living powers, by which things of most importance to mankind are activated, combined and humanized.[20]

Since 'the best part of human language properly so called is derived from reflection on the acts of the mind itself', attention to the combinations, relations and the mutual accommodations of words gives us direct access to the intimate operations of the mind. When there are the words of a great writer, we have the liberalizing experience of being made free, luminously free, of a mind infinitely more subtle, complex and powerful than our own. And by mind, of course, I mean not just intellect but the whole concourse of cooperative mental powers, of thought, feeling, purpose and imagination. I say made free of. But I do not wish to imply that it is easy. It is something we have to struggle towards with discipline and abnegation. Without severity of effort there is no quality of attainment. To mitigate the difficulty Coleridge gives us his own technique of interrogation.

'The first question', says Coleridge, 'we should put to ourselves when we have to read a passage that perplexes us in a work of authority is: What does the writer *mean* by all this? And the second question should be, What does he intend by all this?'[21] That is to say, each part of the text must be interpreted in the light of the intention of the whole. The mean of particular parts is always modified and often constituted by the general intention of the author. The separation of meaning and intention here is made, it is clear, for purposes of discussion; in action they are not divided as we see from Coleridge's explanation of meaning. 'I include in the meaning of a word not only its correspondent object, but likewise all the associations it recalls. For language is framed to convey not the object alone, but likewise the character, mood and intentions of the person who is representing it.'[22] Throughout an analysis we have to be alert to detect confusion and equivocation. 'To expose a sophism, and to detect the equivocal or double meaning of a word, is in the great majority of cases one and the same thing.'[23] We have also to learn to refine our sense of distinction. To appreciate and to make fine – but always relevant – distinctions is the mark of an educated mind. And the subtler the distinctions, the better the mind. 'For one useless subtlety in our elder divines and moralists, I will produce ten sophisms of equivocation in the writings of our modern preceptors; and for one error resulting from excess of distinguishing the indifferent, I could show ten mischievous delusions from the habit of confounding the diverse.'[24] But the distinctions must always be relevant, appropriate that is within the sphere of discourse established by the author's intention. The quality of just and delicate relevance is the hardest come by, the most easily lost, of all the qualities of the educated mind. A leading idea, a quirk of intolerance, some failure in patience or self-restraint, and our analysis ceases to be critical – and educative – and the words of a great writer are made an occasion for rambling meditations of our own.

Probably few would quarrel with the contention that the study of education should be more than a casual gossip about the great, composed of fragments impertinent to one another and unrelated to a whole, or disagree with the view that it would, if undertaken according to Coleridge's prescription, more smoothly collaborate with other agencies of liberal education in helping the student to become a person of finer quality. But one question naturally arises at this point. What is the student likely to gain from the study which will prove of peculiar benefit to him in his vocation as teacher? The answer is an experience of humane learning remarkable for its purity, intelligibility and power. There are those who teach without having learned. There are even more who teach without ever really having known what it is to learn. And institutions of learning of every sort are packed with titular teachers either deficient or wholly lacking in what one would have thought a sense vital for a teacher, the sense of what it is to be a learner.

If we sought an account of the learning hoped for in the study of education, we could find nowhere an exposition more perceptive and convincing than Coleridge's. The act of learning was a main and persistent theme of Coleridge's thought, likely in any context to come to the front of his attention. Its characteristics, therefore, are not detailed in a set piece of analysis but, as one would expect, are scattered in a rich variety throughout his work and letters. Their unity is in their source, in one mastering and decisive conviction, that the mind is an active power. 'To know is in its very essence a verb active.'[25] He had himself a mind unusually gifted with awareness and energy, or rather with awareness of its own energy. (As for his notorious lethargy in action, that is, when his accomplishment is fairly considered partly a legend of his own devising.) From his earliest years he was conscious of his mind shaping and patterning his experience. 'I regulated all my creeds', he wrote of his childhood, 'by my conceptions, not by my sight, even at that age.'[26]

Because of his conviction he rejected the eighteenth-century world, the psychology of Locke and the Newtonian intellectual system, in which the mind is a 'lazy looker-on at an external universe'.[27] In learning 'things take the signature of thought'.[28] Where the mind has the initiative, 'things the most remote and diverse in time, place and outward circumstance are brought into mental contiguity and succession, the more striking as the less expected'.[29] When the mind is passive, human experience, 'the confluence of innumerable impressions in each moment of time',[30] falls asunder into a delirium of inconsequence. The activity of the mind, 'combining many circumstances into one moment of consciousness, tends to produce that ultimate end of all human thought and feeling, unity'.[31] The activity of thought, as of imagination and passion, Coleridge would add, is an activity of unification. What thought, imagination and passion connect is not separated facts, 'not things only or for their sake alone, but likewise and chiefly the relations of things, either their relations to each other, or to the observer, or to the state of apprehension of the hearers. To enumerate and analyse these relations with the conditions under which alone they are discoverable is to teach the science of method'.[32] It is also to teach the art of learning.

Coleridge's insight into learning is not coarsened by any pretension finally to solve what is ultimately insoluble. He is as free from the vulgarity which seeks – to use the idiom of Gabriel Marcel – to degrade a mystery into a problem, as he is from its twin vice, that ignorant lack of reverence for life, which Lawrence bitterly and justly complained of in his contemporaries. All too many, indeed, of the problems of education are mysteries made shabby by the absence of reverence. Coleridge was quick to see and to judge this particularly uncouth kind of provinciality.

I have known [he wrote to Poole in 1797] some who have been rationally educated as it is styled. They were marked by a microscopic acuteness but when they looked at great things, all became a blank and they saw nothing, and denied (very illogically) that anything could be seen, and uniformly put the negation of a power for the possession of a power and called the want of imagination judgement and the never being moved to rapture philosophy.

But in Coleridge himself a miraculous clarity of discernment is inseparable from the restraint and sanity of humility, and the subtlest analytic intelligence from a sense of modesty and wonder. Perhaps nothing illustrates better this mature hospitality of mind than a remark in another letter to Poole, in 1801. 'My opinion,' he wrote, 'is this: That deep thinking is attainable only by a man of deep feeling, and that all truth is a species of revelation.'

Here Coleridge anticipates the modern educational psychologist in that which has come more and more to engross his interests, the non-intellectual aspects of learning, the depth and urgency of its impulses. But at the same time he recognizes that there is always more than the psychological conditions in learning, that learning is always something revealed as well as something performed. Learning as revelation is an idea with Platonic and Christian vibrations which may for some be sufficient to make it unwelcome. But however much these grate upon him, it is important for the teacher to realize that it contains at least an unmistakable negative truth, attested by his daily experience. Learning cannot be guaranteed. To believe that it can, even with every circumstance and effort cooperating, is to regard man as an infallibly adjusting organism, teaching as the cunning manipulation of environment, and learning as producing the appropriate reaction in a specific situation. But human dignity requires us to admit the possibility of failure, the vocation of teacher involves a sense of reverence in the presence of mystery, the role of learner entails patience and stillness in waiting on the event. Learning should begin in wonder, go on in humility, and end in gratitude. It should end in gratitude, that is, if we are persuaded with Coleridge that learning, while it cannot be guaranteed, is certainly not fortuitous. Gratitude is a feeling in place only in the presence of something given. It is the correlate of grace.

Coleridge then, for his insistence on the activity of the mind in learning, was alive to what in it is beyond activity and not to be commanded by effort. Similarly, in spite of his regard for the transcendent or the 'grace' in learning, he could without incongruity offer a test of humane learning arrived at by psychological analysis. (But, of course, for Coleridge psychological analysis meant not a statistical computation but an appraisal, alert, delicate, discriminating, of the drama of concrete feeling and particular thought.) It was in the course of an examination of the intricate mode of learning by which the listener develops acquaintance with the art of music that he formulated his criterion. 'I allude,' he said, 'to that sense of recognition which accompanies a sense of novelty in the most original passages of a great composer. If we listen to a symphony of Cimarosa, the present strain still seems not only to recall but almost to revive some past movement, another and yet the same.'[33]

The sense by which we recognize in the new a fulfilment of our finest experience, if it is felt with remarkably telling force in music, is not confined to that art. As a measure of its worth it is presupposed by Keats's judgement that poetry 'should strike the reader as a wording of his own highest thoughts, and appear almost a remembrance'. It is implicit in the Socratic theory of reminiscence. It informs Eliot's conception of tradition, 'an awareness that the mind of Europe is a mind which changes, and that this change is a development which abandons nothing *en route*, which does not superannuate either Shakespeare or Homer, or the rock drawings of the Magdalenian draughtsmen'. And it is the unspoken standard used by scientists in their collaborative effort to take up partial truths into a larger conciliation. The common ground in each case is a belief in the seamlessness of experience of quality, in the unity of texture between the finest whether familiar or utterly new

The belief that experiences dissimilar in character but alike in quality fit together to make a coherent whole is one with heartening implications for education. It means that there can be a 'progressive transition' between the humblest sorts of these experiences which are relevant for children and the mature discoveries of genius. It means that for all there is an entrance into the world of value, a route through it and no point of necessary and final arrest. And it denies the natural existence of inveterate hostility between experiences of quality belonging to different categories, whether these be scientific, humane, technical or religious.

A mind active in elaborating and unifying more and subtler relations, recollected in a patient attendance on the revelation of learning, possessed of a standard of value with personal significance and a more than personal validity – such is the mind that has profited from the discipline of humane learning as Coleridge conceived it. And such is the mind required of one who would discharge the serious, indeed the terrifying, obligations of a teacher.

CHAPTER 4

THE LITERARY CRITIC AND THE
EDUCATION OF AN *ÉLITE*

COLERIDGE, ARNOLD AND F. R. LEAVIS

EVERY student of the theory of education is sensible of what his study owes to the philosopher. And it is hardly possible for the student of it today not to be aware of the subject's indebtedness to the psychologist. But insufficient acknowledgement is made of the obligations of educational theory to the literary critic.

Perhaps the neglect of the literary critic is to be attributed to the odd pattern of the history of educational theory – or of what is taken to be its history – which, it appears, began as an obscure branch of moral philosophy and turned in the course of time into a subordinate section of applied psychology. But the critic's influence, if unrecognized by the official historians, is none the less real. There is a relationship, natural and intimate, between education and literary criticism, and that this should be so will be no cause for surprise when we recall the nature of the critic's business.

It is so to order his intelligence, so to refine his feelings, that he will respond to particular works with purity and relevance, and at the same time, by reference to the standards implicit in his educated sensibility, make on them judgements appropriate and true. The operation of criticism is a continual exercise in the education of the self and good criticism is a record, inward and articulate, of many acts of self-discipline. The term 'discipline' is a proof that the education of the critic's sensibility is *not* the same as the aesthete's training of a special faculty of appreciation. The critic's mind is not the mind we see sophisticated in Pater, vulgarized in Wilde, and satirized by Henry James in *The Tragic Muse*. His effort is not directed towards what Henry James spoke of as 'multiplying and saving from the dark gulf, happy moments of consciousness'. The critic's career is an education not a cultivation of self, a disciplining not a cosseting of his powers, and it is like all true educational activity in being inseparable from a genuine seriousness, a devoted and troubled earnestness, which must be called moral. A necessary qualification of the important critic is a conscience. He cannot be like the aesthete in *The Tragic Muse* 'willing to assent to any decision that relieves him of the grossness of choice'. Nor does the critic pursue his vocation as a solitary, interested only in one consequence, the finer condition of the self; for the real critics, alive and dead, compose a community, united in purpose, 'the common pursuit of true judgement'. Not only has the critic an obligation to something outside himself, 'which,' as Eliot said, 'may provisionally be called truth', but he has also a duty towards all those other members of his society among whom his office is to be the corrector and improver of taste.

Intelligence, vigorous and subtle, feeling, strong and sensitive, that is a matured sensibility, together with a strenuous concern for the health and tone of civilization – these characters mark the two most influential critics of the nineteenth century, Coleridge and Arnold, just as they distinguish one practising critic, Leavis, whose name can, without incongruity, be joined to theirs. Many in the twentieth century have contributed to the extension of critical capacity. Some like Eliot have enriched the fund of ideas at the critic's command, others like Richards have helped to bring about a reformation of the critical vocabulary, yet others like the groups associated with the *Calendar of Modern Letters* or with *Scrutiny* have given admirable examples of the application of critical method or have acted as mediators and popularizers. But no one who keeps before him a rigorous criterion, no one who has regard for the volume and quality of criticism, no one who considers the range and depth of its influence, can have any serious doubt that these names, Coleridge, Arnold, Leavis, compose the grand line of the modern English critical tradition. And no one who comes after these critics will be able to ignore, or not be compelled to make use of – although he may refuse to acknowledge – the new maps of literature drawn by them. Each has made intelligible the literature of his own age, and the literature of the past as seen by his age, revealing the permanent structure behind the deceptive appearance. The work of each satisfies what one of them, Arnold, declared the canon of important criticism: 'To ascertain the master-current in the literature of an epoch, and to distinguish this from all minor currents, is the critic's highest function; in discharging it he shows how far he possesses the most indispensable quality of his office, justness of spirit.'[1]

In speaking of the connexion between criticism and education, and of the structure of the English critical tradition, I have been at pains to differentiate between the critical and the aesthetic, and to insist that criticism looks to a moral end. Literary criticism has a reference beyond literature to life. But it would be as perverse, if today not so common, an error to suppose that criticism is a form of moral didacticism, and to think of literary criticism as an activity of manœuvre, a means manipulated by an exterior moral fervour. Literary criticism exists in its *own* right and obeys is own laws. The proper conception of the relation of literary criticism and morality in the largest sense is not that which sees the one as the agent or servant of the other, but rather that which recognizes a moral impulse to be part of the *donné* of the critical talent, and a moral criterion as involved, necessarily implicated, in its exercise. The equipped critic is one aware of the moral influence even of what appears to be the most purely aesthetic part of his craft. In Arnold's words, he is able to appreciate 'the ethical influence of style in language – its close relation, so often pointed out, with character'.[2] This capacity Coleridge claimed he had from an early age. 'I am pleased to think that when a mere stripling I had formed the opinion that true taste was virtue and that bad writing was bad feeling.'[3] To accept a moral dimension in the critic's work is to adopt a view of his profession shared by Coleridge, Arnold and Leavis. In none of their critical expositions does the critic end by *not* taking up sides. For them criticism is a matter of affirmations, definitions, judgements, exclusions, of analysis accompanied by decision, and the ultimate sins are neutrality and eclecticism. Criticism must be impassioned as well as acute. It must engage the critic's soul as well as his sensibility.

Each of these critics, therefore, in practising his art performs a double activity. On the one hand, all his resources of perception engaged, all his energies of discernment braced, he attends to the object of criticism, with patience, self-restraint, and an exact sense of relevance. On the other, he summons his own apprehension of that body of values called in the past – even by Hume – the Laws of Taste, and by the *Calendar of Modern Letters* – simply – the Standards of Criticism. The merit of criticism depends then not just on the critic's fineness of tact or the deftness of his analysis but as much on the reality of his possession, the sureness of his grasp, of these standards. 'The strength of applied irony,' said Henry James, and the same is true of criticism, 'is surely in the sincerities, the lucidities, the utilities that stand behind it.' 'These postulates, these animating presences' cannot be specified or codified. But if they are not regulations or laboratory gauges, neither are they arbitrary or chaotic. It is true that the accidents of time and circumstance always exert their formidable influence, that personal predilection and the configuration of talent make for individuality and difference. But none of these is determinative, and the surprising thing is not the variety of difference and originality among these critics but the degree of their consent. Particular judgements may be discrepant, although not nearly so often as the devotees of utter relativity in taste would have us believe, but the grounds for these judgements exhibit, in spite of changing idioms, a singular unanimity. In fundamental matters these critics belong to one party.

This is not to say that Coleridge, Arnold and Leavis maintain a precisely identical relationship of distance between ground and judgement, standard and application. Coleridge's criticism habitually tends to over-explicitness of principle. In him the philosopher is always threatening to break out, with however horrid an incongruity, from the literary critic. And Leavis has been arraigned by philosophers, by René Wellek for example, for too great an inexplicitness about the system of values from which his comparative judgements derive, although it is only fair to add that this is not an accusation made against him by other literary critics. They would find his manner, the manner in which positives are unmistakably implied at every point of the exposition, in keeping with Arnold's dictum: 'Here the great safeguard is never to let oneself become abstract, always to retain an intimate and lively consciousness of the truth of what one is saying, and, the moment this fails us, to be sure that something is wrong.'[4] Perhaps no one excels Matthew Arnold himself in the decorous and easy grace, in the unfought-for control and balance with which he performs the tight-rope walk between the standard and the judgement. In his work – it is probably his greatest critical achievement – there is an uninterrupted, supple flow of movement between principle and fact. But with whatever differences of emphasis or expression, these writers have sustained during the nineteenth and twentieth centuries, when other continuities have lapsed or are falling away, a common order of concepts unifying the past and present, and making possible a concerted effort of communication. They have been, that is, the promoters of consciousness, of connexion, of civilization itself. And they have kept alive the existence of standards and the reality of value, not by debate on the nature of these but by presenting them in operation, in the concrete, in action. It would be hard to find a better example of what Henry James again called 'the civic use of the imagination – a faculty for the possible fine employment of which in the interests of morality my esteem grows every hour I live'.

As a private person the literary critic is the ideal member of the audience which it is his purpose by 'the civic use of the imagination' to create. He is the model, alert, responsive, discriminating, of the qualified and attentive reader. But we have no warrant for supposing that there can be in any age more than a small minority of such readers. The mind, fitted by capacity, training and inclination to make this kind of reading a significant activity, is a rare one, even in periods when the conditions of civilization appear to be all in favour of it. 'It is the privilege of the few', said Coleridge, 'to possess an idea: of the generality of men it might be more truly affirmed that they are possessed by it.'[5] 'It is impossible', thinks Leavis, 'to question the clear fact: only a minority is capable of advanced intellectual culture.' And writing of the organization of education he repeats: 'It is disastrous to let a country's educational arrangements be determined, or even affected, by the assumption that a high intellectual standard can be attained by more than a small minority.'[6] We have no reason for undue dejection therefore when we note how closely Arnold's words apply to our own age: '. . . how little of mind, of anything so worthy and quickening as mind, comes into the motives which alone, in general, impel great masses of men.'[7] Civilization, or 'culture' in Coleridge's and Arnold's sense, has always been the direct concern and the immediate product of minorities. What is disturbing in our time, what has been a strengthening cause for anxiety throughout the nineteenth and twentieth centuries, is not that qualified readers are relatively few but the discontinuity between them and the body of society, and the lack of coherence and agreement among the learned class. The Victorians were probably the last able to address themselves with effect to an audience representative of the whole of society, the last able to assume among their readers both unity and range. These writers partially, writers before them more completely, gave expression to beliefs held by multitudes incapable of formulating them explicitly. But the serious modern writer, and *a fortiori* the modern critic, expresses only his own reconstruction of an evaporating ideal. He has to assemble the readers he would address, to create the audience he would advise.

The fissures so solidly established now, the fractures so brutally present here, were threatening a hundred years ago. In *The Literary Influence of Academies*, Arnold could claim that educated opinion existed here as it did in France; but he had to go on to describe the very different conditions it enjoys in this country. And his description shows that the ground was cracking already. Educated opinion in England was disrupted, 'provincial' from being remote from 'a centre of correct taste', lacking 'the lucidity of a large and centrally placed intelligence', without 'the fitness, the measure, the centrality' that comes from the active influence of 'a sovereign organ of the highest literary opinion, a recognized authority in matters of intellectual tone and taste'.

'It is not,' says Arnold, 'that there do not exist in England, as in France, a number of people perfectly well able to discern what is good in these things, and preferring what is good; but they are isolated, they form no powerful body of opinion, they are not strong enough to set a standard, up to which even the journeyman of literature must be brought if it is to be vendible.' 'A Victorian critic,' he says again, 'feels himself speaking before a promiscuous multitude, with the few good judges so scattered through it as to be powerless; therefore he has no calm confidence and no self-control; he relies on the strength of his lungs, he knows that big words impose on the mob and that even if he is outrageous, most of his audience are apt to be a good deal more so.'

And even before, Coleridge had no doubt but that the origins of dissent were planted deep in the past. 'After the Revolution,' he remarks, 'the spirit of the nation became more commercial than it had been before; a learned body or clerisy, as such, gradually disappeared and literature began to be addressed to the common miscellaneous public.'[8] In his view there were also revolutions of a different sort more disturbing in their effect than the openly political ones: 'There have been three silent revolutions in England: first when the professions fell off from the Church; secondly when literature fell off from the professions; and thirdly when the press fell off from literature.'[9] His account of his own period uncannily anticipates the state of affairs not only in Arnold's time but in our own. 'On the one hand despotism, despotism, despotism, of finance in statistics, of vanity in social converse, of presumption and overweening contempt of the ancient in individuals', on the other, 'government by clubs, committees, societies, reviews and newspapers'. And again, 'acquiescence in history, testimony substituted for faith, and yet the true historical feeling, the feeling of being an historical people, generation linked to generation by ancestral reputation, by tradition . . . this noble feeling . . . openly stormed or perilously undermined.'[10]

From the antecedents laid bare by Coleridge, in the conditions exposed by Arnold, comes the society which forms the context for the efforts of the modern critic and the modern educator, a society so divided within itself, so separated from the past as to suffer from 'a discontinuity of consciousness'.

On the one hand [says Leavis] there is the enormous technical complexity of civilization, a complexity that could be dealt with only by an answering efficiency of co-ordination – a cooperative concentration of knowledge, understanding and will (and 'Understanding' means not merely a grasp of intricacies, but a perceptive wisdom about ends). On the other hand, the social and cultural disintegration that has accompanied the development of the inhumanly complex machinery is destroying what should have controlled the working. It is as if society, in so complicating and extending the machinery of organization, had lost intelligence, memory and moral purpose.[11]

If this statement of Leavis does not exaggerate our plight and if, as we learn from Coleridge and Arnold, disunity of educated opinion is no abrupt arrival but a disorder in train over many generations, what remains to be called on in any effort of correction? We must invoke the remnant of our cultural tradition. 'I assume,' Leavis maintains, 'that the attempt . . . to restore in relation to the modern world the idea of liberal education is worth making because in spite of all our talk about disintegration and decay, and in spite of what we feel with so much excuse in our many despondent moments, we still have a positive cultural tradition.'[12]

If we are to address ourselves to what survives of our cultural tradition, we must do so by a deliberate effort of education. The continuance of tradition, together with the fostering of humane powers and civilized standards which it makes possible, cannot now, as it could once, be left to ancestral pieties, to immemorial rhythms or the intercourse of the like-minded. 'We are committed to consciousness,' says Leavis. What Arnold felt it essential to recommend to his contemporaries was an effort of mind, a quickening and refining of consciousness, the encouragement of a free flexible play of intelligence, without which 'a nation's spirit, whatever compensations it may have for them, must in the long run die of inanition'.[13] 'In an age in which artificial knowledge is received almost at birth, intellect and thought alone can be our upholder and judge,' insists Coleridge. 'Only by means of seriousness and meditation and the free infliction of censure in the spirit of love can the true philanthropist of the present time curb in himself and his contemporaries. . . .'[14] At such a time Coleridge considered it became a moral duty 'to raise into distinct consciousness' what in a more organic age might be left to the inheritance of traditional wisdom.

We have, then, to regenerate a declining tradition of civilization by an education for a finer consciousness. To state the purpose is to define the character of those for whom it could be significant. The object could only appeal to, the method be undertaken by, Leavis's 'intellectually given minority', Coleridge's 'possessors of ideas' and Arnold's 'small circle apt for fine distinctions'. When, as now, intelligence is so little of, so tenuously in touch with, the folk, the direction of remedial effort must be from the top down. 'But you wish for general illumination,' writes Coleridge. 'You would spur-arm the toes of society: you would enlighten the higher ranks *per ascensum ab imis*. You begin with the attempt to popularize science: but you will only effect its plebification. It is folly to think of making all, or the many, philosophers or even men of science and systematic knowledge.'[15] We have the testimony of Wordsworth that Coleridge habitually acted on this belief.

There are obviously, even in criticism, two ways of affecting the minds of men: the one by treating the matter so as to carry it immediately to the sympathies of the many, and the other by aiming at a few select and superior minds, that might each become a centre for illustrating it in a popular way. Coleridge . . . acted upon the world to a great extent through the latter of these processes.[16]

Efforts at indiscriminate education have as an inevitable consequence a debasement of standards; they make worse what they set out to correct.

And contemporary Britain, and America, demonstrate the force of Coleridge's anxiety. We may appropriate to the educational system of these countries what Arnold wrote about the British Constitution. It sometimes looks 'with its compromises, its love of facts, its horror of theory, its studied avoidance of clear

75

thought . . . a colossal machine for the manufacture of Philistines'.[17] Nor should we be much disturbed by the accusation that the view upheld here is 'undemocratic'. Democracy has much to tell us about the equality of moral value of men but very little to say about the equality of intellectual capacity. And capacity, intellectual capacity, is to be the sole measure regulating the composition of the *élite*. No one was a more inveterate opponent of 'the religion of inequality' than Arnold, but on this issue Arnold's opinion is firm and unambiguous:

> the mass of mankind will never have any ardent zeal for seeing things as they are; very inadequate ideas will always satisfy them. On these inadequate ideas reposes, and must repose, the general practice of the world. That is as much as saying that whoever sets himself to see things as they are will find himself one of a very small circle; but it is only by this small circle resolutely doing its own work that adequate ideas will ever get current at all . . . for the practical man is not apt for distinctions, and yet in these distinctions truth and the highest culture greatly find their account.[18]

The special education of an intellectual *élite* can only be 'undemocratic' if it is assumed that democracy entails the lowering of standards. 'And if democratic equality of opportunity,' writes Leavis, 'requires that standards should be lowered, then I am against democracy.'[19]

Nevertheless, it is possible to find some justice in the complaint of an anti-democratic bias. Substance and colour are lent to the charge by the perversion that passes in some places for the education of an *élite*, and not least, it is sad to say, in the ancient English Universities. (It is to the credit of the Scottish and of the provincial English Universities that they are relatively free of this particular malady.) The teaching of some influential members in these ancient institutions, the values they endorse, the aspirations they encourage, suggest that their ideal of an educated *élite* is a form of bogus metropolitan culture represented in a sophisticated guise by the Bloomsbury group. But the character of such a group, the *ethos* in which it flourishes, the ends it serves, the attitudes it professes, are a total betrayal of what the literary critic takes to be the essential properties of a true *élite*. The true *élite* is characterized by a deep sense of the gravity of moral issues as well as by a fineness in other discriminations; secure in its own coherence, it still looks beyond the confines of the initiate and acknowledges a serious obligation to society at large, a duty to promote and refine the quality of living outside as well as within the group. But in such a body as the Bloomsbury group, and even more in its pallid derivatives, strict impersonal standards give way to the pressure for social conformity; it acknowledges no obligation but to itself and cherishes its isolation; to savour the exquisite is its aim in art, to mistake moral obtuseness for neutrality or even superiority to the moral concerns of men is its practice in living.

Arnold felt impelled in his time to reject the lure of the clique and to warn against the infection it could communicate to the idea of the *élite*.

... let us have a social movement, let us organize and combine a party to pursue truth and new thought ... let us all stick to each other, and back each other up. Let us have no nonsense about independent criticism and intellectual delicacy. . . . If one of us speaks well, applaud him; if one of us speaks ill, applaud him too; we are all in the same movement, we are all in pursuit of truth. In this way the pursuit of truth becomes really a social, practical, pleasurable affair, almost requiring a chairman, a secretary and advertisements; with the excitement of a little resistance, an occasional scandal, to give the happy sense of difficulty overcome. . . . It is true that the critic has many temptations to go with the stream, to make one of the party movement, one of these *terrae filii*; it seems ungracious to refuse to be a *terrae filius*, when so many excellent people already are; but the critic's duty is to refuse, or if resistance is vain, at least to cry with Obermann, *Périssons en resistant.*[20]

In our day we note the force of the *élite* enfeebled, the power of the clique increased, and only very few resisting voices to be heard uttering Arnold's protest.

The processes of mass civilization had drastically reduced the number of critical organs and thus virtually abrogated the standards of criticism . . . [declares Leavis]. But it may still be wondered that there should have been, apparently, so little sense of what was happening, no protest, no note of scandal; certainly no resistance in places where one might have expected to find it. . . . And it has to be said further that in the literary world there was already an established tradition of coterie-power and of coterie-power as a dazzling, creditable and proper thing. It was a tradition that, in ways more and less subtle, tended to countenance the intrusion of social and personal values into the field of criticism. In fact, not only conscience, but consciousness in these matters had been gravely weakened.[21]

In these circumstances it is all the more imperative for the critic and the educator to be aware of the distinction between the clique and the *élite*, and to have not only a 'consciousness' of it but a 'conscience' about it. Otherwise the members of the *élite* he hopes to help into being will resemble those Cambridge apostles, of whom Leavis writes: 'They were able to take a fixed and complacent immaturity in themselves for something very different; and to associate an inveterate triviality with a suggestion of intellectual distinction and moral idealism.'[22]

To the literary critic, then, the clique is a substitute – in Coleridge's words – 'marked with the asterisk of spuriousness'; and as a spokesman for life the critic is keen to detect decay. Himself an accredited member of a genuine *élite* whose influence straddles the generations, he knows with the certitude of immediate acquaintance what belongs to and what is outside the *élite*'s true meaning and proper end. The affirmations of Coleridge on the nature and the purpose of the *élite* are argued for by the critic's own existence, are the conclusions of his own experience, proved in his nerves, his feelings and his taste. 'A learned order, a national clerisy . . . is an essential element of a rightly constituted nation, without which it lacks the best security alike for its permanence and its progress.'[23] 'The clerisy of a nation, that is its learned men, whether poets, philosophers or scholars, are the points of relative rest: there could be no order or harmony of the whole without them.'[24] 'The objects and final intention of the order are these – to preserve the stores and guard the treasures of past culture, and thus to bind the present with the past; to perfect and add to the same, and thus to connect the present with the future.'[25]

On this understanding of the idea of the *élite*, and assuming that the *élite* is to be nourished by a conscious effort, what should be the organ of its education? For Coleridge it is the Church, for Arnold the Academy, for Leavis the University. The term Church as used by Coleridge meant both the religious communions, or rather the particular communion Coleridge supported, and the organized body of learned men. 'If the former be *Ecclesia*, the communion of such are called out of the world, that is, in reference to the especial ends and purposes of that communion; the latter might more expressively have been called *Enclesia*, or an order of men chosen in and of the realm, and constituting an estate of the realm.'[26] There was no reason, Coleridge thought, why the ministers of one church should not also be the ministers of the other; indeed there were many reasons why they should be. Not even the most devout Christian could seriously hope to realize Coleridge's suggestion in practice today, the life of the Church now being, however regrettably, eccentric to the main sweep of a secular civilization. Its merit is its implied insistence, in the context of Coleridge's time, on the necessity for having an organ of education which is historically rooted, an active source of values, traditional and alive. The note of actuality is not the one most stressed by Arnold in his apologia for the Academy. Indeed, he concludes his essay by confessing the unlikelihood of our ever having an Academy quite like the French Academy. The best we could hope for were 'academies with a limited special scientific scope in the various lines of intellectual work'. In chaotic and depressing conditions his eye was on ideal possibilities, on the idea of the Academy.

The Academy is the nurse of what was desperately needed in Britain, 'a conscience in intellectual matters', 'a deference to a standard higher than one's own habitual standard'; it is the opponent of what is most at home, aberration, wilfulness, eccentricity, haphazardness, crudity, violence, blundering. The Academy, 'a centre of intelligent and urbane spirit', 'sets standards in a number of directions and creates, in all these directions, a force of educated opinion, checking and rebuking those who fall beneath these standards or who set them at naught'.[27] If we

associate Coleridge's requirement of an historical institution with
Arnold's conception of the educational possibilities of the
Academy, we have the grounds on which Leavis elects for the
University as the one established institution now capable of
educating an *élite*. In spite of Coleridge's dismissal of it as 'a
lecture-bazaar absurdly called a university', it is one of the few –
and among the few the strongest and most esteemed – of the
traditional organs of consciousness remaining in the modern
world. The University, says Leavis, is

society trying to preserve and develop a continuity of consciousness
and a mature directing sense of value – a sense of value informed by a
traditional wisdom. The Universities [he continues] are recognized
symbols of cultural tradition – of cultural tradition still conceived as
a directing force, representing a wisdom older than modern civilization and having an authority that should check and control the blind
drive onward of material and mechanical development. . . . The
ancient Universities are more than symbols; they, at any rate, may
fairly be called Foci of such a force, capable, by reason of their
prestige and their part in the life of the country, of exercising an
enormous influence. Much has been compromised there; there, too,
unconsciousness gains – it both spreads and deepens; but they are still
in more than form representatives of humane tradition.[28]

Within the University there is one discipline peculiarly concerned to encourage a finer awareness of the tradition, a discipline
which engages with the living growing tissue of the tradition
where it is most vividly and insistently present. This is the critical
study of the tradition alive in literature, 'the most intimate kind
of study, that is, of a concrete tradition'. Proposals are sometimes
made in University circles suggesting that our disunity could be
assuaged by the provision of 'general' courses designed to impart
a number of agreed opinions, or even an agreed number of
opinions. But the critical study of literature is neither an ideol-
ogical crusade nor a plan to enlarge a common stock of reference.
Its purpose is to train a certain kind of mind, and through a community of such minds to establish a centre, a centre of intelligence
and communication. There is nothing in this view out of congruity with the thought of Coleridge and Arnold: it follows from

their doctrine as a pertinent consequence in our circumstances. But it was left to our period to make it explicit and coherent. And in our period no one has written on this subject with keener lucidity, with greater persuasiveness or more justifiable authority than Leavis.

The *raison d'être* of the critical discipline in the University is to be, says Leavis, 'amid the material pressure and dehumanizing complication of the modern world, a focus of humane consciousness, a centre where faced with the specialization and distraction in which human ends lose themselves, intelligence, bringing to bear a mature sense of values, should apply itself to the problems of civilization'.[29] The mind required is to be formed, he goes on,

by a training of intelligence that is at the same time a training of sensibility; a discipline of thought that is at the same time a discipline in scrupulous sensitiveness of response to intricate organizations of feeling, sensation and imagery. Without that appreciative habituation to the subtleties of language in its most charged and complex uses which the literary-critical discipline is, thinking – thinking to the ends with which humane education should be most concerned – is disabled. And the process of evaluative judgement, implicit or explicit, that is inseparable from the use of intelligence in that discipline is no mere matter of taste that can be set over against intelligence.[30]

There are other studies, linguistic, semantic, philological, historical, of strictly subordinate and instrumental importance, which claim, or have even attained, the key position within the School of English.

All these candidates, both the more and the less respectable, are in relation to a School of English *Ersatz* [Leavis insists], and are to be resisted as inimical to the recognition and practice of the essential discipline. The essential discipline of a School of English is the literary critical; it is a true discipline; only in a School of English if anywhere will it be fostered, and it is irreplaceable. It trains, in a way no other discipline can, intelligence and sensibility together, cultivating a sensitiveness and precision of response and a delicate integrity of intelligence – intelligence that integrates as well as analyses and must have pertinacity and staying power as well as delicacy.[31]

In an age of illiberal technicians and technical humanists we have to develop a central intelligence, to train the accomplished non-specialist mind. For two reasons literary criticism is eminently qualified to be the discipline by which this mind is perfected. It is of course an integral study, informed by its own ends, possessed of its own methods, expressed in its own idiom. But the complexity of its undertaking is such that it is bound to take a ranging view of its function and to reject any rigid limitation of its sphere of interest. It is impelled at all times to go beyond its own frontiers into the provinces of other disciplines. 'One of the virtues of literary studies,' writes Leavis, 'is that they lead continually outside themselves, and while it is necessary that they should be controlled by a concern for the essential discipline, such a concern, if it is adequate, counts on associated work in other fields.'[32] 'The scrupulous and enterprising use of intelligence' which literary criticism excites and enhances is not to be confined to the literary mode. The criticism, the intelligent reading, of a single poem can set up an inquiry into the whole world which speaks in the poem, and this inquiry, while still answering to the control of every canon of critical relevance (if it doesn't, it isn't literary criticism or anything else worthwhile), is bound to be concerned with much that formally belongs to different studies. Some may offer as an object, what others would regard as a tribute, that this is to favour the merely amateur mind. 'Call him what you will,' Leavis replies, 'we want to produce a mind that knows what precision and specialist knowledge are, is aware of the kinds not in its possession that are necessary . . . and has been trained in a kind of thinking that is of its nature not specialized but cannot be expected without special training.'[33] The other characteristic of literary criticism which fits it so admirably to be the appropriate discipline for educating the free intelligence is that the powers it appeals to, the capacities it exercises, are those deeply involved in the serious conduct of life. Penetration of mind, tact of address, subtlety of response, concern to refer to a mature standard, deliberation in judgement and responsibility in decision – these are the qualities essential in literary criticism as they are those most required in the important commitments and refusals, elections and acceptances of humane living. 'The more advanced the work,' writes Leavis with relation to the literary critical student, 'the more unmistakably is the judgement that is concerned inseparable from that profound sense of relative value which determines, or should determine, the important choices of actual life.'[34] And bringing the whole argument to its climax he concludes: 'It is an intelligence so trained that is best fitted to develop into the central kind of mind, the co-ordinating consciousness, capable of performing the function assigned to the class of the educated.'[35]

But at this point one feels what Henry James called 'a rueful sense of affront to verisimilitude'. Because, as we all know, literary criticism as practised in the Universities is, with a few honourable exceptions, very rarely this or anything like it. The mood of these sentences should be the optative. And since, as Arnold said, 'We like to be suffered to lie comfortably in the old straw of our habits, especially of our intellectual habits, even though this straw may not be very clean or fine,'[36] it is clear that improvement, improvement vital for the health of society, will be brought about only by a determined effort of 'conscience'. But an effort of 'conscience' is blindly ineffective unless illumined by a greater 'consciousness' – to use again Leavis's pair of terms – and this is the justification for speaking of literary criticism as it might be, as it should be. It is to the honour of these critics that one can say of their work with justice and sobriety that on this issue as on so many others it serves both to awaken conscience and to enlighten consciousness.

CHAPTER 5

KEATS AND THE EDUCATION
OF SENSIBILITY

I

A LITERARY education has not been fully effective if Literature still means for the student an array, however splendid, of distinct and independent works, however intimately known. He needs also to cultivate a sense of the way in which many works compose a single literature, a sense of the common mind, imagination and sensibility which they, for all their variety, both express and help to form. Similarly, a reader has responded to no more than a part of the influence of a great poet when the poetry remains for him an assortment of individual poems. He must also come to see them as stages in a poetic career, bound together by their sources, their direction, their continuity and their purposes. This degree of insight into the life and movement of a talent turns a knowledge of the poetry from an acquaintance with it to a penetration into it, and the effort to achieve it is an imaginative experience which is truly educational. In extending one's conception of the range of human possibilities, it offers both a means of attaining and a standard of judging, a discovery of self. Above all it enables one to see, if only in glimpses and according to one's capacity, the total meaning of the work of a genius, to get a view of 'the figure in the carpet'. It renders intelligible the variety, the discrepancy, the stresses which the energy of genius makes it liable to. It is a clue to the allegory of a man's life. And as Keats said, 'A Man's life of any worth is a continual allegory – and very few eyes can see the Mystery of his life – a life like the scriptures, figurative – which such people can no more make out than they can the Hebrew Bible. Lord Byron cuts a figure – but he is not figurative. Shakespeare led a life of Allegory: his works are the comments on it.'[1] Keats's own works are also commentaries upon his life, reports on places gained and on those aspired to as well as acknowledgements of errors and misdirections. And as the word acknowledgements suggests, they have, since they are works of art, this advantage over reports and comments, words denoting opinions formulated at a distance upon events considered as objects: that the self is always implicated in them. Poems are at once chronicles of events and reflections of self. They are even more than revelations 'giving away' the self; they are activities which fashion what they comment on, which form and reform the image they reflect.

My intention in this chapter is to consider Keats's writings as comments on his life, by which I mean his poetic career, that astonishing passage from cockney to classic. An essential clue to the understanding of his poetic life, to the interpretation of the 'allegory', is, it seems to me, an educational one, since Keats's career is the most brilliant example in literature of the education of a sensibility. Rémy de Gourmont defined sensibility in these words:

Par sensibilité, j'entends, ici comme partout, le pouvoir général de sentir tel qu'il est inégalement développé en chaque être humain. La sensibilité comprend la raison elle-même, qui n'est que de la sensibilité cristallisée.

It is the maturing of such complex power that I have in mind when I speak of the education of sensibility – what Keats himself described as the effort 'to refine one's sensual vision into a sort of North Star'.[2]

'I am ambitious of doing the world some good,' Keats wrote to Richard Woodhouse. 'If I should be spared that may be the work of maturer years – in the interval I will assay to reach to as high a summit in Poetry as the nerve bestowed upon me will suffer.'[3] 'The nerve bestowed' upon Keats was a poetic endowment of an exquisite and powerful kind. It would be hard to name anyone in the nineteenth century with natural gifts of genius and character superior to his. Secure in their possession he could even hold as an axiom, 'That if Poetry comes not as naturally as the Leaves to a tree it had better not come at all.'[4] It will be useful here to reflect on the nature of Keats's poetic endowment. We shall then be able to form a clearer idea of the constitution on which 'education' was to operate, and to gain a juster view of the difference it was eventually to make.

Keats had from the first and kept throughout his life a marvellous sense of the particular. If he was in the line of those from Dryden to Hopkins able to release and control the energy of the language, he was also, again like Hopkins, of those who used this energy to reveal differency, oddity, the power of a thing to be itself. It was discrete objects – each glitter on each wave – which blazed for Hopkins with a strange individuality. For Keats it was a complex of events, felt to be one structure, but also suddenly seen as having an utter and fundamental singularity. The vivacity, the force of Keats's verbs, belonged to him as one of those able to unleash the activity of the language, but it was also a means perfectly adapted to press out the unique being, the proper quality, of each event.

Keats's experiences of the particular fed and sustained his poetic power. In a letter to Thomas Keats which describes a scene in the Lake District and which vividly produces the peculiar character of the place, Keats voices this very sentiment. In the same letter he uses an odd phrase, 'the intellect, the countenance' which carries the same meaning as Hopkins's 'inscape'.

At the same time the different falls have as different characters; the first darting down the slate-rock like an arrow; the second spreading out like a fan – the third dashed into a mist – and the one on the other side of the rock a sort of mixture of all these. We afterwards moved away a space, and saw nearly the whole more mild, streaming silverly through the trees. What astonishes me more than anything is the tone, the colouring, the slate, the stone, the moss, the rock-weed; or if I may so say, the intellect, the countenance of such places. The space, the magnitude of mountains and waterfalls are well imagined before one sees them, but this countenance or intellectual tone must surpass every imagination and defy any remembrance. I shall learn poetry here. . . .[5]

The attraction that 'this countenance or intellectual tone' held for Keats meant that he had an acute susceptibility for forms, for the particular self and structure of a thing, even when it was, in his own words, 'smothered with accidents'. This is a habit of mind or rather a specialization of insight often accompanied, as in many of the poems of Marvell or Hopkins, by an unusual intensity of feeling and a concomitant concentration of expression. Keats certainly believed in the theory that the excellence of an art lay in its intensity. But the qualities of intensity and concentration showed themselves only in the best of his poems since there was, as we shall see, another part of his nature which was infatuated by the drowsily vague and the languorously narcotic, which dimmed his clear eye for the object and betrayed him into the cult of 'silken phrases and silver sentences'. Indeed, Keats's career could be read as the history of the friction of these two elements in his nature.

But so vivid and so strong was this sense of the identity of others in his personal life, so intrusive his images of others, that, he reported to Richard Woodhouse, 'when I am in a room with People if I am free from speculating on creations of my own brain, then not myself returns to myself but the identity of every one in the room begins so to press upon me that I am in a very little time annihilated'.[6] And even when he was nursing his beloved brother Tom, so overwhelmingly was the impression of Tom's identity pressing in upon him that he had to leave the house to be free of it. Nor was his plasticity limited to the influence of human beings; 'if a sparrow come before my window I take part in its existence and pick about the gravel', and 'I lay awake last night listening to the rain with a sense of being drown'd and rotted like a grain of wheat'. We should err, however, if we supposed that Keats's extraordinary receptiveness to the identity of other things and persons was a mere quirk of temperament or an odd psychological idiosyncrasy. We should be as wrong to think of him as having an unduly passive or feminine nature. On the contrary his mind had, it seemed to Hopkins, 'the distinctly masculine powers in abundance, his character the manly virtues; but while he gave himself up to dreaming and self-indulgence, of course they were in abeyance'. And we know what Matthew Arnold meant when he said in his indispensable essay, 'the thing to be seized is, that Keats had flint and iron in him, that he had character'. His receptiveness was not just an accident of his life as a person but it entered into the substance of his life as a poet, as it did, we may remember, into the artistic lives of Wordsworth and Lawrence. Keats made an explicit connexion between this capacity for sensitive openness and the essential character of the poet.

As to the poetical character itself (I mean that sort of which, if I am anything, I am a member; that sort distinguished from the Wordsworthian or egotistical sublime; which is a thing *per se* and stands alone) it is not itself – it has no self – it is every thing and nothing – it has no character – it enjoys light and shade. . . . What shocks the virtuous philosopher delights the camelion Poet. . . . A Poet is the most unpoetical of any thing in existence; because he has no identity. . . .[7]

The poet's anonymity is far from being a mere vacancy, a weakness or a defect. It is the quality which goes 'to form a man of Achievement especially in Literature' and its varying intensity is what distinguishes the greater from the lesser writer. 'I mean *Negative Capability*, that is, when a man is capable of being in uncertainties, mysteries, doubts, without any irritable reaching after fact and reason – Coleridge, for instance, would let go by a fine isolated verisimilitude caught from the Penetralium of mystery, from being incapable of remaining content with half-knowledge.'[8] Upon the poet so endowed there lay, thought Keats, the duty, almost the moral duty, to be still, to contemplate, to wait upon the event. When he had written the following comment Keats with characteristically wry and pleasing self-dismissal observed that he might well have been deceived into offering as a general truth what was no more than a sophistical defence of his own indolence. Even so, he believed, his remark was the neighbour to the truth. 'Let us not therefore go hurrying about and collecting honey, bee-like buzzing here and there impatiently for a knowledge of what is to be aimed at; but let us open our leaves like a flower and be passive and receptive.'[9] And elsewhere he wrote: 'The genius of Poetry must work out its own salvation in a man. It cannot be matured by law and precept, but by sensation and watchfulness in itself. That which is creative must create itself.'[10]

In mentioning Keats's characteristic self-dismissal I am referring incidentally to something, in part a gift of intelligence, in part a disposition of character, which is sufficiently important – in that it brought an added strength to Keats as poet – to be considered expressly. I mean an unusual degree of self-awareness. To say this is not to impute to Keats a narcissistic self-interest. He does indeed offer many proofs in his letters of an ability for self-analysis, but it is of a detached and clinical sort, uncoloured by prejudice, touchiness or self-love. Nor was his self-knowledge distorted, as it was with Shelley by an excessive pre-occupation with the public or messianic role of the poet. No one was more purely or deeply dedicated to his art than Keats; yet he could write on occasion, 'I am sometimes so very sceptical as to think Poetry itself a mere Jack a lanthern to amuse whoever may chance to be struck with its brilliance';[11] or again, 'For although I take Poetry to be the chief, (yet) there is something else wanting to one who passes his life among Books or thoughts on Books.'[12] The tone of these remarks is as significant as the overt burden. In the one the nicely sceptical, lightly ridiculing note gives the impression of being the utterance of a sane and realistic mind. In the other the deliberate and reflective air of the judgement endorses the suggestion that there must be more than poetry to make the full life. In both we see poetry and the vocation of poet accepted as serious and important, and yet placed in a larger hierarchy.

The general characteristics of Keats's self-awareness are both humorous sanity and humility, a combination which permitted him a sturdy independence of merely fashionable influences or ill-disposed critics. 'I refused to visit Shelley that I might have my own unfettered scope,'[13] he wrote on one occasion; and on another, 'My own domestic criticism has given me pain without comparison beyond what Blackwood or the Quarterly could possibly inflict, and also when I feel I am right, no external praise can give me such a glow as my own solitary reperception and ratification of what is fine.'[14] Its particular features are quickness in recognizing the mixture of motives which impelled him and willingness not to rush to tidy them up into a neat and 'rational' pattern. He was confident enough to let his thoughts and motives lie in their puzzling ambiguity and patient enough not to thrust them into a false coherence. He could see the inadequacy of a Dilke 'who cannot feel he has a personal identity unless he has made up his mind about every thing. . . . Dilke will never come at a truth as long as he lives; because he is always trying at it.'[15]

The habit of mind revealed in these remarks derives from a fundamental quality of Keats's genius, a scrupulous fidelity to the object of attention whether this be a landscape, a constellation of feelings as in a poem, or the characters displayed in a quarrel between Reynolds and Haydon. It is perhaps not without significance that what I never called the *object* of attention Keats should habitually refer to as the *subject*. Poetry itself, he generalized, 'should be great and unobtrusive, a thing which enters into one's soul, and does not startle it or amaze it with itself, but with its subject'.[16] When he was conscious that he was deserting the subject, he rebuked himself in terms which show that keeping to it was for him a principle of his own intellectual life and a mark by which he judged the quality of other minds. 'I am continually running away from the subject – sure this cannot be exactly the case with a complex mind – one that is imaginative and at the same time careful of its fruits – who would exist partly on sensation partly on thought. . . .' A complex mind, thriving on sensation and thought, imaginative and careful, is shown in these lines from the beginning of the posthumous *Fall of Hyperion* :

> Fanatics have their dreams, wherewith they weave
> A paradise for a sect; The savage too
> From forth the loftiest fashion of his sleep
> Guesses at heaven; pity these have not
> Traced upon vellum or wild Indian leaf
> The shadows of melodious utterance,
> But bare of laurel they live, dream and die.

The tone of this passage has the unmistakable note of authority, the unstrained confidence belonging to a mind fully in possession of an idea, and aware with precision of its every implication. The opening announcement – 'Fanatics have their dreams' – is made with axiomatic certainty, and the body of the piece follows with the firmness of a logical conclusion. There is a significant structural alteration within the first four lines. The phrase 'wherewith they weave A paradise for a sect' follows unbrokenly on the first completed general statement; the corresponding phrase, 'From forth the loftiest fashion of his sleep', is interpolated into the second general statement, 'The savage too guesses at heaven.' The lines begin with an unqualified statement, are then enriched by the detail of two supporting but contrasting phrases – there is an element of deliberate design in 'wherewith they weave' opposed to the uncalculated process of 'From forth the loftiest fashion of his sleep' – and come to an end again on an unconditioned fact. The effect of certitude anchored in particulars is corroborated by the varying inflections of the rhythm. The pulse at first is strong and regular, quickens at 'wherewith they weave', slows at 'the savage too', accelerates for 'From forth the loftiest fashion of his sleep', and diminishes its pace to a collected conclusion with 'Guesses at heaven'. At the same time the sudden inversion of the beat at 'guesses' pulls the reader up, and subtly recalls the effort of the savage's guessing. The dry regret compressed into one word, 'pity', has been prepared for by the faint irony of 'A paradise for a sect'; and the subdued diction of 'pity these have not' makes an effective entrance for the mellow and peculiarly Keatsian music of

> Traced upon vellum or wild Indian leaf
> The shadows of melodious utterance

which here works vividly to recall the poetic tradition without which, 'bare of laurel' – the classical reference is beautifully in place and evokes no sense of the literary – men 'live, dream and die'. The last line is terse and severe and aptly so after the elaborate euphony of the preceding couplet. The restrained vocabulary and the rhythm broken by repeated implacable pauses increase the feeling of finality and deepen the power of the concluding word. By this point we have felt with intense conviction how the absence of literary tradition reduces the most human acts of the savage and fanatic to meaningless gestures, we have realized how man without it is no more than an unhistorical organism, casual and impermanent.

This is an illustration of Keats at the height of his powers 'keeping to the subject', an illustration of his capacity for apprehending fully and elaborating completely a poetic idea, and above all of following its every movement with utter fidelity. It takes a great poet to give the appearance – but here appearance *is* the reality – that he is allowing the impulse of his original conception to work itself out without intrusion, direction or manipulation, as though it were obeying some evolutionary law. In observing the operation of a mind of such stature one has very strongly the impression of the strange innocence of genius – strange in that it is aware of but unexposed to the temptations of the lesser artist. It is aware of them because it avoids them; it is unexposed to them because being avoided they are inconceivable. This experienced innocence, this impersonal serenity was far from being given to Keats. It was something he had to struggle towards painfully and through successive renunciations.

For Keats began his poetic life with a corrupted sensibility. The career of most artists moves from simplicity to complexity, or from uncertainty to assurance, or from illusion to reality. The direction of Keats's progress, in ironic contrast with that of his body, was from sickness to health. We often think of corruption as a state supervening on a period of health, or of decadence as the aftermath of vigour; but for the artist himself it can be corruption which comes first and health which has to be agonizingly striven for. And sensibility, a mode of perceiving, ordering, valuing and realizing experience, in part a cognitive, in part an affective operation, is far from being wholly within the control of the individual. It is very much an effect of collaboration both of the living and the dead. It is largely inherited from tradition, remote and immediate, and it is modified, not only by personal effort, but by family, formal education and contemporaries. When, as with Keats, tradition is in decline, family ineffective, education inadequate and contemporaries supine or uncomprehending, it requires gifts of genius and heroism of character, and both arduously and perseveringly developed, to arrive at that health and order which other poets in more fortunate times have started from.

The first works of a young poet are more frequently expressions of the intent to be a poet than exercises of a poet's powers. They are also, almost necessarily, derivative; in Keats's case the influence of Spenser is pervasive, not the homely, English and moral Spenser but the cultivator of the enamelled and the musical. These early poems also exhibit, often with pitiless clarity, the modes of sensibility current at the time. The character of those of Keats's time may be inferred from a remark in a letter from Haydon to Keats. (The remark was in fact made about *Endymion*.) 'I have read your delicious poem with exquisite enjoyment.' The influence of Spenser is one likely to play quite happily on poetry which is 'delicious' and designed to provide 'exquisite enjoyment'. The poems published in 1817 are generally notable for their lack of organization: of structure they have little more than the external verse pattern and a single generalization or introductory remark followed by a long catalogue of more or less pertinent examples. The characteristic mood is one of romantic pain, ''sweet desolation' – 'balmy pain'; the characteristic pose is one of indulgent relaxation,

> So when I am in a voluptuous vein
> I pillow my head on the sweets of the rose;

the characteristic place

> Some flowery spot sequester'd, wild, romantic;

those moments of the past are significant which produced an intoxicated retreat from the rough edges of reality:

> But many days have passed since last my heart
> Was warmed luxuriously by divine Mozart;

the staple of the idiom is composed of such phrases as these, warm desires, coy muse, quaint jubilee, curious bending, luxuries bright, milky, soft and rosy, luxurious wings, pleasant smotherings. The unexpressed premise of these poems is that poetry is a drug, a more refined form of alcohol. But 'art', says Santazana 'so long as it needs to be a dream, will never cease to prove a disappointment. Its facile cruelty, its narcotic abstraction, can never sweeten the evils we return to at home; it can liberate half the mind only by leaving the other half in abeyance.'[17]

Undoubtedly a part of Keats's mind, the more critical and intelligent part, was in abeyance during the composition of these poems. But not wholly so. There are moments when the indolence gives way to a more energetic, a more keenly apprehensive grasp, when the fumes of indulgence are dispersed by a fresher air. At these moments the verse shows a more biting sense of reality, a firmer rhythm, a more particularized sort of imagery, and a use of language at once more strenuous and more controlled. Here is an example of such a moment:

> A pigeon tumbling in clear summer air;
> A laughing schoolboy without grief or care
> Riding the springy branches of an elm.[18]

And here are other lines enlivened by an unpretentious gaiety and simplicity in the manner of Herrick.

> The stalks and blades
> Chequer my tablet with their quivering shades.
> On one side is a field of drooping oats,
> Through which the poppies show their scarlet coats,
> So pert and useless, that they bring to mind
> The scarlet coats that pester human-kind.[19]

There is that more modest, objective and very successful poem *On the Grasshopper and the Cricket*. The significance of these stirrings of a more complete, a more responsible mind and a less partial response to experience is corroborated by evidence of a more explicit sort. Keats was becoming aware that a poet could not remain content to loll a prisoner of his own senses; his sensations must be filtered through a judging mind and be informed by deliberate thought.

> though no great ministering reason sorts
> Out the dark mysteries of human souls
> To clear conceiving: yet there ever rolls
> A vast idea before me, and I glean
> Therefrom my liberty;[20]

(The trouble, of course, is that a due poetic relation of sensation to thought is not achieved by mulling over specific sensations in the light of a vast idea, as *Lamia* and *Hyperion* sufficiently show. A relationship more intimate and more informing is required, in which sensation and thought are not divided by the discrepancy implied in Keats's lines but exhibit what Coleridge called 'a coincidence of subject and object'.) Again in the Preface to *Endymion* Keats confesses himself troubled by just the imperfections we have noted:

the reader . . . will soon perceive great inexperience, immaturity and every error denoting a feverish attempt, rather than a deed accomplished. . . . The imagination of a boy is healthy, and the mature imagination of a man is healthy; but there is a space of life between in which the soul is in a ferment, the character undecided, the way of life uncertain, the ambition thick-sighted: thence proceeds mawkishness. . . .

Mawkish is too severe an epithet to apply to *Endymion*. It is not gross in any way. It is fluent, facile, sweetly insipid. There is no leading idea, unless we call Endymion's search for pleasure one, and little that is remarkable in the detail. It appears to be the result of no particular pressure and engages nothing that exists at a deeper level than the decorative. Its structure is vague, its development sketchy, its length (except that Keats took length as a test of a poet's powers) pointless. 'Long passages,' says Santayana, 'in Keats's *Endymion* and Shelley's *Revolt of Islam* are poetical in this sense, the reader gathers probably no definite meaning but is conscious of a poetic medium, of speech euphonious and measured, and redolent of a kind of objectless passion which is little more than the sensation of movement and the sensuous richness of the lines.'[21] The poem is without any intrinsic distinctions, the effect is mellifluous and trivial, it is impossible to take it seriously. It is a florid exhibition of that 'love of the picturesque' which Keats was later to abjure.[22] That it should be based on a classical myth is readily comprehensible. The classics, during the nineteenth century, as they ceased to have any real ground in the life of the nation, came more and more – and particularly for the half-educated and the emotionally immature – to be a source book of elegant grandeur and a reposi- tory of models of lofty greatness. They were incapable of being a spring of life or a means of realizing the deepest sorts of experience. The gods were reduced to literary jargon. This state of affairs is as different from that obtaining in the eighteenth century when the classics embodied a system and a traditional wisdom sanctioned by society, as the shapeless couplets in which *Endymion* is written are from Pope's.

There would be no need to qualify these remarks very radically to have them apply with equal force to *Isabella, or the Pot of Basil*. This is a poetical version of an anecdote drawn from one of Keats's favourite books, *The Anatomy of Melancholy*, itself an essentially literary and academic work, the purposes of which conform closely to the ends that Keats conceived at this time as proper to poetry. *Lamia* also derives from Burton and uses a myth with a long history stretching back in English literature to the late fourteenth or early fifteenth century *Thomas of Ercel-doune*. But *Lamia* differs from *Isabella* in that it is meant to present a serious idea; it is a poem written to the formula of the 'vast idea'. It is still plangent and melancholy but slower and fuller in movement. The poem endeavours to represent – but as in a tableau rather than a drama – the conflict between illusory beauty and the hallucination of pleasure and the life of the intel- lect and moral dignity. Lycius, the normal man, is caught and destroyed between the two. But there is an excessive dispropor- tion between the important ideas formally involved and the essentially literary idiom and manner. That discrepancy is abolished in *The Eve of St Agnes*. The poem is much less pre- tentious than *Lamia*: no vast idea rolls before the poet's eye. He remains within the limitations of a subject which gives him with- out pressing or manipulation natural opportunities for realizing his extraordinary perception of glow, richness and colour in the physical world. The exigencies of the narrative, slight as they are, control his delight in luxury and give it due subordination as one element in experience. Keats successfully resists the temptation merely to indulge his 'sensual vision'. The figure of Madeline, delicate and uncharacterized as it is, is more than an example of what Keats called the 'tendency to class women in my books with roses and sweetmeats'.[23] Throughout the poem the imagery has, even in those scenes which could easily become occasions for uncritical, relaxed indulgence, a certain quality of coolness and crispness and a scope of metaphorical reference which save it from any descent into the ludicrous or into mere sensuality.

> And still she slept an azure-lidded sleep,
> In blanched linen, smooth, and lavender'd,
> While he from forth the closet brought a heap
> Of candied apple, quince, and plum, and gourd;
> With jellies soother than the creamy curd,
> And lucent syrops, tinct with cinnamon;
> Manna and dates, in argosy transferr'd
> From Fez; and spiced dainties, every one,
> From silken Samarcand to cedar'd Lebanon.

'Azure-lidded' is keen and exact; 'blanched' and 'lavendered' introduce more than the purity of the linen; the gesture of bringing forth the gorgeous fruits from a closet encloses them in reality; the word 'lucent' really lets in light, and 'tinct' is minutely precise – signs that the eye is on the object; the references to Fez and Samarcand have a generalizing, idealizing effect, and 'cedar'd Lebanon' supports the whole with the grave authority of the Bible. The total effect is both rich and severe.

Between *The Eve of St Agnes* and the great Odes Keats was, it is clear, astonishingly transformed, advancing from the status of a charming minor talent to that of a genius of the first order. As I see it, that development is in essence a brilliant, profound and exemplary exercise in self-education. The fact that in this instance we speak of genius makes Keats's development more and not less suitable as a model for the rest of us, since genius is not a uniquely different form of humanity but rather a finer and fuller organization of it. I want now with the help of Keats's letters and largely in Keats's own words to trace the course of this development.

2

First, then, there is the primary poetic sensibility corresponding to the ordinary man's original endowment, 'the knowledge of contrast, feeling for light and shade, all that information (primitive sense) necessary for a poem'.[24] There is no doubt that there is delight to be had, both for the poet and readers, in the uninhibited play of this 'primitive sense'; but it is like the graceful, fluent gestures of childhood, supple but not subtle, free but not disciplined, exquisite but not serious. But no young poet any more than any young person becomes adult by the mere progression of original endowment. It also requires effort, conscience, thought. The man at a certain point in his life, the poet at a certain point in his career – it may be earlier or later – must make a fundamental choice, a moral decision. For Keats this radical election assumed a variety of forms. 'I think a little change has taken place in my intellect lately – I cannot bear to be uninterested or unemployed, I who for so long have been addicted to passiveness.'[25] Or again: 'I hope I am a little more of a Philosopher than I was, consequently a little less of a versifying pet-lamb.'[26] Or in another place: 'Some think I have lost that poetic ardour and fire 'tis said I once had – the fact is perhaps I have: but instead of that I hope I shall substitute for it a more thoughtful and quiet power.'[27] Perhaps these words put the choice most nakedly: 'I must choose between despair and energy – I choose the latter.'[28]

For every man who wishes to discipline his sensibility and refine his sensual vision, who wishes to graduate into adulthood, this choice lies at the roots of progress. It is a choice impossible to evade. If a person thinks he has evaded it, it merely means that he has chosen the lesser side, he has opted for passivity, despair and the perpetual arrestment of development. In and by this choice, a man decides against the volatility of impulse and for the life of reason which is, says Santayana, 'simply the unity given to all existence by a mind in love with the good'. The good will show itself to various people in their different roles under a number of forms, as poetry to the poet, as science to the scientist or to the ordinary man just as a happy and useful life; each of these may quite properly be a fit object of the life of reason. And to say that the life of reason belongs to a mind in love with the good is to indicate the two great streams of personal development. They are moral and intellectual. Sensibility itself is matured not by efforts aimed directly at sensibility but by becoming more piercingly informed by intelligence and less precariously an instrument of morality. (And what is true of sensibility for the poet is true for every interest and every brand of scholarship.)

When I speak of the double course of personal development, I would not wish to be taken as meaning that intellectual and moral development are parallel but independent. It is rather that morality becomes intellectually enlightened, and intelligence dignified by morality. Keats himself explicitly connected them. Describing his life's purposes, he wrote in sentences immediately succeeding one another: 'I find that I can have no enjoyment in the world but continuously drinking in knowledge. I find that there is no worthy pursuit but the idea of doing some good to the world.'[29] An interest, or taste, a category of scholarship, a poetic sensibility become disciplined in so far as they produce the peculiarly intellectual virtues, in so far as they lead to 'the ultimate morality of mind', which, significantly enough, Whitehead defined as 'style'. Sensibility, the intellect, the moral sense develop as a single existence, flow in and out of one another till they are indistinguishable. Or in Keats's idiom: 'Then I should be the most enviable – with the yearning passion I have for the Beautiful connected and made one with the ambition of my intellect.'[30]

What are these peculiarly intellectual virtues which compose the morality of the mind? The first is that consistent moral attitude which we call integrity. Whether in art or science, philosophy or religion, this is the recognition and acceptance of an order which must never be compromised by mere expediency, or disturbed by personal caprice, or sacrificed to any interest outside itself. It is the moral correlative of the coherence of reason itself, and the primary virtue of the mind. As Keats said : 'For that sort of probity and disinterestedness which such men as Bailey possess does hold and grasp the tip-top of any spiritual honours that can be paid to anything in the world.'[31] To preserve integrity – but of course it is not preserved, only continually recreated – is hard enough. It is harder still to maintain it without succumbing to the temptation it is very prone to expose one to, the temptation to make a holocaust of one's humanity before it. The danger of making integrity itself an abstraction, the danger of receding from the warmth of humanity into icier, remoter spheres, was a very present one to Keats. And perhaps to be aware of this danger is to anticipate it. 'All I hope,' he says, 'is I may not lose all interest in human affairs – that the solitary indifference I feel for applause even from the finest spirits will not blunt any acuteness of vision I may have.'[32]

It is the second great intellectual virtue which most effectively keeps the integrity of a discipline within its proper limits. This virtue is a double quality combining generosity and disillusion, tolerance and a tonic sense of reality. We find the two themes in perfect equilibrium, in the following comment: 'Men should bear with one another: there lives not a man who may not be cut up, aye lashed to pieces, on his weakest side. The best of men have but a portion of good in them, a kind of spiritual yeast in their frames, which creates the ferment of existence by which a man is propelled to act and strive and buffet with circumstance.'[33] Again in this passage we hear a cool dismissal of the pretensions of men: 'Very few men have arrived at complete disinterestedness of mind: very few have been influenced by a pure desire of the benefit of others – in the greater part of the Benefactors to Humanity some meretricious motive has sullied their greatness – some melo-dramatic scenery has fascinated them.'[34] But Keats's recognition of the impurity of human motives and of the part that *amour-propre* plays in human affairs never descends into a superficial cynicism of the Rochefoucauld sort. He goes on: 'As Wordsworth says, we have all one human heart – there is an electric fire in human nature tending to purify – so that among these human creatures there is continually some birth of new heroism.'

Keats's realistic diagnosis of human fact, his generous estimation of human possibility, goes, as one would expect, with a corresponding account, equally acute, equally liberal, of the specifically intellectual advance of the kind of mind which could become strengthened by these virtues. The following words, for example, are not a defence of universal scepticism – Keats was constantly making up his mind – but a vivid plea for range and catholicity, for intellectual sympathy and suspended judgement. 'The only means of strengthening one's intellect is to make up one's own mind about nothing – to let the mind be a thorough-fare for all thought, not a select party. All the stubborn arguers you meet with are of the same brood. They never begin upon a subject they have not preresolved on.'[35] 'An extensive knowledge is needful to thinking people', but there is no merit in it as such. It is an instrumental good; it is to be valued in Keats's view be-cause 'it takes away the heat and fever; and helps by widening speculation to ease the burden of the Mystery'.[36] On the other hand an extensive knowledge, when it is enlightened and arti-culated, is a demonstration in one mind, or better, a minute exemplification of the unity of all knowledge. To be aware of this truth is an intimate and personal way ('for axioms in philosophy are not axioms until they are proved upon our pulses'[37]) is both a stage in and a sign of intellectual maturity. 'When the mind is in its infancy a Bias is in reality a Bias,' Keats says, 'but when we have acquired more strength, a Bias becomes no Bias. Every de-partment of knowledge we see excellent and calculated towards a great whole.'[38]

But the knowledge which exists in any mind is never a mere aggregation of components. It makes a structure, even if only a fragmentary and disorderly one. It is also true, as Keats realized, that no matter how extensive the knowledge and how excep-tional the mind, its knowledge is organized under only one or two fundamental themes or interests: 'the two uppermost thoughts in a man's mind are the two poles of his world, he revolves on them and everything is southward and northward to him through their means. We take but three steps from feathers to iron.'[39] The intelligent acceptance of this limitation together with the sense of modesty and realism which it argues is a check to fana-ticism. 'The points of leaves and twigs on which the spider begins her work are few, and she fills the air with a beautiful circuiting. Man should be content with as few points to tip with the fine web of his soul. . . .'[40] Nor is this fact about the human mind anything which should lead to division either of man from man or of the specialist from the general body of the educated. 'But the minds of mortals are so different, and bent on such diverse journeys, that it may at first appear impossible for any common taste or fellowship to exist between two or three under these suppositions. It is, however, quite the contrary. Minds would leave each other in contrary directions, traverse each other in numberless points, and at last greet each other at the journey's end.'[41] Moreover, 'every point of thought', Keats insisted, 'is the centre of an intellectual world',[42] and 'when man has arrived at a certain ripeness of intellect any one great and spiritual passage serves him as a starting point towards all "the two-and-thirty palaces" '.[43]

Keats in describing his own intellectual development again and again stresses the need for activity, for effort and energy. He goes so far as to say that 'every mental pursuit takes its reality and worth from the ardour of the pursuer'. This insistence, which is, of course, related to what he feels to be the importance of the truth he is recommending, is also in part explained by the conformation of his own character and the disposition of his own talents, which were unduly susceptible to the attractions of luxurious indolence. But we should not be having Keats's full view if we failed to consider his insight into the other side of the question, namely, the importance in intellectual development in waiting, of not forcing the issue, of patience. Keats believed too that nothing is 'finer for the purpose of great productions than a very gradual ripening of the intellectual powers';[44] and although this may seem odd to us as we observe his own extraordinarily quick transformation, no doubt to him, a genius, it felt like a slow and painful progress. As well as the ardour of energy, a man, to advance intellectually, requires the quality I have already referred to, which he terms negative capability, and which is partly defined as the 'absence of any irritable reaching after fact and reason', the capacity to be still and receptive without any 'buzzing here and there for a knowledge of what is to be arrived at'. The ability to attend calmly on the gradual ripening of the powers of the mind is the intellectual equivalent of an attribute we find repeatedly referred to in Keats's letters as proper to a mature mind. That is the virtue of a rational humility. I say 'rational' because there is nothing servile or unmanly in Keats's idea of humility. 'I have not,' he writes, 'the slightest feeling of humility towards the public, or to anything in existence but the Eternal Being, the Principle of Beauty and the memory of great men.'[45] Humility, as Keats understood it, was positive and selective, neither a mere absence of pride nor a generalized feeling of inferiority. But if he stood in a position of dignified independence towards his audience, his attitude to it was also free from any infection of arrogance. 'I have not the slightest contempt for my species, and though it may sound paradoxical, my greatest elevations of soul leave me every time more humbled.'[46] To be humble towards those with a more inclusive view of life and finer vision of perfection, Keats thought, was to preserve the health of one's soul with the salt of sanity. Without it, a man was guilty of a mortal sin. 'There is no greater sin, after the seven deadly, than to flatter one's self into the idea of being a great poet, or one of those beings who are privileged to wear out their lives in the pursuit of honour.'[47] And since humility is a wide-eyed view of reality, to be without it is also to fall into the illusory and the unreal. 'Every man has speculations, but every man does not brood and peacock over them till he makes a false coinage and deceives himself.'[48]

Humility was part of the criterion – the names he gives themselves suggest it – by which Keats made a fundamental division of states of mind; and since there is a sense in which it is true of mental life that being follows on action, in which the mind is what it thinks, we may add by which Keats made a fundamental division of kinds of minds. Keats distinguished the frivolous from the serious, the anarchic from the disciplined mind in these words: '. . . there are two distinct tempers of mind in which we judge of things – the worldly, theatrical and pantomimical; and the unearthly, spiritual and ethereal. In the former, Bonaparte, Lord Byron and Charmian hold the first place in our minds; in the latter, John Howard, Bishop Hooker rocking his child's cradle, and you, my dear sister, are the conquering feelings.'[49] What the other part of Keats's criterion was *not* may best be conveyed by a phrase he used of a contemporary, Dilke, 'a Godwin-perfectibility man'.[50] Keats himself was not, nor was anyone he approved of, 'a Godwin-perfectibility man'. 'But in truth,' he said, 'I do not at all believe in this sort of perfectibility – the nature of the world will not admit it – the inhabitant of the world will correspond to itself.'[51] In spite of Keats's belief that there had been between Milton and Wordsworth 'a grand march of intellect', he did not interpret the experience of history nor his own life as a necessary, upward drive to the millennium. His sight was free from the myopia of unqualified optimism. Keats's letters are strewn with remarks critical of, sometimes caustically critical of, religion; which is perhaps not surprising when we remember the face religion wore in the early nineteenth century. But Keats himself had this in common with the religious mind: he was not con-vinced that even the most liberal intentions, the most candid cooperation, the best of goodwill could ever usher in an earthly paradise. For him, human experience could never be wholly and just a comfortable context for man to develop in. He believed in a certain constancy and permanence in human nature which would always transform human experience into something more diffi-cult and more intransigent. Human nature was such that human experience would always be liable to assume the form of a painful predicament. And the inescapable conditions of that pre-dicament were tension, strain and conflict within the soul. He held a conception of human nature and an idea of the significance of human life which were integral with those expressed in the greatest literature. He held, that is, the tragic view of life. It is the view of life which marks off the minds in Keats's second from those in his first category. And it is this conception of human existence, held not as an abstract proposition but as part of the stuff of its being, which Keats believed distinguished the mature from the undisciplined, the developed from the arrested mind. The tragic view of man modified Keats's attitude to the practical affairs of daily life, just as it provided the principle under which he organized his picture of the human situation. I will quote two passages in support of this last contention, the first a comment on the instability of human affairs, and the second Keats's famous simile of the human situation:

Circumstances are like clouds continually gathering and bursting – while we are laughing the seed of some trouble is put into the wide arable land of events.[52]

I will put down a simile of human life as far as I now perceive it; that is, to the point to which I saw we both have arrived at – well – I compare human life to a large Mansion of many apartments, two of which I can only describe, the doors of the rest being as yet closed upon me. The first we step into we call the infant or thoughtless chamber, in which we remain as long as we do not think. We remain there a long while, and notwithstanding the doors of the second Chamber remain wide open, showing a bright appearance, we care not to hasten to it; but are at length impelled by the wakening of the thinking principle within us – we no sooner get into the second Chamber, which I shall call the Chamber of Maiden-Thought, than we become intoxicated with the light and the atmosphere, and think of delaying there for ever in delight. However, among the effects this breathing is father of is the tremendous one of sharpening one's vision into the heart and nature of men – of convincing one's nerves that the world is full of misery and heartbreak, pain, sickness and oppression – whereby this Chamber of Maiden-Thought becomes gradually darken'd and at the same time on all sides of it many doors are set open – but all dark – all leading to dark passages – we see not the bal(l)ance of good and evil. We are in a mist. We are now in that state – We feel the burden of the mystery.[53]

These, then, according to Keats's reading of his life are the stages in the education of the sensibility; first a fundamental moral decision on the side of seriousness and maturity; next the long effort 'to refine one's sensual vision' by acquiring the virtues of the disciplined mind, integrity, generosity, disillusion or a sense of reality, patience, humility; then the recognition and acceptance of a mature conception of man, the view of man as at least potentially responsible and moral and therefore tragic and not wholly passive, conformist and perfectible. Some writers, as for example Coleridge with his philosophical bent, take such a development to be a growth in self-knowledge – which of course it is: an increasing understanding both of a common human nature as well as of that peculiar modification of it which makes each individual unique, a deepening apprehension of 'the all in all and the each in each'. But for Keats as poet the ontological preceded the cognitive; being was the ground of recognition. And in Keats's eyes the education of sensibility, the qualities engendered in the course of it, the interplay of various elements of human nature, even the circumstances of our life – all these are preparatory and subordinate not just to a fuller discovery of self but to its actual constitution. Every human life was spent in the struggle to establish what Keats called 'a sense of identity': the education of sensibility and the disciplining of intellect are only the most advanced, the least wasteful and most economically organized forms of a universal human effort, the effort to become a person, the effort of every character to become 'personally itself'. We are accustomed today, using a kind of discourse which has become thoroughly impregnated with psychological presupposition, to think and speak of human life as the development of 'personality'. (This misty, impalpable word was one that Henry James, an expert in the most exact shades of meaning, never used except tentatively and hesitantly inside inverted commas.) We are apt to suppose when we employ this idiom that personality is a more or less completed structure lying within us clogged by symptoms of immaturity and obscured by malformations of our nature, which it is our life's purpose to reveal in a clean and articulated coherence. Keats, however, placed his emphasis elsewhere. He did not think of the world as a clinic for correcting psychological disturbances nor as a dressing-room for stripping off various concealing veils, nor as an obstacle race in which we attempt to carry our formed personality through and over the irritatingly awkward conditions of our particular autobiographies. He thought of it rather as a place in which we alter nature, where we construct from our experience and whatever lies to hand a personal identity, in which we school an intelligence and make it a soul. Human life was 'a vale of soul making'.

I will conclude this section of the argument by quoting at length a remarkable passage in which Keats with a characteristic combination of enthusiasm and subtlety, buoyancy and acuteness gives his analysis of the genesis of a soul.

Call the world if you please The Vale of Soul Making. . . . I say Soul Making, Soul as distinguished from an Intelligence – There may be intelligences or sparks of the divinity in millions – but they are not souls till they acquire identities, till each one is personally itself. . . . How are these Souls to be made? . . . How but by the medium of a world like this? . . . This is effected by three grand materials acting the one upon the other for a series of years : These three materials are the intelligence – the human heart (as distinguished from intelligence or mind) and the world or Elemental Space suited for the proper action of the mind and Heart on each other for the purpose of forming the soul or Intelligence destined to possess the sense of Identity. I will call the world a School instituted for the purpose of teaching little children to read – I will call the human heart the horn book used in that School – and I will call the Child able to read the soul made for that School and its horn book. Do you not see how necessary a world of Pains and troubles is to school an intelligence and make it a Soul? A place where the heart must feel and suffer in a thousand diverse ways. Not merely is the Heart a Horn book, it is the mind's Bible, it is the mind's experience, it is the teat from which the mind or intelligence sucks its identity. As various as the Lives of men – so various become their souls, and thus does God make individual beings souls, identical souls of the sparks of his own essence. I began by seeing how man was formed by circumstances – and what are circumstances? – but touchstones of his heart – and what are touchstones? – but provings of his heart, but fortifiers or alterers of his nature? and what is his altered nature but his Soul? – and what was his soul before it came into the world and had these provings and alterations and perfectionings? – An intelligence – without identity – and how is this identity to be made? Through the medium of the heart? And how is the heart to become this medium but in a world of circumstance?[54]

3

The fruit of Keats's maturing mind and sensibility is the set of four poems, *Ode on Melancholy*, *Ode to a Nightingale*, *Ode on a Grecian Urn* and *To Autumn* written in 1819, the first three during the early months of the year. (The *Ode to Psyche* was also written in April 1819, but it does not belong in the same class with the others.) These poems are different in kind from their predecessors; while the earlier ones are merely decorative, these are tragic: they are enlarged, complicated by a dimension of human experience unknown in the former. Their distance from the earlier poems may be indicated by saying that while Spenser is the dominant influence there, here it is Shakespeare; and not Shakespeare as the supplier of external literary tricks like Shelley's Shakespeare in *The Cenci*, but a Shakespeare who is grasped, subordinated to Keats's purposes and dissolved in Keats's own idiom. To say this is not to claim for these poems, or for all of them, a complete maturity. Leavis defined the sort of inadequacy which persists in them when he said: 'It is as if Keats were making major poetry out of minor – as if, that is, the genius of a major poet were working in the material of minor poetry.'[55] And there are, without doubt, positive weaknesses in these poems, remnants of decay, touches of nostalgic softness and moments of regression to a less disciplined past. I can best illustrate this combination of strength and relaxation, order and impurity, by a detailed consideration of one of these poems, and for this purpose I will choose the *Ode on a Grecian Urn*. But first I must refer to the third great literary influence on Keats's poetic career and to the poem in which it is manifest, to Milton and *Hyperion*.

It is easy to see why Milton should have appealed as a model to a poet of Keats's character, and one engaged like Keats in an effort, intense and sustained, 'to refine his sensual vision'. (Not that Milton appeared as an artist actually undergoing this process of self-redemption, but rather that he showed what might be hoped for at the end of it.) There was a strong Miltonic current running in the eighteenth century, especially among those minor writers who were later to be thought of as writers of 'true poetry', the predecessors of Romanticism. Then, with the rejection of Augustanism, Milton came to stand for all that was lofty, epic and severe in the English tradition. He was the solitary giant, looming and self-sufficient, and the distracted second generation Romantics were profoundly impressed by his heroic individuality, his calm assumption of the poet's public robes, and the untroubled confidence with which he undertook his enormous theme. Above all he represented a poet in his role as moral teacher and spiritual healer. But although we can see *why* Milton should have attracted Keats, we can also see *how*, in the event, Keats's choice of Milton as an exemplar was a disastrous one, as Keats himself admitted when he abandoned his project: 'Life to him would be death to me.' No two poets could have been so radically different, so constitutionally unsympathetic to one another, no two poetic styles could have been so naturally antagonistic. While Milton was a man of solid certainties whose slightest prejudices were liable to be erected into dogmas, Keats was one who arrived at his convictions with difficulty and held them tentatively and fluidly. Keats's use of language which accommodated itself so easily to the influence of Shakespeare was denuded of all its proper virtue when associated with Milton's. The idiom which Keats elaborated – or fabricated – for *Hyperion* was neither genuine Milton nor true Keats; it had neither the 'beautiful curiosity' of Milton's language nor the palpable embodying power of Keats's. It was, says Leavis, 'a very qualified Miltonic – Miltonic as transformed by a taste for "Spenserian vowels that elope with ease". . . . The attitude towards the verse, the handling of the medium reminds us strongly of Tennyson.'[56] This is a judgement which the following lines vividly confirm :

> Goddess benign, point forth some unknown thing:
> Are there not other regions than this isle?
> What are the stars? There is the sun, the sun !
> And the most patient brilliance of the moon ![57]

The association of these names Keats, Milton, Spenser, Tennyson points to a discrepancy which lies at the heart of this poem. *Hyperion* was intended to be an extension of Keats's poetic experience, an effort in a new direction, and also a stage in his spiritual progress, an exercise in moral discipline; in fact, it turned out to be a contraction of the one and a retrogressive step in the case of the other. What was meant to be as strict and ascetic as Milton proved to be as ornamental as Spenser, as relaxed as Tennyson. What was designed to be a central commentary on human life disclosed itself as merely marginal and elegiac, not a vehicle for wisdom but a symptom of weakness.

The true line of Keats's development, lost in *Hyperion* in a waste of misdirected energy, misguided submission and frustrated purpose, is recovered in the Odes. These are the poems of a sensibility both powerful and exquisite, on the point of attaining its majority, on the point of completing its self-education. And because of this Keats is liable momentarily to be guilty of certain imperfections. But our recognition of these will only make us wonder all the more at the triumph of the spirit, the triumph of the lacerated spirit, which these poems, written at an unpropitious time and in the most tragic conditions, represent. I will attempt to substantiate this view by considering in detail one of these poems, the *Ode on a Grecian Urn*.

The *Ode on a Grecian Urn* was written during April 1819 at an agonizing time in Keats's life, when his money was nearly gone, his health undermined, his love-affair a cause of pain, his family dispersed or dead. If at moments the poem's lucidity as a work of art is muddied by unabsorbed personal feeling, this is hardly surprising. In Keats's circumstances the degree of detachment attained is not less than heroic. Such objectivity is not come by without a rare effort of character, together with an apt choice of the proper technical means. Here the remoteness of a part of the subject – the projection of imagination, that is, required to realize the Greek element in it – the complicated stanza pattern, the whole elaborate and formal structure of the Ode itself, are some of the means Keats chose in order to achieve distance and control.

But these comparatively external conditions imposed by the poet on himself carry only a general and predisposing influence. Closer to the poet's purpose, because more intimate with the substance of the poem, is the structure formed by the different kinds of statement out of which the poem is made. There are three sorts of statement used in the Ode, address, question and something vaguer which I shall call generalization or reflection. These three modes of statement are alike in this, that they all direct the flow of attention on to the object and away from the speaker. A vivid address, a provocative or surprising question, a brooding generalization compose a kind of discourse in which the pivotal points are the second and third persons, and the first is reduced to anonymity. This poetic use of syntax brings to Keats's rich language the authority of a more austere form of utterance, just as it gives the experience embodied in it a more than subjective validity. It is also an example of what Matthew Arnold spoke of in Keats as 'character passing into intellectual production'.

Of course, when I speak of a statement producing a general effect throughout a poem, I am speaking of a secondary function. The first function of each statement, phrase or even word is to produce a precise effect in a particular place. Look at the opening address of the poem:

> Thou still unravish'd bride of quietness!
> Thou foster-child of silence and slow time.

What this does is to provide a first term for the violent contrast which is the ground of the first stanza and the source of the rest of the poem: the contrast between the form of the vase, a perfect and unchanging definition, and the tumult of action inscribed upon its surface. The images in the first part of the poem combine to stress – but that is too harsh a word – subtly to present the vase's character of arrested and timeless perfection. In doing so they call, paradoxically, on a contribution from the three dimensions of time, from the immediate, the momentarily present in 'still unravish'd bride', from the possible and the future in 'foster-child of silence', from the past in 'Sylvan historian'. But Keats's symbols, like Shakespeare's, are habitually charged with more than single significance. The word 'still' keeps in simultaneous operation both the notion of enduring in time and that of tranquillity; the phrase 'still unravish'd bride' keeps in play both the idea of the present and that of uncorrupted innocence, a note which is continued in 'foster-child'. It is a foster-child too because it is from the hand of man, an artefact adopted by time; a natural object presumably would be just a child of time. The human quality is registered again in 'Sylvan historian', which also alerts the mind to the urn's expressive function, the urn as an organ of communication, something that is consequent on but different from its self or being, the theme of the opening couplet. The narrative or telling function of the vase introduces the next three lines, which present the content of what is told. There is another note sustained in this passage: 'Sylvan' is connected with 'flowery' and 'flowery' with 'leaf-fringed', the frame of the carvings of the urn upon the detail of which the poet's attention is now fixed.

> What leaf-fringed legend haunts about thy shape
> Of deities or mortals, or of both,
> In Tempe or the dales of Arcady?

'Legend' suggests first the mythical content, a development this of the sense latent in 'historian'; but legend also implies the intricacy of the carving – it is to be read to be interpreted and not just seen; the lightness of sound of 'legend' is carried on in the aerial and ghostly 'haunts about thy shape' and evokes the fineness and delicacy of the carving, a suggestion which is strengthened by the muted and exact rhythm of the whole phrase and by the sense in 'haunts about thy shape' of hardly touching the surface; the word 'about' involving a slight labial effort in speech and with a full and open sound rounds out for us the circle of the vase's shape.

The next two lines

> Of deities or mortals or of both,
> In Tempe or the dales of Arcady

make explicit the hint in 'legend'; they also quicken the pulse of the rhythm and prepare us for the extreme agitation of the last three lines; simultaneously, and this is a good example of the use of double and opposed potentialities of words, their cool freshness (as well as all that tangle of suggestion in Arcady) acts as a foil for the Dionysiac conclusion.

> What men or gods are these? What maidens loth?
> What mad pursuit? What struggle to escape?
> What pipes and timbrels? What wild ecstasy?

These six peremptory questions in a broken and tempestuous

rhythm powerfully enforce the sexual suggestiveness of the language, and complete, as it were by opposition, the note announced in 'Thou still unravish'd bride'. At this point the stanza has described a great unerring circle from peace to violence and from innocence to passion.

There is another quality of this magnificent stanza I want to call attention to. That is the marvellously plastic use of language by which the system of apprehensions assumed by the reader in response to the poet's words is a kind of model or metaphor of the physical structure of the vase, from its still centre to its turbulent surface. The language traces in the responsive mind the shape of the vessel; there is a second brilliant example of this essentially poetic power:

> Heard melodies are sweet, but those unheard
>   Are sweeter; therefore, ye soft pipes, play on;
> Not to the sensual ear, but, more endear'd,
>   Pipe to the spirit ditties of no tone:

These lines have not only a musical reference but a musical structure. The theme – the pre-eminence of the unrealized possibilities of silence – is announced in a generalization like a ground or bass; it is elaborated in a middle key, quicker, less deliberate, and then pointed in the words, 'Pipe to the spirit ditties of no tone', which have the clear and nimble melodic line of composition for the flute.

The word 'therefore' in the second line, 'therefore, ye soft pipes, play on', concludes a poetic and not a logical argument, or more correctly it completes a piece of characteristically poetic logic. In the first stanza silence symbolizes the timeless and unmoving, and music activity and passion. Now the poet reflects that this music carved on the urn is itself soundless, a possibility, never realized, of actual sound, a distillation of silence. At this point, music comes to stand for the perfection of the possible, for all that is superior to 'the sensual ear'. The second half of this stanza and the whole of the third stanza detail the conclusion and connect it with the instances cut in the vase, the fair youth, the trees, the bough, the happy melodist.

In this section, and particularly in the passage beginning 'More happy love! more happy, happy love!' there is, it seems to me, a decided slackening in the tightness of the poem's organization, a softening and blurring of its energy and precision. This is seen in the litter of Keatsian clichés (happy love for ever warm, a heart high-sorrowful and cloyed) and an unwarranted amount of repetition (the word 'happy' occurs six times in the stanza). The shrill insistence of the repetition shows, or rather shows up, the poet's anxiety to project a desperately desired state on to the object; he is betrayed under the pressure of his private condition into deserting his heroic detachment from self and fidelity to the object for the sake of personal psychological relief. There is a corresponding dimming of his critical conscience which leaves him unaware of the touch of caricature, of absurdity, in the table of the lover's symptoms (it seems the right term) which concluded the stanza. It is not without significance that these are of the hectic and feverish kind associated with Keats's own disease.

We must, I think, be conscious of an inartistic and too personal presence of the poet's self in this last part of the stanza; but we must also recognize the supple recovery of poise in the next one. There we detect the taint of sickness, here we feel vitality and control, the qualities of health. We are aware of vitality in the intensely realized, vividly rendered scene and in the deep, organic movement of the rhythm; we are aware of control in the poet's pure and disinterested attitude, in the kept distance and the designed succession of effects. The initial question – 'Who are these coming to the sacrifice?' – works both within and without the frame of events in the stanza; it voices both the bystander's awe and the reader's wonder, and its effect is to place the reader there in the front rank of the spectators. From that viewpoint he sees the procession as a brilliant figure on a darker ground – first the priest and the animal, then, less clearly, the more generalized crowd, 'those coming to the sacrifice', and more distantly still, the town, the generic town, 'by river or sea-shore or mountain-built' from which the procession comes. The detail is rich enough to establish the reality of the procession, and it is complex enough to be a verbal equivalent of the intricate decoration on the vase. It is also so finely, so economically organized, as to carry with complete lucidity a complex symbolic meaning. A commentator can only point clumsily at the meaning the poet offers with utter precision. I will call it fumblingly, inadequately, an association of the natural and the numinous. The business of associating these two starts at the beginning of the stanza: 'Who' quietly touches a note of surprise at the unusual; 'these' identifies them with us, the ordinary natural occupants of the world; 'sacrifice' is the destination which gives a tone to the whole journey; 'green altar' fuses the two elements; and 'mysterious priest' intensifies the feeling of religious solemnity. The association is completed in the following couplet, when the 'heifer lowing', the familiar farm beast richly suggestive of terrestrial good, modulates easily ('at the skies' is the transitional phrase) into the elected, sacramental victim, 'all her silken flanks with garlands drest'.

Keats now turns to contemplate the town, the point of departure of the procession and the familiar centre of a communal life which is intimate, explicable, accustomed. The idea connecting the natural and the numinous here, the small town and the dedicated victim, is contained in the phrase 'this pious morn'. Piety is a settled, traditional, humanized habit of religion, the bridge between the ultimate mysteries and the simple immediacy of everyday life, symbolized in the 'little town'. And how tactfully the poet lodges the suggestion that is to be the impulse of the next movement of the poem. The town is desolate, emptied of its folk, and appropriately silent. And it is this image of silence which the poet uses as a means of transferring our attention from the decorated surface of the urn, 'with brede of marble men and maidens overwrought', to its total pattern, the silent form which teases us out of thought and the cold pastoral which holds a permanent communication for men. Keats's reading of that communication, 'Beauty is truth, truth beauty', has been the subject of endless comment. For some it is meaningless, for others an utterance of a New Testament or Dantesque grandeur. But it seems to me that a modest and attentive reader, careful not to import his metaphysics or his prejudices into the poem, can accept it as something neither so outrageous nor so formidable. Keats distinguished between fact and truth; it was the business of the organizing imagination to transfigure the one into the other. And the equivalence of beauty and truth which he asserts here is an elliptical way, in place at this point in the poem, since this, the transfiguring of brute fact into imaginative or poetic truth, is what the poem has been doing all along, of making the same assertion. There is a relevant remark on this theme in a letter to Bailey. 'What the imagination seizes as beauty must be truth whether it existed before or not . . . the Imagination is like Adam's dream – he awoke and found it true.'[58]

But we are, I think, quite rightly disappointed by the intrusive and over-anxious last line and a half.

> that is all
> Ye know on earth, and all ye need to know.

Even if we interpret the statement as sympathetically as possible, taking 'that is all' to mean 'that is the finally important thing', it still looks like an effort, ungainly and unjustified, to inflate the dignity of the poem's conclusion. It is ungainly for it suddenly puts on the poet the necessity of taking up quite a new stance and arguing a case directly. It is unjustified because it doesn't issue irresistibly from what has gone before. Keats's design on us may not be palpable at this moment but it certainly leaves us suspicious and uneasy.

The complete maturity so earnestly laboured at in Keats's life, so lucidly and persuasively theorized about in his letters, is wholly realized in Keats's art in the ode *To Autumn*. In this poem we see genius having at its disposal a perfected sensibility. Keats's meditations on maturity, his efforts to achieve it, here issue into a disciplined poetic act. The poem exhibits, like the best romantic poems, a radically original, first-hand response to experience, and exhibits it moreover with the characteristic Keatsian virtues of density and definition, weight and pressure. Autumn in this poem is neither attenuated by customary perception or conventional expectation, nor idealized away – as in other romantic poetry – into a thin and misty abstraction. Keats's art shows us not an ideogram, not the pictured structure of the season, but its dimensions and complex savour. For it gives us not only the full-ness and softness of autumn – the ripeness of it – but also its more masculine qualities, the acrid, the rough and the vigorous. Or rather it embodies a more inclusive conception of ripeness. Not only does it offer mellow fruitfulness and clammy cells, the fume of poppies and the last oozings, but also the moss'd cottage-trees, the granary floor, the brook, the cyder press, the stubble-plains, the small gnats and the river sallows. By this point in his career, it is clear that ripeness had come to be for Keats both a varied and an ordered concept. It represented a rich fund of experience which had been examined and weighed by a scrupulously just and delicately balanced mind. It is no accident that the ripeness which is the theme of the poem should stand in so close an analogy to the maturity which is the theme of Keats's moral and intellectual life. In this poem maturity is both achieved and trans-cended. Keats's poem gives us the right to use a dangerous and difficult word. It gives us a sanction for saying that here maturity is transformed into wisdom.

CHAPTER 6

G. M. HOPKINS AND A SENSE
OF THE PARTICULAR

PROBABLY most of us would agree that the purpose of a teacher is to guide his pupil towards new and richer experience, towards eliciting the meaning of that experience and composing it into a coherent pattern, with the aim finally of increasing the pupil's power of action. Education, that is, begins with the particular, goes on to theory in the widest sense, namely the study of structure and organization, and concludes again in a heightened sense of the particular. If it does not begin with the particular, then it will not be personally significant to the pupil; if it does not go on to a general explanation, then it will not extend consciousness and promote the grasp of principle but merely inculcate a clumsy rule of thumb; if it does not bring about increased power over the particular, then it will be no more than theoretical and academic in the worst way. In this chapter I want to discuss what is meant by a sense of the particular as the origin and conclusion of educational activity. I propose to do this by inquiring into the mind and practice of Gerard Manley Hopkins, a poet endowed in the most extraordinary way with the strong and subtle feeling for the concrete and particular.

If we examine a characteristic passage of Hopkins, even of his simpler verse, we see a highly developed sense of the particular operating poetically. Look for instance at the familiar *Pied Beauty*.

Glory be to God for dappled things –
  For skies of couple-colour as a brinded cow;
    For rose-moles all in stipple upon trout that swim;
Fresh-firecoal chestnut-falls; finches' wings;
  Landscape plotted and pieced – fold, fallow, and plough;
    And all trades, their gear and tackle and trim.

> All things counter, original, spare, strange;
>   Whatever is fickle, freckled (who knows how?)
>   With swift, slow; sweet, sour; adazzle, dim;
>   He fathers-forth whose beauty is past change:
>   Praise him.

The imperative (a significant mood in Hopkins which I shall comment on in a moment) in the opening phrase, 'Glory be to God', performs a double duty; it is first and emphatically a desire that glory be accorded to God, but it is also an implied statement that glory is in fact given to God. What yields Him glory is the peculiar blend of existence, the oddly composite and distinctive character possessed by each of the details in the body of the piece. These details, each with its singularity and difference exquisitely evoked, are not arranged according to any rules of formal or discursive logic. And yet there is implicit in their combination an order of sensibility, a poetic logic which is, as Coleridge says, 'the more severe because the more fleeting'. That logic, one can see, provides a double principle of organization.

In the first place each detail is so qualified as to make us conscious of it at the moment of its first discovery by the eye: 'couple-coloured as a brinded cow' and 'rose-moles all in stipple' are phrases which expose each a unique and intimate form of being as it is originally apprehended by the delighted sight. Moreover, the succession of details rehearses the movement of the eye as it flickers over the landscape inward from the horizon and downward from the sky, striking on the trees and the birds and coming to rest on 'fold, fallow and plough'. In the second place these details compose a tiny, vivid image of a tradition of thought, the traditional conception of the scale of being. In a terse, compressed and yet sufficient manner, many rungs of the ladder of reality are touched or pointed to here, inanimate nature and vegetation, the sentient world of birds and animals, and the crown of creation, man, the plotter of the landscape and the user of gear and tackle. The same set of words succeeds in presenting to us the object of the primary, untutored sensibility *and* an array of objects organized and informed by 'thought' or 'theory', by an intellectual tradition. We see the original sense experience, then the theory, the explanation which gives it coherence, and finally the result, a more penetrating sense of the 'counter, original, spare, strange'.

The structure – or rather the action in the dramatic sense, for it is a vital, moving structure – implicit in these lines is repeated and amplified in the poem as a whole. It is amplified in that it begins at a stage further back and concludes at a stage further on. It starts with feeling and ends with action. The opening imperative – a device not uncommon in Hopkins – works to convey that strength of feeling, of delight and excitement (or 'interest' as we should say in the colourless language of education) which first sets the sensibility and the mind in motion. An intense and relevant feeling is, as Hopkins says in his *Sonnet to R. B.*, the force that generates mental experience:

> The fine delight that fathers thought; the strong
> Spur, live and lancing like the blowpipe flame.

Then the provoked and directed eye comes to grips with its various, highly individualized objects, and we are shown these slowly being informed by an organizing theory, by implicit generalization in the lines I have commented on, by explicit generalization in those which follow:

> All things counter, original, spare, strange;
> Whatever is fickle, freckled (who knows how?)
> With swift, slow; sweet, sour; adazzle, dim;

And lastly with all this ancestry of experience caught up and made available, with thought prepared for by sensibility and sensibility enlightened by explanation (a continuity beautifully realized in the complex and flowing syntax of

> He fathers-forth whose beauty is past change:)

the poem concludes decisively in action: 'Praise him'. That abrupt concise phrase wheels round on the grammatical intricacy preceding it and renders the simplicity and finality of action.

Pied Beauty shares in a community of intention with other poems of Hopkins in which an important part of the purpose is to present the mind grappling with reality. These poems – *The Windhover* is probably the greatest example – delineate, or dramatize, the action of understanding, from its inception in the particular, through its use of generalization, up to its issue into concrete action. In the act of knowing, as it is rendered in these poems, we find engaged two distinct impulses of the mind which are related by a mutual tension and support. They are an eagerness to light on the highest degree of individuality of things and a concern to generalize, to establish an order of thought among the particulars. On the intimacy of union of these two, the richness of the first, the relevance and adequacy of the second, depends the completed act of understanding. It is the nature of the poetic intelligence, as we see with great clarity in the poetry of Hopkins, to give us the wholeness of the act of knowing. It is this which makes it so salutary a corrective in education, where we fall continually into the error of identifying understanding – and especially trains of understanding or reasoning – with one component of understanding, the generalizing, systematizing element, and neglect what it should be grounded in, a sense of the particular, as well as what it should return to, a still more heightened sense of the particular.

Not that the mere remarking of details is any guarantee of a sense of the particular, either as that out of which knowing begins or that to which, in a finer form, it returns. This may be no more than 'minute upholstery' as Hopkins called it, 'an impotent collection of particulars'. Each detail must be so seen, and in art so presented, as to imply an essential truth about its own being, and there must be some significance in the aggregate of details, some point which raises it from a collection to an order (as there wasn't, Hopkins pointed out, when Browning observed that the names Wiseman, Manning, Newman, all contained the word man). It is its closeness to the essential object and its part in contributing to a significant whole which give any one detail a claim to express a true sense of the particular. The essential reality of the object will be more muffled, less clearly and precisely revealed, the significance of the pattern less inclusive, in a primary than a secondary sense of the particular (to distinguish it before and after generalization). But these marks will still be present, partially and imperfectly, it is true, but still there, the active residue of former acts of understanding.

With this said, it still remains the case that our primary sense of the particular – our observation of a new fact, our response to a new person or truth – is relatively gross, relatively erratic. It may be blurred by inappropriate preconception, or distorted by conventional expectation, or dimmed by reminiscence, by those echoes which Hopkins said were 'a disease of education'. 'When a new thing . . . is presented to us our first criticisms,' Hopkins wrote to Bridges, 'are not our truest, best, most heartfelt, or most lasting but what come easiest on the instant. They are barbarous and like what the ignorant and the ruck say.'[1] It is reflection and generalization – or reasoning – which rescue our first impression from being what it often is, an echo of 'what the ignorant and the ruck say'.

It is a common misapprehension that we go to poetry not for reasoning but for feeling. The ground of this belief is our tendency to narrow the meaning of 'reasoning' to the more abstract and technical uses of intelligence like the logician's or the scientist's. But we are all reasoners, and few of us are logicians.

For everyone [said Hopkins] arrived at the age of reason asks Why and sometimes says Because and Although. Now when we use these three words we reason. Longer trains of reasoning are rarer, because life does not present the need or opportunity for them; but as soon as the matter requires them they are forthcoming. Nor are blunders in reasoning any proof that man is not a rational or reasoning being, rather the contrary: we are rational and reasoners by our false reasonings as we are moral agents by our sins.[2]

Everyone reasons, and not least the poet. Indeed, our dissatisfaction with some poetry comes from our sense of its lacking swift and active intelligence: such poetry, said Hopkins – he said it of Morris – is 'desolately limited'. And the poet's kind of reasoning, just because it is unprofessional and untechnical, because it is dense with particulars, and moves on a pulse of feeling, because it is sinuous and circling, is a better model of, corresponds more closely to, the actuality of human reasoning than the cooler, more directed and systematic reasoning of the philosophic or scientific mind. Or, as Lawrence said in his essay on Verga:

> It is a psychological fact that when we are thinking emotionally or passionately, thinking and feeling at the same time, we do not think rationally: and therefore, and therefore, and therefore. Instead the mind makes curious swoops and circles. It touches the point of pain or interest, then sweeps away again in a cycle, coils round and approaches again the point of pain or interest.[3]

It is such informal, untechnical reasoning that we find in poetry, and it is a similar use of intelligence which in the mass of our experience transforms our first raw response into a surer and more exact sense of the particular. A developed sense of the particular is the mind's instrument for discovering in what is new, and for recovering in what is familiar, that in any object of attention which marks it off from every other form of existence. It strives to light on the singular and the distinctive. This general human capacity was heightened in Hopkins to such a degree that it became the centre of his genius. His sense of nuance and distinction was extraordinarily acute, and he conveyed it, unlike many similarly endowed, with a masculine authority and force. Power in communication, delicacy in discrimination – these were, he thought, two essential qualities of the poet. He describes the first, which he calls 'masterly execution', as a kind of male gift, 'the begetting one's thoughts on paper; the life must be conveyed into the verse and displayed there, not suggested as having been in the artist's mind'.[4] The second, the sensitive feeling for individuality, he recognized as the peculiar note of his own talent. 'But as air, melody, is what strikes me most in music and design in painting, so design, pattern or what I am in the habit of calling "inscape" is what above all I aim at in poetry. Now it is the virtue of design, pattern or inscape to be distinctive.'[5] And he continues with his accustomed lucidity and refreshing frankness about himself to recognize further that his bias also contained possibilities of weakness. 'And it is the vice of distinctiveness to become queer. This vice I cannot have escaped.'

Certainly some of Hopkins's verse exhibits the vice of queerness – a riot of uncontrolled detail – but as much, or more, brilliantly exemplifies the virtue of distinctiveness. Here is a passage of the latter sort which has the added advantage in the present context of dealing explicitly with the theme of singularity and distinctiveness, the power of a thing to be its own unique, marked-off self.

> As kingfishers catch fire, dragonflies draw flame;
> As tumbled over rim in roundy wells
> Stones ring; like each tucked string tells, each hung bell's
> Bow swung finds tongue to fling out broad its name;
> Each mortal thing does one thing and the same:
> Deals out that being indoors each one dwells;
> Selves – goes itself; *myself* it speaks and spells,
> Crying *What I do is me: for that I came.*

We ought in attending to these lines to recall Hopkins's advice to Bridges as to how his poetry should be read, 'but take breath and read it with the ears, as I always wish to be read, and my verse becomes all right'. I say this because, as in speech, the unit of meaning and of rhythm here is the phrase, which is to be detected and measured chiefly by the ear. And what connects the phrases in these lines, what is the principle of progression in the piece, is the increasing volume and resonance of sound. The light treble of 'As kingfishers catch fire', the alto of 'dragonflies draw flame' enacts in sound the clean flight of the brilliant bird, the slightly more impeded motion of the gleaming insect. This treble-alto differentiation is subtly enforced by the muscular effort of articulation; the k and c in the first phrase being formed higher in the mouth than the dentals in the second phrase. 'As tumbled over rim in roundy wells Stones ring' is in the middle register, and the sound and the strong break in the phrase reproduce the diminishing clatter of the falling stone. Then 'each tucked string tells' is a viola sound preparing the ear for the great bass of the swung bell.

Having established his array of particulars, and having by these 'musical' means indicated an implicit organization among them, the poet then by a natural movement of intelligence goes on to unify them more closely by an explicit generalization.

> Each mortal thing does one thing and the same:
> Deals out that being indoors each one dwells;
> Selves – goes itself; *myself* it speaks and spells,
> Crying *What I do is me: for that I came.*

The form the generalization takes – the impetuous utterance, the emphatic but broken rhythm, the urgency disturbed by check and hesitation, and the final clinching certainty – reconstructs the action of Lawrence's 'impassioned intelligence', 'thinking and feeling at the same time'. There is, the poet realizes, a truth latent in the details so vividly summoned in the first quatrain, and the second gives us not a conclusion deduced from premises but the process of realization itself. The variety of effect which the senses appreciate is an extension into the common world of a host of different identities; it is proof of what Lawrence again speaks of as 'the marvellous plurality of being'. There is a comment in another letter of Hopkins which although it represents only part of the 'meaning' of the poem, yet throws light on the conception the poet is bringing to birth here. He calls it, in his odd, personal idiom, 'sake'. 'I mean by it the being a thing has outside itself, as a voice by its echo, a face by its reflection, a body by its shadow, a man by his name, fame or memory, *and also* that in the thing by virtue of which especially it has this being abroad, and that is something distinctive, marked, specifically or individually speaking. . . .'[6]

A matured sense of the particular, then, meant for Hopkins having a double consciousness towards an object: an awareness of 'the being a thing has abroad', its echo, reflection, effect, together with an awareness of 'that being indoors each one dwells', a sense of the thing's distinctive self. To us this may seem rather too fine, rather too brittle a distinction. But the care with which Hopkins drew it both in prose and verse, and the force with which he expounded it, suggest that it is in keeping with a strong bias of Hopkins's nature. And my feeling is that this tendency is present, no doubt clumsily and obscurely present, in every man. In the case of Hopkins we may take it as a metaphysical preoccupation; in the rest of us it will be more accurate to call it a metaphysical groping. It is said that the problems of metaphysics may all be reduced to the fundamental problem of the one and the many. Certainly the tension between the two is a frequent theme, often submerged, sometimes overt, in Hopkins's verse. (Hopkins may indeed be called a metaphysical poet in the strict sense defined by James Smith in his well-known essay *On Metaphysical Poetry*[7] where he lays down a concern with this theme as the distinguishing note of the true metaphysical poet.) The mind, Hopkins believed, even when it is wrestling with the finest kind of particularity, simultaneously aspires to the most abstract and general realization; the manifold shades and differences of existence are supported and held together by an ultimate unity. The unique depends upon the universal. To Hopkins, of course, as a poet, it is not a 'problem', but a state of affairs which adds immensely to the significance and richness of life. His habit is to indicate the intimacy of the two by making a statement about one which is equally a statement about the other. For example, the line in the present poem, 'Each mortal thing does one thing and the same', is both an exact declaration about a particular thing and a statement of the highest generality. Or again in *Pied Beauty* the lines

> All things counter, original, spare, strange;
> Whatever is fickle, freckled (who knows how?)

convey with great dexterity the double movement of the mind. The epithets, counter, original, spare, strange, etc., are at one and the same time limiting, confining predicates, carrying the meaning, All things *which* are counter, original, spare, strange; but they are also enlarging, generalizing epithets carrying the further meaning, All things *are* counter, original, spare, strange. In the most developed sense of the particular the first understanding is transformed into the second, or rather the two are held in a creative tension.

It was thus that Hopkins showed the mind, at its most intent and acute, engaging with reality. His best poems are a dramatic analysis of the moment of engagement. Reality is a word impossible to avoid when one is speaking of Hopkins. Duns Scotus, the philosopher he preferred to Aristotle and to 'a dozen Hegels', appealed to him so much because he was 'Of realty the rarest-veined unravellers'. His conception of reality was a governing influence on his poetry. For Hopkins, the world for all its mystery (and he had a keen sense of that) and all its horror (and no one who has read his accounts of his pastoral work in industrial Lancashire or the ignominy of the working class in Victorian Britain can doubt his acquaintance with this side of life), the world for all that was still a rational order. Even his intense and ecstatic religious experience had its place in a reasonable scheme of things. The presence of God – 'The world is charged with the grandeur of God' – which he felt so strongly did not dilute or obliterate any savour of the natural world; God was its ground or cause or purpose, but always the divine was connected to the material order by an intelligible relation. When Hopkins writes:

> Summer ends now; now, barbarous in beauty, the stooks arise
> Around; up above, what wind-walks! what lovely behaviour
> Of silk-sack clouds! . . .

nothing could be more natural, more reasonable, than the beginning of the next part of the poem,

> I walk, I lift up, I lift up heart, eyes,
>   Down all that glory in the heavens to glean our Saviour.

A vigorous air of sanity breathes through all that Hopkins wrote. It is in part the product of his general conception of the reasonableness and order of reality, in part the consequence of his own sense of the particular, a faculty which was in him a fine and inclusive sense of reality, a genius for actuality. Hopkins brought this idea and this sense into play in a multitude of ways, for both were deeply implicated in his standard of value. 'The worst fault a thing can have,' he said, 'is unreality';[8] and again he remarked, 'This leads me to say that a kind of touchstone of the highest or most living art is seriousness: not gravity but the being in earnest with your subject – reality.'[9] It was his concern with actuality which made him so opposed to archaism in art – 'we do not speak that way; therefore if a man speak that way he is not serious, he is at something else than the seeming matter in hand, *non hoc agit, aliud agit*'.[10] And so, he insisted, 'the poetical language of an age should be the current language heightened, to any degree heightened and unlike itself, but not . . . an obsolete one'.[11] Only in a contemporary language – the actual verbal equivalent of reality – could the poet practise an essential part of his art, 'the art or virtue of saying everything right *to* or *at* the hearer, interesting him, holding him in the attitude of correspondent or addressed or at least concerned, making it everywhere an act of intercourse'.[12] It was his conviction of the unrivalled capacity of literature to sharpen a sense of concrete realities which led him to utter a warning on the dangers of the exclusive study of the physical sciences. And it must be remembered that Hopkins was a man intensely interested in science, one of the few poets surely ever to have had communications published in *Nature*.

The study of physical science has, unless corrected in some way, an effect the very opposite of what one would suppose. One would think it might materialize people . . . but in fact they seem to end in conceiving only of a world of formulas, with its being properly speaking in thought, towards which the outer world acts as a sort of feeder, supplying examples for literary purposes. And they go so far as to think the rest of mankind are in the same state as themselves.[13]

Those who want a literary component in the scientist's education do so not from any vague idea of general education or the rounded man but because they see it as an essential preservative of the sense of complex actuality in an education apt to dissolve existence into 'a world of formulas'.

In a letter to Canon Dixon he discusses the quality of feeling – 'that true humanity of spirit', he calls it – which in a mature mind accompanies an exact sense of the particular, distinguishing it from brashness on the one side and from sentimentality on the other. He condemns what he describes in Browning as 'a way of talking . . . with the air of a man bouncing up from the table with his mouth full of bread and cheese and saying that he means to stand no blasted nonsense'.[14] But where we find real 'humanity of spirit', as in Shakespeare, we find a true relevance of feeling to object, a state of justice and equipoise between them, 'neither mawkish on the one hand nor blustering on the other'. Nor is this propriety of feeling merely a function of the sensibility in a narrow sense. It is more than a technical, artistic capacity. It is part of a larger order, a more complete personal discipline. It includes a reference – the mind being integral – to a person's values and standards. At its best it belongs to 'that chastity of mind which seems to lie at the very heart and be the parent of all other good, the seeing at once what is best, the holding to that, and the not allowing anything else whatever to be heard pleading to the contrary'.[15]

It would be hard to find a better instance of the 'chastity of the mind' than Hopkins himself. It shows itself in his dedicated life, in his purity of purpose, in his never allowing his vocation as a Jesuit to be subordinated to his art as a poet. There was nothing faked or fabricated in Hopkins's life. Nor was there in his art. His chastity of mind showed itself there in an asceticism of attitude which, in spite of his intense desire – 'but it kills me to be time's eunuch and never beget' – kept him from composing when it was clear to him that the verse would not be issuing from a genuinely vital source, or when that source was too sacred to be made public. 'I cannot in conscience spend time on poetry, neither have I the inducements and inspirations that make others compose. Feeling, love in particular, is the great moving power and spring of verse and the only person that I am in love with seldom, especially now, stirs my heart sensibly, and when he does I cannot always "make capital" of it, it would be a sacrilege to do so.'[16]

His chastity of mind is also shown in his art in a quality which I will call integrity of sensibility. By this I mean both an unusual consciousness of the peculiar modification made on the sensibility by an object and a remarkable power to communicate it. The sense of the particular in Hopkins, that is, combined awareness of the self of the object and awareness of the self of the subject. Examples of acuteness of registering and fidelity in communicating – not that they can be separated in the verse – abound in his work. I will take two. The first is from *Spring*:

> Nothing is so beautiful as spring –
>> When weeds, in wheels, shoot long and lovely and lush;
>> Thrush's eggs look little low heavens, and thrush
> Through the echoing timber does so rinse and wring
> The ear, it strikes like lightnings to hear him sing;
>> The glassy peartree leaves and blooms, they brush
>> The descending blue; that blue is all in a rush
> With richness; the racing lambs too have fair their fling.

The strength of this evocation depends on a system of exact sensory impressions. Each object is, as it were, constituted by the individuality of the sense brought to bear on it, or rather each object is a blend of the complex of senses attending to it, since we experience anything not as an aggregate of several notes but in many dimensions simultaneously. The poem begins with the effect of motion (here a symbol of new life which is sustained throughout), the vegetable movement of quickening growth, and it ends with the nimble hilarity of the lambs. In between comes the action of the eye and the ear. 'Thrush's eggs look little low heavens.' We notice how the curve of the heavens – a curve, a dynamic shape – is repeated in miniature in the eggs, and how the blue is 'descending', that is moving and alive. And the metaphor of 'rinse and wring' is beautifully appropriate for the thrush's song cascading through the canals of the ear. Despite its rich and thronging vocabulary there is nothing merely decorative in this piece. Every word is working, in the interests of precision.

My second example is one of Hopkins's most impressive Sonnets.

> I wake and feel the fell of dark, not day.
> What hours, O what black hours we have spent
> This night! what sights you, heart, saw; ways you went!
> And more must, in yet longer light's delay.
>> With witness I speak this. But where I say
> Hours I means years, mean life. And my lament
> Is cries countless, cries like dead letters sent
> To dearest him that lives alas! away.

I am gall, I am heartburn. God's most deep decree
Bitter would have me taste: my taste was me;
Bones built in me, flesh filled, blood brimmed the curse
    Selfyeast of spirit a dull dough sours. I see
The lost are like this, and their scourge to be
As I am mine, their sweating selves; but worse.

Here again 'the bone, frame and *charpente*' of the poem – to use
a phrase of Hopkins – is an organization of unerringly noted sense
impressions. The poem begins with the sense of touch, one of the
most present, the least reminiscent, of our senses, and therefore
well fitted to convey the actual instant when the poet awakes to
the enclosing darkness, a suffocating fur of despair. Then the poet
casts his mind backward to the black hours endured and forward
to 'yet longer light's delay'. He does so by means of images of
sight (black hours, sights you saw) and sound (cries countless,
cries like dead letters). These are senses which operate at a distance and aptly communicate both the duration of the night and
the feeling of God's remoteness. In 'dead letters' this feeling is
strengthened to one of God's utter and appalling absence. We are
brought shockingly back to the present in the daring, Shakespearean metaphor of taste, again one of the most momentary of
our senses, 'I am gall, I am heartburn'. So intense and universal
is the bitterness of the taste that it is no longer something the
poet has but something he is, 'my taste was me'. The poem ends
with a characteristic Hopkins stroke in the words, 'but worse'.
On the point of identifying his own sweating self with that of the
damned, he draws back to make a comparative judgement. This
rational act lets the coolness of sanity into the fevered atmosphere. It doesn't lessen the poet's agony, but it saves it from
hysteria.

In concluding my brief comment on this poem, I should like to
direct the reader's attention to the phrase in it which runs 'With
witness I speak this'. These words are important in the poem.
They make a claim for the first-hand, the underivative quality of
the experience in question, for its immediacy and freshness; they
testify to an advanced and tested sense of the particular; and we
feel the poet has every right to make the claim. But these words

are also more generally significant They indicate what Hopkins took to be an essential part of the act of knowing; and it will be recalled that many of Hopkins's best poems dramatically reconstruct the act of knowing. His opinion has a decided educational importance too, for what is education but the sustaining, the disciplining and articulating of many acts of knowing? I can best explain what Hopkins had in mind by quoting a passage from one of his letters. He writes to Canon Dixon: 'The world is full of things and events, phenomena of all sorts that go without notice, go unwitnessed. . . . And if we regret this want of witness in brute nature, much more in the things done with lost pains and disappointed hopes by men.'[17] To notice an object isn't merely to give it recognition; it is to bring it into existence in a new way, to endow it with additional being. The witnessing by the mind, this investing a thing with an extra existence, is essentially a creative art. It saves part of the miraculous variety of the universe from waste. To know a thing – above all to know it through that finely developed sense of the particular which reveals unblurred a unique individuality – is a birth of new life, a release of possibility and an increment to being.

It is this conception which we find working powerfully in Hopkins's superb poem, *The Windhover*, a poem which rehearses the action of the mind in the instant of knowing. The beginning of the poem masterfully impels on the reader a vision of the falcon, which is both at one with the element it inhabits as it halts in the air or flows smoothly through it, and different from it when it strikes against the almost solid wind. And the image of the skater incisively establishes the intent and elegant energy of the hawk, its controlled, formidable and fluent power. Then follows the great statement of the theme of the human mind as the witness to creation.

>   My heart in hiding
> Stirred for a bird, – the achieve of, the mastery of the thing!

> Brute beauty and valour and act, oh, air, pride, plume, here
>   Buckle! AND the fire that breaks from thee then, a billion
> Times told lovelier, more dangerous, O my chevalier!

'My heart in hiding' at once opens out the theme. *In hiding*: the mind is a watcher, a hidden witness to 'the achieve of, the mastery of the thing!' In the act of witnessing, all that power and distinction are grasped, *buckled*, and clasped *here*, that is, in the mind itself; AND, that is to say, immediately, on the instant, the beauty and the being of the bird are immeasurably and *dangerously*, excitingly, breath-takingly multiplied. In the moment of intercourse of the known and the knower, 'the lagging lines' of a natural event achieve 'the roll, the rise, the carol, the creation'.

If that is true of the secret acts of ordinary minds, how much truer is it of the testimony to the richness of life afforded by works of art. For works of art make public and permanent the finest knowledge of the most gifted minds, minds which we may qualify with words Hopkins applied to another, 'so mature, so masculine, so fresh, and so fastidiously independent'. They offer us standards by which we may judge the incompleteness and the poverty of our own knowledge, but they also supply us with the means to emulate them. They give us what we need to appreciate them and the life embodied in them. For what, Hopkins asks, are works of art meant to do? 'To educate, to be standards. Education is meant for the many, standards are for public use.'[18] Their 'not rivalled insight' gives us, like the poems of Hopkins, innumerable, civilizing experiences of the sense of the particular. But they also, again like Hopkins, keep vividly alive a humane conception of the nature of man.

CHAPTER 7

THE WRITER AND THE CHILD

MARK TWAIN, HENRY JAMES, D. H. LAWRENCE
AND WALTER DE LA MARE

As I said above when writing of Coleridge and the Age of Child-hood, we think of our period as being in a special way the age of childhood. We feel ourselves more aware of the child, more sympathetic in his troubles, more intimate with and more responsive to his nature. What truth there is in our feeling of knowing so much more about the child is more than anything else the effect of the remarkable development of the science of psychology during the last fifty years and the dissemination among a larger and larger audience of psychological ideas. But psychological ideas are general ideas, psychological doctrines are general doctrines. When psychology teaches us about children, it gives us abstract categories which we may endeavour to apply in our relationships with children. (Of course, with a trained and skilled psychologist these general conceptions enter into and modify his sense of the concrete, give him a finer and more delicate feeling for the individual – but psychology does this only with those for whom it is the main discipline of their life; for the rest of us psychology is a set of rules and findings and general propositions.) It must also be remembered that psychological study has developed in such a way as to be concerned almost exclusively with the differences between adults and children. The similarities occupy only the tiniest part of its attention. Because of this we are immensely impressed with the uniqueness and autonomy of childhood, so that in a sense all our psychological knowledge has led us to think of childhood as a different and peculiar state, almost as something remote and alien to us.

In this chapter I want to suggest another source of knowledge about children, namely great novels. The novelist is an artist with a deep intuition of his oneness with his characters. They are all certainly marked off from him by some special modification of human nature, but they still all share with him a common human nature. The novelist's conception of human nature is general or universal, but also intensely concrete and individual. Every great novel is a lesson for us, not a didactic lesson, not just good advice, but a lesson in the sense that it embodies a literary idea. The lesson of a work of art, to repeat a phrase of Henry James, is the idea that lurks in any vision prompted by life. It is the complex truth distilled by the great writer's intricate apprehension of reality. The literary idea is mastered not when we know it, as it were at arm's length, but when it is incorporated into our being, when it modifies our sensibility and makes our eye juster and more delicately accommodated to its object. This is essentially the kind of knowledge about children which parents and teachers need – the kind of knowledge that makes a difference to a person's relation to children because it alters the quality of the person's self.

Let me give a few examples. In *Huckleberry Finn* Huck is the child who is, like all children in some ways, a stranger in and a critic of the adult world. The adult world is governed very much by appetite and by conventional illusion, and very often the child's voice is the voice not of fantasy but of reality and his remarks have a sharp and shocking justice as criticisms of the illusion by which adults live. Maisie in Henry James's *What Maisie Knew*, like every child to some degree, is the child exposed to adult corruption, a corruption which is accepted as the routine commonplace of ordinary life. But the child has not yet come to acquiesce in this routine, hardly recognized evil and often, like Maisie, has an instinct for life and spiritual health. Ursula in Lawrence's *The Rainbow*, on the other hand, is the child too intensely loved, too passionately possessed. This is a love which is the expression of an inadequacy, a want of maturity in the adult, and it brings a radical distortion into the character of the child and into the way it sees the world. Every child has something in him of Huck, of Maisie and of Ursula, just as every adult, and especially every parent, has something in him of the illusion, the corruption and the self-centred love of the adults these children had to deal with. In this chapter I propose to examine these novels from this point of view. I have also added, in order to extend the range of children considered, a note on the child in the poetry of Walter de la Mare.

Huck in *Huckleberry Finn*

There are those who look on the presence of Tom Sawyer at the beginning of *Huckleberry Finn* as evidence of the author's uncertainty, as though he were unsure exactly what kind of novel he was undertaking. Such a view seems to me not at all to square with the effect on the reader of these Tom Sawyer episodes. The relations of Tom and Huck – and especially the various contrasts between the ebullient fancy of the one and the unromantic sobriety of the other – perform a function essential at that point in the novel, and they perform it rapidly and with telling economy. These scenes set up the system of assumptions on which the novel is to operate, and elucidate the law of Huck's world, which is a law of detached and disillusioned reality. From the start small, flicking, needle-like touches define the area in which the action is to take place, and establish the very solid sort of reality that Huck is to represent. When, for example, Tom and Huck are creeping on hands and knees out of the widow's garden, Tom wants to tie up the sleeping Jim to the tree for fun. 'But I said no; he might wake up and make a disturbance, and then they'd find out I warn't in.' Again, when they reach the edge of the hill-top, 'we looked away down into the village and could see three or four lights twinkling, where there were sick folks, maybe'. Huck's refusal to cooperate in the 'adventure' of binding Jim, his qualified suggestion as to the reason for the late lights, dispel the atmosphere of unreal fantasy always generated by Tom. Their effect is to place these episodes in the world of everyday reality, and to make of Huck, who remains an utterly convincing boy, an inhabitant of a solid and existing world. The same deflationary effect is produced when a conversation between Tom and Ben Rogers, who are inclined to rule Huck out of the gang because he hasn't a family that can be found, and 'everybody must have a family or somebody to kill', is followed by Huck's unemphatic comment, 'Pap he hadn't been seen for more than a year, and that was comfortable for me; I didn't want to see him no more', a mild but astonishingly effective communication of the horror of Huck's father. Having succeeded by this sort of dramatic implication in confirming Huck as the voice of sanity, Mark Twain then allows himself, through that voice, to make an explicit judgement on the contrast I have suggested. The passage occurs where Huck is bringing some of Tom's advice – how to conjure a genie – to the test of practice. 'So then I judged that all that stuff was only just one of Tom Sawyer's lies. I reckoned he believed in the A-rabs and the elephants, but as for me I think different. It had all the marks of a Sunday school.'

In Huck's world all, both children and adults, think like Tom Sawyer, and are only too willing to believe his 'lies'. Perhaps the adults require an extra degree of sophistication, but they too, like the Dauphin and the Duke, bask in illusion, or like the assembly at the camp-meeting, ache to be deceived. Between Huck – 'but as for me I think different' – who cares only for the actual, and a society avid of the fanciful there lies a deep difference of mind, a wholly dissimilar response to life. It is his love for reality which makes Huck an alien in a world infatuated with appearance. It is this too which makes it so beautifully appropriate that Huck should be, what he so thoroughly is, a boy. His role as outsider is the perfect analogue of the part played by the child as critic of adult society, and his comments on the communities along the river, which he observes but never in any final way enters, have the justice we are disconcerted by in the child's undrilled, un-answerable judgements on the fictions of the adult world. His opinions are sharp (Huck has the outcast's keen telescopic vision), but temperate (he is the detached observer who expects little and is surprised by nothing). His views have the relevance of the undistracted and the impartiality of the disengaged. He is the wanderer with the cool observant glance who never allows him-self to be entangled, whose tactics are always evasive, who with his horror of the trap of adult illusion continually keeps open a track back to the free, detached life of the river. 'I was powerful glad to get away from the feuds, and so was Jim to get away from the swamp. We said there warn't no home like a raft, after all. Other places do seem so cramped up and smothery, but a raft don't. You feel mighty free and easy and comfortable on a raft.'

The burden of Huck's views on the people he comes in contact with – in contact with, one says, not in touch with – is that they all in some important respect live by an illusion, by a sham which is invariably connected with some degree of evil. Not that evil is simply the result of a failure of the sense of reality. Huck's is no comfortable *philosophe's* theory that evil is just the product of ignorance. It is rather that moral disorder always works itself out in, protects itself under, illusory value. It may be the social code observed by Miss Watson and her friends in the village, a mechanism for giving the sanction of law and custom to trivial vanities. It may be the love of money as the only reality which made it impossible for Judge Thatcher to understand the plain sense of Huck's offer to resign the fortune. It may be some professional pretension like that of the preacher and the doctor, devastatingly dismissed in a remark like this: 'Rev. Hobson and Dr Robinson was down at the end of the town, a-hunting together; that is, I mean the doctor was shipping a sick man to t'other world, and the preacher was pinting him right.' It may be the bogus conception of chivalry which governs the lives of Colonel Grangerford and his family. Here was a man, one would have guessed, with everything likely to bring a dignified and happy life: position, wealth, popularity, respect. But he and his family are self-destroyed. The heart of the tradition by which he lives, so formal and civilized in appearance, is in reality a vicious and atavistic greed for revenge. (It is significant that Buck, the youngest Grangerford, doesn't even know what started the feud, the one event that might lend it some measure of reality.) The romanticism of the Grangerfords is an extreme and stylized version of 'Tom Sawyer's lies'. Less extreme in evil but equally fantastic in illusion are the two confidence-men, whose whole lives are a masquerade, under which lurks, or – when it doesn't matter if it is seen – parades, a deep, corrupting selfishness.

If the confidence-men show the intimacy of evil and illusion, their dupes exhibit the same connexion, but in the social sphere. I have referred to the instance at the Pokeville camp-meeting where the voracious credulity of the congregation goes more than half-way to meet the calculated trickery of the 'pirate-captain'. There is a second, still better example in a superb passage later in the novel where we see comic genius at the service of a serious intention, and of course all the more brilliantly comic for that. The swindlers arrive as the Reverend Harvey and William Wilks, English brothers of the recently deceased Peter Wilks. The relatives and neighbours are gathered round the coffin as they appear, attended by Huck, their 'valley'.

And when they got there, they bent over and looked in the coffin, and took one sight, and then they burst out a-crying so you could a heard them to Orleans, most; and then they put their arms around each other's necks, and hung their chins over each other's shoulders; and then for three minutes, or maybe four, I never see two men leak the way they done. And mind you, everybody was doing the same; and the place was that damp I never see anything like it. Then one of them got on one side of the coffin and t'other on t'other side, and they kneeled down, and rested their foreheads on the coffin, and let on to pray all to theirselves. Well, when it come to that, it worked the crowd like you never see anything like it, and so everybody broke down and went to sobbing right out loud – the poor girls, too; and every woman, nearly, went up to the girls, without saying a word, and kissed them solemn on the forehead, and then put their hand on their head, and looked up towards the sky, with tears running down, and then busted out and went off sobbing and swabbing, and give the next woman a show. I never see anything so disgusting.

Well, by and by, the King he gets up and comes forward a little and works himself up and slobbers out a speech, all full of tears and flap-doodle about its being a sore trial for him and his poor brother to lose the diseased, and to miss seeing the diseased alive, after the long journey of four thousand mile, but it's a trial that's sweetened and sanctified to us by this dear sympathy and these holy tears, and so he thanks them out of his heart, and out of his brother's heart, because out of their mouths they can't, words being too weak and cold, and all that kind of rot and slush, till it was just sickening; and then he blubbers out a pious goody-goody Amen, and turns himself loose and goes to crying fit to bust.

And the minute the words was out of his mouth somebody over in the crowd struck up the doxolojer, and everybody joined in with all their might, and it just warmed you up and made you feel as good as church letting out. Music *is* a good thing; and after all that soul-butter and hogwash, I never see it freshen up things so, and sound so honest and bully.

In this passage we see exposed both the duplicity of the conspirators and the hysterical and perverse desire of the audience to be deluded. By 'exposed' I mean both dissected and constructed in the form of art. Mark Twain shows himself, at least in this novel, to be gifted with a fine faculty for moral analysis, that is, to be expert in the logic of motives, and at the same time possessed of standards mature enough and complex enough to put on them their true value. But such a faculty could not realize itself as art without the marvellously supple and responsive medium which the author created from several forms of local speech. Despite the care with which the idiom is composed – 'painstakingly', says Mark Twain, 'and with the trustworthy guidance and support of personal familiarity' – from a number of Missouri and South-Western dialects and sub-dialects, it wears an air of unforced and casual spontaneity, a natural litheness of spring and run. Huck has a remark in the novel on his own words which applies very justly to the language of the novel: 'I went right along, not fixing up any particular plan, but just trusting to Providence, to put the right words in my mouth when the time come; for I'd noticed that Providence always did put the right words in my mouth, if I left it alone.' The language has the exciting vivacity of folk speech, an effortless flowing energy which makes the laboured-at vigour of later American prose writers look febrile and insubstantial. It has, too, the intimacy of peasant talk. The phrase, 'And mind you', fits beautifully into the tone of personal confidence. And like folk speech too it breaks naturally into imagery. A great part of the meaning of this passage is carried by the images. They are versatile, nicely modulated to each inflection of the narrative. For example, the two men 'leak', the place is 'damp', the women go off 'sobbing and swabbing'. At the same time the images are remarkably consistent with one another. One element, the liquid or watery, is sustained through-out. But the images are so organized as to convey a mounting intensity of grossness and moral squalor. This is very evident if we look at the way in which they succeed one another. At first the images are fairly mild and neutral – 'leak', 'damp', 'sobbing', 'swabbing'. Then at the point in which the next woman is given a 'show', a word which suggests both a turn and a sham, the images begin to be more and more repulsive. 'Slobbers' is fol-lowed by 'tears and flapdoodle', and 'sweetened and sanctified' communicates a flavour of greasiness and unction, which is strengthened in 'rot and slush' and 'blubbers'. Then we have in conclusion the brilliant contrast between the freshness and whole-someness of the music of the 'doxolojer' and the nauseating hypocrisy of 'all that soul-butter and hogwash'.

The situation described in this scene is sufficiently outrageous to allow Huck an open indignation. 'I never see anything so disgusting.' In general, the tone of the novel is more restrained, the mood ironic, the judgements implied. Irony is indeed a mood very appropriate to a character so collected and detached as Huck, observing a world dedicated to unreality. The habitual technique of the author is to render a scene with the sharpest clarity, while the persons and objects in it are so arranged as to make the relations between them speak the author's mind. The radical comments are concealed, as it were, in the interstices of the narration. It isn't necessary to bring them into the open. What overt comments there are are made directly on some detail in the foreground of the story. But underneath they refer to another order of reality. A nice instance occurs at the beginning of the novel. 'After supper she got out her book and learned me about Moses and the "Bulrushers" and I was in a sweat to find out all about him; but by and by she let it out that Moses had been dead a considerable time; so then I didn't care no more about him; because I don't take no stock in dead people.' The 'dead people' in whom Huck takes no stock include more than Moses; it is a company which counts in it also the widow and Miss Watson and their friends in the village mummified by convention. Again with what obliqueness the following passage comments on the lot of Jim – and of man – and with an effect all the more telling and serious for the very absurdities which he and Huck are so gravely canvassing. 'I had heard about some of these things before, but not all of them. Jim knowed all kinds of signs. He said he knowed most everything. I said it looked to me like all the signs was about bad luck, and so I asked him if there warn't any good-luck signs. He says: "Mighty few – and *dey* ain't no use to a body. What you want to know when good luck's a-coming for? Want to keep it off?" '

'It is Huck,' says Eliot, 'who gives the book style. The River gives the book its form. But for the River, the book might be only a sequence of adventures with a happy ending.' Throughout the novel we are aware of the river as a shaping, unifying form. To the solitary Huck, who in the village 'felt so lonesome I most wished I was dead', the river offers a natural environment. 'Two or three nights went by; I reckon I might say they swum by, they slid along so quiet and smooth and lovely.' When he cannot sense its current supporting and carrying him forward, he is uneasy and disturbed. 'I never felt easy till the raft was two miles below there and out in the middle of the Mississippi.' At a distance from the river he is not only unsettled; his identity itself is uncertain. One remembers how often circumstances compel him to assume some other identity. It is only on the river that he is fully himself. Clothes for Huck are always a sort of disguise, the properties of a part played in an unnatural society. 'She put me in the new clothes again; and I couldn't do nothing but sweat and sweat, and feel all cramped up.' On the raft, however, 'we was always naked, day and night, whenever the mosquitoes would let us – the new clothes Buck's folks made for me was too good to be comfortable, and besides I didn't go much on clothes nohow'.

But the river is more than a home for Huck, more than a school where he learns resource and versatility. It is more than a natural force. The character of Huck, his words and actions, constitute a profound commentary on human life, and they do so because behind them, communicating significance and richness to them, stands the great 'animating presence' of the river. The river in *Huckleberry Finn* represents life unconstrained by artifice, and value uncomplicated by pretence. Away from the river and its controlling influence, men live according to abstract systems or by illusions of greed or profit or power. But to those on it or near it the river, following the law of its own nature, brings the irresistible rush and swirl of reality. The meaning of the river in *Huckleberry Finn* has been stated magnificently by Eliot at the beginning of *The Dry Salvages*, a poem, we must believe, which draws some of its strength from this very novel.

> I do not know much about gods; but I think that the river
> Is a strong brown god – sullen, untamed and intractable,
> Patient to some degree, at first recognized as a frontier;
> Useful, untrustworthy, as a conveyor of commerce;
> Then only a problem confronting the builder of bridges.
> The problem once solved, the brown god is almost forgotten
> By the dwellers in cities – ever, however, implacable,
> Keeping his seasons and rages, destroyer, reminder
> Of what men choose to forget. Unhonoured, unpropitiated
> By worshippers of the machine, but waiting, watching and waiting.

The river is Huck's 'strong brown god', his life a kind of service paid to it. Because of it Huck too becomes a 'reminder of what men choose to forget'.

The most important inner event in the course of Huck's voyage on the river is the growth of his moral life. The critical influence in that growth is his relationship with the runaway negro, Jim, the one human being he loves, the one person with whom he is completely himself.

> But I . . . set there thinking . . . And got to thinking over our trip down the river; and I see Jim before me, all the time, in the day, and in the night-time, sometimes moonlight, sometimes storms, and we a-floating along, talking, and singing, and laughing. But somehow I couldn't seem to strike no places to harden me against him, but only the other kind. I'd see him standing my watch on top of his'n, stead of calling me so I could go on sleeping. And see him how glad he was when I come back out of the fog . . . and such-like times; and would always call me honey, and pet me, and do everything he could think of for me, and how good he always was.

Indeed one of the greatest lessons of *Huckleberry Finn*, in Henry

James's sense of lesson, 'the idea that deeply lurks in any vision prompted by life', is that the child lives what is in essence a moral life. Huck's choices have a reference to standards. His 'strong brown god', the river, is his standard. In the great scene in which Huck debates with himself whether he should give up Jim to the hunters, we hear not only the continual murmur of conscience, but with perfect naturalness and propriety the word conscience itself. 'I couldn't get that out of my conscience . . . no how nor no way . . . it got to troubling me so I couldn't rest . . . but it wasn't no use, conscience up and says. . . . That was where it pinched. Conscience says to me . . . my conscience got to stirring me up hotter than ever. . . .' Then in the climactic passage Mark Twain presents with extraordinary finesse both the moral argument and the standard by which Huck resolves it.

They went off and I got aboard the raft, feeling bad and low, because I knowed very well I had done wrong, and I see it warn't no use for me to try to learn to do right; a body that don't get *started* right when he's little, ain't got no show – when the pinch comes there ain't nothing to back him up and keep him to his work and so he gets beat. Then I thought a minute, and says to myself, hold on – s'pose you'd done right and give Jim up: would you felt better than what you do now? No, says I, I'd feel bad – I'd feel just the same way I do now. Well, then, says I, what's the use you learning to do right, when it's troublesome to do right and ain't no trouble to do wrong, and the wages is just the same? I was stuck. I couldn't answer that. So I reckoned I wouldn't bother no more about it, but after this always do whichever come handiest at the time.

I went into the wigwam; Jim warn't there. I looked all around; he warn't anywhere. I says:

'Jim !'

'Here I is, Huck. Is dey out o' sight yit? Don't talk loud.'

He was in the river, under the stern oar, with just his nose out. I told him they was out of sight, so he come aboard.

Here the subtlety consists in the simultaneous rendering of the apparent and the real conflict as well as of the apparent criterion by which it is decided and of the actual one. Huck appears to be arguing the claims of current social morality against peace of mind, and comes to a decision on the grounds of expediency, 'whichever comes handiest at the time', but in fact the tension, the intolerable tension, is between an inhuman and brutal code and a morality with sources deep in human nature. And the standard – 'whichever comes handiest at the time' – turns out to be, as Huck's decisive action shows, not expediency at all but a genuine, unforced moral impulse, the moral correlative of the free, flowing life of the river. It is no accident that Jim was in the river with just his nose out. He is covered by the river, but also protected by the freedom, decency and respect for which the river stands.

Huck, I have said, is the voice of sanity. Nowhere is that title more firmly justified than in his final comment on conscience which occurs towards the end of the novel. It expresses not only the coolest sanity but also a high degree of maturity. Moreover, quoting it gives me the opportunity to conclude these pages on *Huckleberry Finn* on an appropriately wry and self-deflating note, on a cadence which is characteristic both of the humour and the seriousness of this great work.

So we poked along back home, and I warn't feeling so brash as I was before, but kind of ornery and humble, and to blame somehow – though *I* hadn't done nothing. But that's always the way; it don't make no difference whether you do right or wrong, a person's conscience ain't got no sense, and just goes for him *anyway*. If I had a yaller dog that didn't know no more than a person's conscience does, I would pison him. It takes up more room than all the rest of a person's insides, and yet ain't no good, nohow.

Conscience, that is, although the essential mark of a human being, is no easy or comfortable possession. But to ignore it is to commit what is for *Huckleberry Finn* the ultimate sin, the denial of reality.

Maisie in *What Maisie Knew*

The way in which the child performs his role as a critic of adult society certainly confirms us in the belief of the existence in children of a moral life however simple and tentative. But, of course, it is true that for a much larger part of his life, and therefore for most of his moral experience, the child is intimately engaged with adult society. The centre of the child's moral endowment is a candour which has not yet come to be an acquiescence in the routine corruption of the adult world. The relation between the child's single-mindedness and the hypocrisy of conventional valuation, between his spontaneous honesty and the stock response, offers a difficult and therefore attractive theme to the morally discerning writer. Such a theme we might expect would appeal to Henry James. And in two stories, works it must be said of unequal importance, he was concerned with different forms of this relation. In *The Turn of the Screw*, 'that wanton little tale', his intention was, he says, 'to give the impression of the communication to children of the most infernal imaginable evil and danger – the condition on their part of being as *exposed* as we can humanely conceive children to be'. 'Ah!' he cries, 'the exposure indeed, the helpless plasticity of childhood that isn't dear or sacred to somebody!' It would be hard for any child to be less dear or sacred than the heroine of *What Maisie Knew*, and certainly no one could be more exposed, but Maisie is far from exhibiting a helpless plasticity. On the contrary, Maisie is remarkable above all for 'activity of spirit and vivacity of intelligence', for what James calls her 'truth of resistance', the refusal to be pliant and accommodating before the infection of a thoroughly diseased environment.

The technical problem of presenting the relation of child to adult, of such a child to such adults, was one that delighted James with its difficulty. The elements of his novel, he decided, were to be a child of quick but not unnatural intelligence, and adults who were the contemporary version of cocktail-party society, empty, vulgar and selfish. The parents and the step-parents belonged to a society in which, for the most part, people were occupied only with chatter, and with clothes, of course. Of her mother, Mrs Farange, he says, 'Like her husband, she carried clothes, carried them as a train carried passengers.' And of her father, 'contemporary history . . . somehow had no use for him, had hurried past him and left him in perpetual Piccadilly'. James had to make articulate what is almost inarticulate, the child's misty guesses and troubled glimpses at the mysteries of adult behaviour – an undertaking all the more difficult when the behaviour is of that sophisticated, fashionable brand at the furthest move from reality. 'She was taken into the confidence of passions on which she fixed just the stare she might have had for images bounding across the wall in the slide of a magic-lantern. Her little world was phantasmagoric – strange shadows dancing on a sheet.' The field of action was to be the limited consciousness of the child, 'the register of the whole complexity, the child's confused and obscure notation of it'. At first he decided to restrict his design to just what the child understood. But he saw that this method would leave great gaps and inconsistencies. He determined, therefore, to present not only what the child understood but also what she saw, however uncomprehendingly, but only through 'the occasions and connections of her proximity and attention'. A great part of the vitality of the novel comes from the growing correspondence between what Maisie sees and what she understands. At the same time, then, we see the action through the eyes of the child and we are aided by an adult commentary which extends and amplifies what Maisie grasps of its meaning. In the main the adult commentary is finely related to Maisie's experience, even if 'we inevitably note this in figures which are not at her command'. There are occasional lapses. Everyone remembers the notorious passage, a caricature of James's hyper-subtlety, about a meeting of Maisie and her father : '. . . there was an extraordinarily mute passage between her vision of this vision of his, his vision of her vision, and her vision of his vision of her vision'. A less calamitous example of James going rather too far in explanation occurs when Maisie finds Mrs Wix's elation at Sir Claude's condescending kindness rather pathetic, which gives rise to the remark: 'it brought home to Maisie the way her humble companion had sidled and ducked through life'. These words seem to have floated off from any connexion with a child's experience and understanding.

The plot has the characteristic symmetry of a Jamesian scheme. The court has assigned Maisie to each of her divorced parents to spend six months first with one, then with the other, so that she had 'a positive certitude . . . that the natural way for a child to have her parents was separate and successive, like her mutton and her pudding or her bath and her nap'. They treat her as a mere object, useful for inconveniencing or exasperating the other. Maisie's family multiplies when the parents marry their current lovers, Mrs Farange Sir Claude, and Mr Farange Miss Overmore, who was formerly Maisie's governess in her mother's house. The child's relationships become even more entangled and bewildering when the two step-parents begin a liaison and then set up a separate establishment in which they wish to instal Maisie, now deserted by her real parents. This is the unsavoury *milieu* in which Maisie grows up, 'a rattling void filled with relinquished step-parents'. Its exact shade of moral shadiness is conveyed in a comment on the word 'compromised'. 'Hadn't she lived with her eyes on it from her third year? It was the condition most frequently discussed in the Faranges' house, where the word was always in the air, and where at the age of five, amid rounds of applause, she would gabble it off.' Maisie's life is spent in a complexity of temporary arrangements utterly lacking in essential elements of constancy and security. 'The mutability in the little girl's career . . . was naturally unfavourable to accumulation. She stayed long enough only to miss things, not half long enough to deserve them.' And it is an environment even more desperately denuded of love. To Maisie her fashionable mother's embrace was like 'being suddenly thrust into a jeweller's shop-front', and she could face the possibility of her mother's leaving her with 'the unformulated fatalism in which her observation of her own career had long since taken refuge'. ' "You mean if Mamma doesn't come back ever at all?" The composure with which her face was presented to that prospect would have shown a spectator the long road she had travelled.' Her life hasn't even the support of some consistent system, even if a strict and unfeeling one. 'The child's discipline had been bewildering – it had ranged freely between the prescription that she was to answer when spoken to and the experience of lively penalties on obeying the prescription.' Consequently she had habitually to conceal her true feelings: the uninhibited chatter of the happy child was something Maisie could not permit herself. 'For Maisie, moreover, concealment had never seemed deception, and she had grown up amongst things as to which her foremost knowledge was that she was not to ask about them.'

Maisie reminds us that children can sometimes be more fully, more truly human than the most sophisticated adult; and that they can sometimes even be begetters of spiritual help. Maisie's part,' says James, 'is really keeping the torch of virtue alive in an air tending infinitely to smother it . . . drawing some stray fragrance of an ideal across the scent of selfishness'. Only a novelist richly gifted both with psychological discernment and poetic power could have created so convincing and significant a character as Maisie. In his rendering of her mind and development James displays a refinement of response to the most delicate movements of a child's thought together with a mastery of figurative language equal to expressing it. Maisie can perform a symbolic role with such unforced naturalness because she is so completely 'an interesting small mortal'. She can be 'the striking figured symbol' because she is 'the thoroughly pictured creature'.

Both elements will, I hope, be sufficiently demonstrated in the passages I mean to quote. I ought to add that they do not appear in the novel in the more 'logical' order in which I have arranged them. To say this is to call attention to James's precision of observation and fidelity to life. A child can be younger tomorrow than it was last week, and older today than it will be tomorrow. Nevertheless, beneath these currents and reverses there is an irresistible onward drift. It is this which I want to illustrate.

The consciousness of the young child is occupied with events and objects vividly observed and joined together with the minimum of complexity in one of the simple relationships intelligible to the child. These relationships are modelled on the child's limited but intensely emotional experience. Things hardly associated at all by the adult, or judged to have a merely neutral connexion, are linked by the child with a strong bond of feeling. The child sees the world through forms which intensify the relaxed connexions of events and which dramatize the relations of even natural objects. Moreover, these relationships are endowed by the child with a fixed and unalterable status; it is inconceivable to him that the connexions he posits to manipulate his experience *could* be other than they seem to him. The objects which compose his universe trail behind them no cluster of implications; they are free of ambiguity. They are what they are, utterly. It is these features of the child's thought, vividness of impact, simplicity of relation, absoluteness of status, which James chooses to accentuate in *What Maisie Knew*; together they make a world which is remarkable for its positiveness and definition of presence and for its absence of implication. The development of the child's mind, as James analyses it, lies in the strengthening of the sense of implication, the quickening of doubt and the multiplication of possibilities.

It is remarkable with what success James, a novelist noted above all for his concern with the subtlest shades of adult relationships and for his mastery of the method of obliquity, presents the absolute, totally present life of the child. A good example of his skill is his notation of Maisie's response to her first visit to France. 'She was "abroad" and she gave herself up to it, responded to it, in the light air, before the pink houses, among the bare-legged fish-wives and the red-legged soldiers, with the instant certitude of a vocation.' The minute accuracy of the scoring, the primary colouring, the simplicity of the phrasing – the body of the sentence is just a list of dazzling details – all arrange before the reader's eyes the scene which Maisie stares at entranced. It is round the modification of Maisie's 'lively sense of the immediate' that James constructs his version of the progress of the child's inner life. He divides that development into three fairly distinct phases. To begin with, meaning for Maisie is exclusively a function of the present, and importance attaches itself wholly to the instant. 'In that lively sense of the immediate which is the very air of a child's mind the past, on each occasion, became for her as indistinct as the future: she surrendered herself to the actual. . . .' 'She was at the age for which all stories are true and all conceptions are stories. The actual was the absolute; the present alone was vivid.' In a scene between Maisie and her father, where Beale tells Maisie of his intention to begin a new life in America, James has an image which applies not only to the particular information the child is receiving but to all this brilliantly direct, instantly dissolving world of the child. 'This affected her for a moment like some great flashing dazzle in one of the pantomimes to which Sir Claude had taken her: she saw nothing in it but what it directly conveyed.'

Maisie, like every child, begins to release herself from the dominance of the present as more and varied images throng her mind and as the range and relevance of her vocabulary increase. Images and words bring into the child's life a measure of continuity and regularity. An image is more than a representation of an object: in it also lurk dim meanings and indistinct connexions which together form mental patterns long before the child can elaborate them rationally. 'By the time she had grown sharper, she found in her mind a collection of images: echoes to which meanings were attachable – images and echoes kept for her in the childish dusk, the dim closet, the high drawers.' If images initiate understanding, words complete it. When Maisie hasn't words even remotely adequate to her experience, when she hasn't the basic 'arithmetic' to solve the sum, she is left groping helplessly in the dark. 'She put it together with a suspicion that, had she ever in her life had a sovereign changed, would have resembled an impression, baffled by the want of arithmetic, that her change was wrong.' But when she has a name or an analogy she is able to make some sort of order out of the chaos of her feeling. 'The child had lately been to the dentist's and had a term of comparison for the screwed-up intensity of the scene.' Maisie, says James, 'had ever of course in her mind fewer names than conceptions'. By 'names' here, James means words which are part of what he calls in the *Preface* a child's 'prompt, at all producible vocabulary', which is to be distinguished from a much larger store of comprehended but not serviceable words. It is true that all a child's experience which is in any way understood has some faint reference to language. But it is to the degree that its active vocabulary corresponds to its experience, that 'names' in this sense belong to 'conceptions', that the child is moving towards maturity.

As images multiply in Maisie's imagination, as her tongue more easily frames appropriate names, the present stretches and enlarges itself. Each moment is no longer utterly and shockingly new; it begins to fit into a familiar pattern and to be recognized as having some element in common with what has gone before. The child's sense of novelty is tempered by repetition. As she passes from one selfish and corrupt relative to another, 'Maisie could only have a sense of something that in a mature mind would be called the way history repeats itself'. Just as the past comes to qualify the present, the present now alters the past. A vivid experience, like Maisie's delight in the *plage* at Boulogne, changes all that led up to it.

She had grown older in five minutes and had by the time they reached the hotel recognized in the institutions and manners of France a multitude of messages and affinities. . . . For it appeared to her that no one since the beginning of time could have had such an adventure or, in an hour, so much experience; as a sequel to which she only needed, to feel with conscious wonder how the past was changed, to hear Susan, inscrutably aggravated, express a preference for the Edgware Road. The past was so changed and the circle it had formed already so overstepped. . . .

The third stage in Maisie's mental development, in James's analysis, is that in which she begins to realize what is implied in the present. She comes to see both the thing and its shadow, to feel that the surface of an event is entangled with its depths, to sense both the act and the nimbus of suggestion around it. This is how James describes Maisie's beginnings in what he calls 'the art of not thinking singly'. 'Everything had something behind it: life was like a long, long corridor with rows of closed doors. She had learned that at these doors it was wise not to knock – this seemed to produce from within such sounds of derision. Little by little, however, she understood more. . . .' With this more complex consciousness, Maisie's life is more difficult and more deceiving. The lucidities of the younger child are coloured by doubt, her clear-cut assurance blurred by ambiguity. Her life is also more dangerous. Accustomed simplicities are seen to mask treacherous pitfalls; apparent love, as between Sir Claude and her mother or between Beale Farange and Miss Overmore, disguises latent hostility so that Maisie, 'with her inveterate instinct of keeping the peace', has to act the part of a prudent ambassador, and James speaks of 'the small strange pathos on the child's part of an innocence so saturated with knowledge and so directed to diplomacy'. But if Maisie's life, under the burden of implications revealed, is more difficult, it is also more exciting – 'She held her breath with the sense of picking her steps among the tremendous things of life' – and also more independent – 'It may indeed be said that these days brought on a high quickening of Maisie's direct perception, of her satisfied sense of arriving by herself at conclusions.'

It is in these circumstances and at this stage of her development that Maisie makes the discovery which is the prerequisite of the moral life, the discovery of the self. It is in character with Maisie's situation that she has to make that discovery in conditions which, but for the sweetness and soundness of her nature, would certainly make for slyness and hypocrisy. 'She had a new feeling, the feeling of danger; on which a new remedy rose to meet it, the idea of an inner self, or in other words, of concealment.' Concealment is natural to one like Maisie compelled to adapt herself to the varying tones and colours of a shifting, and shifty, underworld of quarrelling parents and plotting relations. When she is open, her candour shocks them, since they prefer children to live in a cosy make-believe world; and the concealment to which she is then forced only persuades them that she is sly and devious. This is what she is accused of more than once by her mother, by Miss Overmore, even by Mrs Wix. 'There had been times when she had to make the best of the impression that she was herself deceitful; yet she had never concealed anything bigger than a thought.' Hiding her thoughts came easily to Maisie, wanting love in an unloving world, and trying to keep the peace in a suspicious and dissenting circle. 'For Maisie, moreover, concealment had never necessarily seemed deception, and she had grown up amongst things to which her foremost knowledge was that she was not to ask about them.'

The experience of finding her own thoughts so much at odds

with what is expected of her brings Maisie to a sharper consciousness of her own self as an entity different from and discontinuous with the world outside. This, and 'the art of not thinking singly', which means habitually referring – however vaguely and tentatively – particular acts to a more persisting standard, are the beginnings of Maisie's moral life.

The existence of Maisie's moral sense is the main, the organizing theme of the second half of the novel. The theme is sharply pointed up in three scenes in which the protagonists are Maisie and her mother, Lady Ida, then Maisie and Mrs Wix, and thirdly Maisie, Mrs Wix, the second Mrs Beale and Sir Claude. In each of these scenes one of Maisie's interlocutors is dismayed or despairing at what he takes to be a defect of moral sensibility in the child. It is on this note that the conversation between Maisie and her mother concludes. Lady Ida appears suddenly at Folkestone and persuades Sir Claude to let her talk to Maisie alone.

It suited her to convey that Maisie had been kept as far as *she* was concerned or could imagine in a holy ignorance and that she must take for granted a supreme simplicity . . . the scene had a style of its own that would have qualified it for presentation, especially at such a moment as that of her letting it betray that she quite did think her wretched offspring better placed with Sir Claude than in her own soiled hands. There was at any rate nothing scant in her admissions or perversions, the mixture of her fear of what Maisie might undiscoverably think and of the support she at the same time gathered from a necessity of selfishness and a habit of brutality. This habit flushed through the merit she now made, in terms explicit, of not having come to Folkestone to kick up a vulgar row. She had not come to box any ears or to bang any doors or even to use any language: she had come at the worst to lose the thread of her argument in an occasional dumb, disgusted twitch of the toggery in which Mrs Beale's low domestic had had the impudence to serve up Miss Farange.

What she had in fact come for was to break finally with Maisie, and to soothe the severance with a ten-pound note. Maisie, however, is neither simple nor ignorant. How could she be? By nature she is not the first, and by circumstances she is not allowed to be the second. In her pleasure at this free intercourse with her mother, the fullest and the friendliest she had known, Maisie forgets that she had never been safe with her mother unless she had pretended to be stupid. She makes the correct assumption that her mother is off to South Africa with a lover. Unfortunately she blurts out her hope that it is 'the Captain', the only one in the long list of her mother's lovers who had impressed Maisie as disinterested, loyal and good. But 'the Captain' had long been discarded; he is now 'the biggest cad in London'. And Maisie's remark is met by her mother with 'one of the looks that slammed the door in her face; never in a career of unsuccessful experiments had Maisie had to take such a stare'. ' "You're a dreadful, dismal, deplorable little thing," ' she tells Maisie as she goes, giving up Maisie as a sort of precocious moral monster, and incidentally thriftily withdrawing the ten-pound note.

Lady Ida is appalled at her daughter's indifference to conventional moral attitudes as well as at her easy familiarity with her own irregular mode of living. But Maisie's indifference and precocious knowledge are really no more than a child's inability to make sense either of the social code which formally rules the lives of Lady Ida and her like, or of the selfish casuistry which whittles down even social obligations to the merest expediency. It is Maisie, in her passionate defence of 'the Captain', who appeals to a serious and genuine morality, to kindness, fidelity and disinterestedness. The effectiveness of the scene depends a great deal on this ironic transposition of the substance and accidents of morality: not having the second, Maisie is condemned for lacking the first. But it is only in relation to the substance of morality represented by Maisie that the gross and vulgar lives surrounding her have any importance or can be made at all tolerable to the reader. 'She has,' says James in the *Preface*, 'the wonderful importance of shedding a light far beyond any reach of her comprehension; of lending to poorer persons and things, by the mere fact of their being involved with her and by the special scale she creates for them, a precious element of dignity.'

As we might expect from the close texture of a Jamesian story, this scene contains the impulse of the next. In a unique spasm of motherly concern, Lady Ida dispatches Mrs Wix to Maisie so that she may have 'at least one decent person about her'. The opposition in the last episode was between Maisie's unaffected goodness and the gross immorality of Lady Ida; here the tension is between Maisie and Mrs Wix, a very different sort of person. Mrs Wix, who plays in Maisie's life something of the part of Jim in Huck's, is a masterly creation, a character worthy of a wittier Dickens.

Her hair had originally been yellow, but time had turned its glow to ashes, to a turbid, sallow, unvenerable white. Still excessively abundant, it was dressed in a manner of which the poor lady appeared not yet to have recognized the supersession, with a glossy braid, like a large diadem, on the top of the head, and behind, at the nape of the neck, a dingy rosette like a large button. She wore glasses which, in humble reference to a divergent obliquity of vision, she called her straighteners, and a little ugly snuff-coloured dress trimmed with satin bands in the form of scallops and glazed with antiquity. The straighteners, she explained to Maisie, were put on for the sake of others, whom, as she believed, they helped to recognize the direction, otherwise misleading, of her glance; the rest of the melancholy attire could only have been put on for herself. With the added suggestion of her goggles it reminded her pupil of the polished shell or corslet of a horrid beetle.

Poor Mrs Wix with all her disadvantages worked for next to nothing. She was uneducated, and a figure of fun, laughed at, ironically described and imitated. She was snobbish in a simple-minded way, dazzled by the 'brilliance' of the social life of her employers and overwhelmed by the attentions of Sir Claude. 'Neither this, however, nor the old brown frock, nor the diadem, nor the button, made a difference for Maisie in the charm put forth through everything, the charm of Mrs Wix's conveying that, somehow, in her ugliness and her poverty, she was peculiarly and soothingly safe; safer than any one in the world, than papa, than mamma.' Even when Mrs Wix was separated from Maisie, she remained strongly present to Maisie's mind:

Her very silence became after this one of the largest elements of Maisie's consciousness; it proved a warm and habitable air, into which the child penetrated further than she dared ever to mention to her companions. Somewhere in the depths of it the dim straighteners were fixed upon her; somewhere out of the troubled little current Mrs Wix intensely waited.

The touch of Dickensian caricature about Mrs Wix (like the reference to her little girl Clare Matilda 'who was in heaven and yet, embarrassingly, also in Kensal Green') diminishes as the novel goes on. She comes to seem a stronger, a much more positive and serious person. It is her relationship with Maisie, the deep concern it causes her, the way it engages and draws out the best in her, which strikingly increases her stature. This is a fact of which, says James, Maisie herself has an inkling. 'I am not sure that Maisie had not even a dim discernment of the queer law of her own life that made her educate . . . those elders with whom she was concerned. She promoted as it were, their development.' We realize that the epithets in James's description of her, 'her old-fashioned conscience and her dingy decencies', are meant in qualification and not in contempt of the reality of her conscience and her decencies.

Someone like Mrs Wix, so securely in possession of a moral sense, is bound to be worried about Maisie's. The question is presented to Mrs Wix in a particularly horrifying form by Maisie's response to the situation brought about when Mrs Beale, Maisie's stepmother, is cast off by the profligate Mr Beale and is thereby 'freed' to take up with Sir Claude, Maisie's protector at this point. The prospect of this couple being the child's guardians naturally appals Mrs Wix. She is even more shocked by Maisie's answer when the child realizes that she is being required to choose between Sir Claude and Mrs Wix on the one side and Sir Claude and Mrs Beale on the other. 'Why after all should we have to choose between you? Why shouldn't we be four?' And when Maisie wants to know why it should be wrong for Mrs Beale to join the household since she is now 'free', Mrs Wix replies that no one is free to commit a crime. 'Is it a crime then?' asks Maisie. 'Branded in the Bible,' gloomily assents Mrs Wix. 'Haven't you really and truly *any* moral sense?' Mrs Wix despairingly inquires of Maisie. For Maisie her moral sense is a mysterious entity. 'She began, the poor child, with scarcely knowing what it was; but it proved something . . . that she could strike up a sort of acquaintance with.'

There is a beautiful passage in which Maisie does her best to produce the response expected of her. She and Mrs Wix are discussing the probability of Mrs Beale's being unkind to Maisie's adored Sir Claude, should she come to live with them. Maisie:

'If I thought she was unkind to him – I don't know *what* I should do !'

Mrs Wix dropped one of her squints; she even confirmed it by a wild grunt. 'I know what *I* should do.'

Maisie at this felt that she lagged. 'Well, I can think of *one* thing.'

Mrs Wix more directly challenged her. 'What is it then ?'

Maisie met her expression as if it were a game with forfeits for winking. 'I'd *kill* her.' That at least, she hoped as she looked away, would guarantee her moral sense.

Mrs Wix is not satisfied with what Lawrence calls 'the instinct for life' in Maisie, wholesome and thriving as it is. She wants her also to have 'a theory of right and wrong'. She is trying to force Maisie prematurely to take up a stand about theoretical moral issues, to choose between ethical abstractions which are almost meaningless to the child. Such theoretical understanding is the last stage in moral growth; insisted on too early it distorts and falsifies the conscience. That Maisie (like many other children) can withstand this unnatural forcing is a tribute to the health and vitality of her 'instinct for life'. It is also evidence of the genuine honesty of Mrs Wix's intentions, which is in some obscure way sensed by the child; the virtue of honesty can redeem many lamentable errors of tactics.

The final phase of the novel is concerned with Maisie's great decision, an act which signals the end of her young childhood and brings her to the edge of another age, after which, as James says, 'her situation will change and become another affair, subject to other measurements and with a new centre altogether'. We see the preparations for Maisie's choice – her choice of a guardian that is – the impulse from which it springs and its peculiar quality and character. A variety of influences is brought to bear on the child with the aim of influencing her judgement.

Each of her connexions in turn, Mrs Wix, Mrs Beale and Sir Claude, brings an adult's energy and guile to the shaping of the child's will. Maisie has to resist the clumsy honesty of Mrs Wix, who wants to get her to make a public declaration on the side of 'morality'. She has to resist the florid beauty, the hard glitter and the ruthless opportunism of Mrs Beale, who wants Maisie to come with her to lend a respectable colour to the household she proposes to establish with Sir Claude. But the influence hardest to withstand because belonging to one she loves deeply is Sir Claude's, who wants her to sacrifice Mrs Wix. Sir Claude is a man of some acuteness of sensibility and some capacity to appreciate the marvel, in those squalid conditions, of the child's undamaged integrity. He gives Maisie an affection as intense as a parent's and as casual and easy as a friend's. He has a spontaneous charm to which Maisie, surrounded by people who are harsh or unpleasant or gauche, is very susceptible. He has, with Maisie, a 'pleasant fraternizing, equalizing, not a bit patronizing way which made the child ready to go through anything for him and the beauty of which, as she dimly felt, was that it was not a deceitful descent to her years but a real indifference to them'. But he suffers from a kind of moral impotence. He sees the evil in Mrs Beale, but he is still helplessly infatuated with her. He wants to be reasonable, but the conditions of life are always impossibly hampering to him. He is a man whose external grace covers an emptiness of spirit, the irresponsible aristocrat, well-bred, superficial and selfish. His character is in his voice, 'his jesting, postponing, perverting voice'.

But when the moment comes for Maisie to choose, she disentangles herself from the whole tissue of influences enveloping her, and in the realization that it must be her own makes her difficult decision with an astonishing degree of independence. 'The question of the settlement loomed larger to her now: it depended, she had learned so completely on herself. Her choice, as her friend had called it, was there before her like an impossible sum on a slate.' And her choice is neither the application of a moral theory nor the routine consequence of a rule of thumb. It issues from a more profound level, from Maisie's 'instinct for life' '. . . as if she were sinking with a slip from a foothold, her arms made a short jerk. What this jerk represented was the spasm within her of something still deeper than a moral sense.' Her answer to the impossible sum is not a simple but a qualified one. She will give up Mrs Wix if Sir Claude will give up Mrs Beale. The qualification, like the conditional clause which the child at a certain point in its development inserts into a plain statement, testifies to the more complex mastery, the more intricate attainment to which Maisie has come. Maisie's condition is not, of course, one that Sir Claude could accept. But now that does not seem to Maisie to matter so much. 'Somehow, now that it was here, the great moment was not so bad. What helped the child was that she knew what she wanted. All her learning and learning had made her at last learn that.' What Maisie has learned, what she knows now, is that an important decision must come from the depths of one's being. It must be what one *really* wants.

The final words are an apt conclusion for the beautifully lucid, richly ironic structure of the novel. They remind us that many adults, while they want to hasten the child on to what they think it ought to know, yet fix much too rigid a limit to what it does indeed, in a very true sense, 'know'.

They caught the steamer, which was just putting off, and, hustled across the gulf, found themselves on the deck so breathless and so scared that they gave up half the voyage to letting their emotion sink. It sank slowly and imperfectly; but at last, in mid-channel, surrounded by the quiet sea, Mrs Wix had courage to revert. 'I didn't look back, did you?'

'Yes. He wasn't there,' said Maisie.

'Not on the balcony?'

Maisie waited a moment; then, 'He wasn't there,' she simply said again.

Mrs Wix also was silent awhile. 'He went to *her*,' she finally observed.

'Oh, I know!' the child replied.

Mrs Wix gave a sidelong look. She still had room for wonder at what Maisie knew.

Ursula in *The Rainbow*

James's purpose in *What Maisie Knew* is to picture the child utterly exposed. Part of the rich and varied intention of *The Rainbow* is to render the life of the too intensely loved, the over-possessed child. A deep, not fully conscious disharmony between her parents is a predisposing cause of Ursula's relationship with her father. It makes itself felt again immediately the child is born. 'It was a girl. The second of silence on her face when they said so showed him she was disappointed. And a great blazing passion of resentment and protest sprang up in his heart. In that moment he claimed the child.' The intemperance of Will Brangwen's response – his resentment and his angry 'claim' – is more than a passing irritation with Anna's remark or fury at an imagined slight on himself. It derives also from a profound inadequacy in himself.

He was aware of some limit to himself, of something unformed in his way of being, of some buds which were not ripe in him, some folded centres of darkness which would never develop and unfold whilst he was alive in the body. He was unready for fulfilment. Something undeveloped in him limited him, there was a darkness in him which he *could* not unfold, which would never unfold in him.

From the first a very special relationship existed between Ursula and her young father, a strong and intense intimacy that he hardly dared acknowledge. When the child cried in the night, he was shaken intolerably: it seemed to him that the crying came from 'the awful, obliterated sources which were the origin of his living tissue'. He was moved by the baby's strange, new beauty. 'He saw the lovely, creamy, cool little ear of the baby, a bit of dark hair, rubbed to a bronze floss, like bronze-dust.' And the child, too, was as stirred by his presence. Its eyes lit up and dilated when he was by. ''It knew its mother better, it wanted its mother more. But the brightest, sharpest little ecstasy was for the father.' When he saw 'the tiny living thing rolling naked in the mother's lap . . . in a world of hard surfaces and varying altitudes . . . vulnerable and naked at every point', he saw it as an image, a living analogy with his own vulnerability, 'the terror of being so utterly delivered over, helpless at every point'.

Persistently, one idea threads its way in and out of these pages recording the beginnings of Ursula's life. It is the idea of possession, of the father's ownership of the child. His original 'claim' issues from this sense of possession, and insistently the same note is repeated. 'He waited for the child to become his. . . . It was his own. . . . So that the father had the elder baby. . . . She was a piece of light that really belonged to him, that played within his darkness.' The ownership implicit in these phrases is not that involved in the possession of an object outside and at some distance from the possessor. It is much closer to that mysterious and uneasy proprietorship which a person has over himself. Theoretically, the father recognizes that the child has a life different from his own, but that recognition is absorbed in his passion of possession. 'It had a separate being, but it was his own child. His flesh and blood vibrated to it.' The root of this almost desperate sense of possession is the father's deep uncertainty about himself and his need therefore to be constantly reassured. The child, he feels, in its vivid response to him, is a kind of proof of his own being. 'As the newly-opened, newly-dawned eyes looked at him, he wanted them to perceive him, to recognize him. Then he was verified.'

In this too charged, overstrained atmosphere Ursula's life begins. Probably not since Wordsworth has a writer conveyed with such essential justice the first stirrings of consciousness, the first movements of the body. Some of the subtlety of Lawrence's portrayal is to be attributed to his having been brought up himself in similar circumstances with his mother filling the role of Ursula's father; more to his extraordinary sense of otherness, his capacity to enter into wholly different natures; but most is to be attributed to his genius for transmuting his experience and ordering his capacities so as to make them both serve with delicate rightness the purposes of his art. And his art is above all an art which uses poetic means to reveal the universal human substance, the permanent, impersonal energy which in other novelists we find almost dissolved in 'character' or encrusted with accidents. How exactly and how convincingly, for example, Lawrence in the following passage catches that generic motion of childhood, the strange drifting movement of a young child hurrying, when it seems hardly tethered to the ground and when, with an odd mixture of confidence and uncertainty, it performs miracles of balance and accommodation.

At evening, towards six o'clock, Anna very often went across the lane to the stile, lifted Ursula over into the field, with a: 'Go and meet Daddy.' Then Brangwen, coming up the steep round of the hill, would see before him on the brow of the path a tiny, tottering, windblown little mite with a dark head, who, as soon as she saw him, would come running in tiny, wild, windmill fashion, lifting her arms up and down to him, down the steep hill. His heart leapt up, he ran his fastest to her, to catch her, because he knew she would fall. She came fluttering on, wildly, with her little limbs flying. And he was glad when he caught her up in his arms.

As convincing, equally exact, and profound in a way that recalls Wordsworth's subterranean explorations of the mind, is Lawrence's record of the beginnings of the child's thought. At first Ursula's life is just an aggregation of incidents, each sliding unemphatically into the next; to the child an event is neither provoked by the one before nor productive of the one after. In this world, bare shadows and suggestiveness, the brightness and prominence of reality belong only to the immediate and the explicit.

The child ran about absorbed in life, quiet, full of amusement. She did not notice things, nor changes nor alterations. One day she would find daisies in the grass, another day apple-blossoms would be sprinkled white on the ground, and she would run among it, for pleasure because it was there. Yet again birds would be pecking at the cherries, her father would throw cherries down from the tree all round her on the garden. Then the fields were full of hay.

The child's consciousness, which is partial and successive, does not include a sense of the past or the future. It has to be discovered, and the provocation to learn it is love. Affection is the seed of time. It is love – intensifying the delight in the present and correspondingly bringing discomfort in absence – which introduces an element of permanence into the child's experience, and the first faint notion of time into its mind.

> She did not remember what had been nor what would be, the outside things were there each day. She was always herself, the world outside was accidental. . . . Only her father occupied any permanent position in the childish consciousness. When he came back she remembered vaguely how he had gone away, when he went away she knew vaguely that she must wait for his coming back. Whereas her mother, returning from an outing, merely became present, there was no reason for connecting her with some previous departure.

The love between father and daughter is the first organizing influence in Ursula's mental life, shaping even those essential ideas of time, permanence and change, the self and what lies outside it, which henceforth order all human thoughts and render all experience intelligible. But there is something strained and distorted in the father's love – it is too narrow, too possessive, too personal. It is the kind of love which consumes its object, which cannot keep its distance or allow its object any degree of autonomy. The father's love springs from some incoherence in his own nature, an absence of serenity or self-acceptance; it is a projection of his own need, his own tension and inadequacy. And so intricately is the child involved with him that it is impossible for him to make the painful and wrenching effort necessary for regarding Ursula as another being, separate, autonomous and sufficient. In Will, Lawrence presents us with an extreme example of that failure of nerve and of that want of clarity of being present in every parent for whom the umbilical cord is never cut. This quality in the father's love conditions the affection Ursula returns to him. His is dependent, hers protective, a strange reversal of natural roles. 'When he was disagreeable, the child echoed to the crying of some need in him, and she responded blindly. Her heart followed him as if he had some tie with her, and some love which he could not deliver. Her heart followed him persistently, in its love.' To base one's life, like Will Brangwen, on the support and accord of a young child is to put an intolerable strain on the child. The relaxed rhythm of childhood is shattered, and the child, like Ursula, is jerked too early into a too sharpened awareness. As in a premature birth, she is pulled from a mindless tranquillity towards a too urgent, a too personal concern.

Her father was the dawn wherein her consciousness woke up. But for him, she might have gone on like the other children, Gudrun and Theresa and Catherine, one with the flowers and insects and playthings, having no existence apart from the concrete object of her attention. But her father came too near to her. The clasp of his hands and the power of his breast woke her up almost in pain from the transient unconsciousness of childhood. Wide-eyed, unseeing, she was awake before she knew how to see.

Will Brangwen's love for his daughter is a narrow and therefore narrowing love. It has an exclusive character which inspires in the child a corresponding jealousy and resentment for anyone outside the magic alliance who attempts to break into it. In particular, Ursula's resentment is directed against her mother's influence and authority. And this is so even when her mother intervenes in her defence against the sporadic, senseless acts of cruelty which her father, in a kind of angry impotence, commits against her. There are several examples of these negative, destructive impulses into which Will's frantic unbalanced love seems to drive him almost against his will. There is, for example, the violence with which he attacks Ursula when in her play about the church she disturbs the hymn-books and cushions, or again there is the sadistic cruelty with which he terrifies and sickens the child by driving her unbearably high on the swing-boat at the fair. The demands of her father's love come out of his own weakness. So exigent a love diminishes and damages its object, which can never feel adequate to the immense claims made upon it. Ursula is overwhelmed by her vast, vaguely grasped responsibility towards her father. She is filled with 'the painful, terrified helplessness of childhood'.

Still she set towards him like a quivering needle. All her life was directed by her awareness of him, her wakefulness to his being. . . . But there was the dim, childish sense of her own smallness and inadequacy, a fatal sense of worthlessness. She could not do anything, she was not enough. . . . This knowledge deadened her from the first.

'It deadened her.' The image of mortification is the one through which Lawrence expresses his deepest judgement on Will's relationship with Ursula. Love is the generator and protector of life. But Will's is a killing love. It hardens the child. It puts a blight, a frost on her. It brings disillusion, 'something cold and isolating'. The scene in which Lawrence's judgement is most powerfully and dramatically realized is that in which Ursula is helping her father to plant potatoes in his garden. It is beautifully appropriate that the occasion for the scene should be a collision between what is most intensely real and important to the child – the universe of play and fancy – and what is to her the mystery of the grown-up power to work deliberately, something the child dreads because it is impossible for her and because it makes her father a stranger to her. Ursula was delighted and excited when Will asked her to help him. ' "Ay," he said, "you can put some taters in for me. Look – like that – these little sprits standing up – so much apart, you see." And stooping down he quickly, surely placed the spritted potatoes in the soft grip, where they rested separate and pathetic on the heavy cold earth.' But the operation was too difficult, too serious and too long for the child. She fumbles and becomes afraid and overcome by her responsibility. Her father works on confidently, ignoring her as she stands 'helplessly stranded on his world'. When he came by he said to her, ' "You didn't help me much." The child looked at him dumbly. Already her heart was heavy because of her own disappointment. Her mouth was dumb and pathetic. But he did not notice. He went his way.'

Then the next day he smashes even more destructively into her sensitive child's world. 'He turns on her shouting, "Who's been tramplin' an' dancin' across where I've just sowed seed? I know it's you, nuisance! Can you find nowhere else to walk, but just over my seed-beds? But it's like you, that is – no heed but to follow your own greedy nose." ' The vulnerable child is shocked. 'She stood dazzled with pain and shame and unreality. Her soul, her consciousness seemed to die away. She became shut off and senseless, a little fixed creature whose soul had gone hard and unresponsive. The sense of her own unreality hardened her like a

frost. She cared no longer.' And when, inflamed by her indifference, he threatens to strike her, 'the child did not alter in the
least. The look of indifference, complete glancing indifference, as
if nothing but herself existed to her, remained fixed. Yet far
away in her the sobs were tearing her soul. And when he had
gone, she would go and creep under the parlour sofa, and lie
clinched in the silent, hidden misery of childhood.'

It takes a very great writer to make us feel, as we do here,
beneath the simple surface of a familiar domestic event, like a
father's anger with his child because her play interfered with his
work, the vibrations of a deep and complex human disaster. And
disastrous is not too extravagant a way to describe the effect of
these experiences with her father on Ursula's life. As well as the
child's natural mortification at her father's brutality, she suffers
another kind of mortification – 'a deadening of the soul' – more
permanent and injurious in its consequences. After such bitterness the child's instinctive response is to blot out the memory of
what has happened

so that the pain and the insult should not be real. She asserted herself
only. There was now nothing in the world but her own self. So very
soon she came to believe in the outward malevolence that was against
her. And very early she learned that even her adored father was part
of this malevolence. And very early she learned to harden her soul in
resistance and denial of all that was outside her, harden herself upon
her own being.

A healthy love helps the child to accept the order and justice of
the world and to recognize the fundamental goodness and sanity
of life itself. But one like Will's communicates its distortion to
the child's very sensibility so that it sees a disturbed and malicious
world from which it must flee into itself. Nor is this all. A child
can tolerate a malevolent world only by denying its reality, and
so like Ursula it becomes convinced of, and tortured by, the
illusion and trickery of everything beyond its own identity.

But she was always tormented by the unreality of outside things.
The earth was to walk on. Why must she avoid a certain patch, just
because it was called a seed-bed? It was the earth to walk on. This was

her instinctive assumption. And when he bullied her, she became hard, cut herself off from all connexion, lived in the little separate world of her own violent will.

As she grew older the relationship between Ursula and her father did not cease. But it was tense and anxious, always straining to break. Her father remained for Ursula 'a centre of magic and fascination', so that 'she seemed to run in the shadow of some dark potent secret of which she would not, of whose existence even she dared not become conscious, it cast such a spell over her, and so darkened her mind'. And yet the child was continually striving for her own separate identity, 'always relaxing on her own violent will into her own separate world of herself'. 'When she returned to her love for her father, the seed of mistrust and defiance burned unquenched, though covered up far from sight. She no longer belonged to him unquestioned. Slowly, slowly, the fire of mistrust and defiance burned in her. . . .' But they were never wholly separated, never cleanly broken apart into their own different identities, which would have been the condition of a true and sound relationship. 'There was this curious taunting intimacy between them.' With it persisted Ursula's sense of the world, whether the world of home or of school or of neighbours or of authority, as illusory and menacing.

There was always this menace against her. This strange sense of cruelty and ugliness always imminent, ready to seize hold upon her, this feeling of the grudging power of the mob lying in wait for her, who was the exception, formed one of the deepest influences of her life. Wherever she was, at school, among friends, in the street, in the train, she instinctively abated herself, made herself smaller, feigned to be less than she was, for fear that her undiscovered self should be seen, pounced upon, attacked by brutish resentment of the commonplace, the average Self.

There are three influences on Ursula which qualify her father's, which to some degree mitigate the harm to the child of Will's excessive, too personal attachment, and which help her 'to move out of the intricately woven illusion of her life'. They are her grandmother, the Grammar School and religion. Each of them represents an order, larger and more enduring, calmer and wiser than the nervous, stormy life at home. Each accords a measure of dignity and a recognition of her own self to the young girl. Each of them helps to satisfy her craving 'for some spirituality and stateliness'. The power and the delicacy with which Lawrence exhibits the exact character of each of these influences must be one of the great fictional and poetic achievements of modern literature.

Lydia Brangwen had retired from the stress and violence and the interested passion of the young. 'She wanted at last her own innocence and peace.' At her grandmother's Ursula found gentleness, understanding and a completely disinterested affection. 'The little girl and the musing fragile woman of sixty seemed to understand the same language. . . . So that for the eldest child the peace of her grandmother's bedroom was exquisite. Here Ursula came as to a hushed, paradisal land, here her own existence became simple and exquisite to her as if she were a flower.' The sense of restraint and civilized order is implicit in each tiny detail of Ursula's meetings with her grandmother. 'Ursula had a special green and gold cup kept for herself at the house. There was thin bread and butter, and cress for tea. It was all special and wonderful. She ate very daintily, with little fastidious bites.' That the civilization – 'the spirituality and stateliness' – which she loved in her grandmother was ancient and rooted and remote was a marvellous thing to the child. Her heart beat as she listened to her grandmother's stories of the family and its origins. 'She could not understand, but she seemed to feel far-off things. It gave her a deep, joyous thrill to know she hailed from far-off Poland, and that dark-bearded impressive man.' It was to her grandmother that Ursula addressed 'her deepest childish questions'.

'But when I am grown up, will somebody love me?'
'Yes, some man will love you, child, because it's your nature. And I hope it will be somebody who will love you for what you are, and not for what he wants of you.'

She clung to her grandmother. Here was peace and security. Here, from her grandmother's peaceful room, the door opened on to the greater space, the past, which was so big that all it contained seemed tiny; loves and births and deaths, tiny units and features within a vast horizon. That was a great relief to know the tiny importances of the individual, within the great past.

If her grandmother brings Ursula into the presence of an ancient civilization and the comfort of the past, the Grammar School at Nottingham to which she goes at the age of twelve gives Ursula a great liberation in the present. Ursula's life at home as the eldest of a large family was onerous and responsible. The little ones depended on her, hunted her out when she wished to be alone and swept her along in 'a storm of movement' from which there was no escape. 'She hated so much being in charge', and was continually fretted by her responsibility to the others. The small house filled with the press and swirl of babies and young children became a nightmare to her. 'When she saw, later, a Rubens picture with storms of naked babies and found this was called "Fecundity", she shuddered and the word became abhorrent to her. She knew as a child what it was to live amid storms of babies, in the heat and swelter of fecundity.' From all this the Grammar School afforded her a retreat, a space to collect herself in. It also rescued her from the village school with its 'meagre teachers' and the niggardly and begrudging companionship of the village children. Above all it introduced her to the life of learning and intelligence. Lawrence brilliantly communicates the joy and excitement and the deep sense of liberation of the intelligent child's first discovery of the forms of educated thought.

She was happy. Up here, in the Grammar School, she fancied the air was finer, beyond the factory smoke. She wanted to learn Latin and Greek and French and mathematics. She trembled like a postulant when she wrote the Greek alphabet for the first time. She was upon another hill-slope, whose summit she had not scaled. There was always the marvellous eagerness in her heart, to climb and to see beyond. A Latin verb was virgin soil to her: she sniffed a new odour in it; it meant something, though she did not know what it meant. But she gathered it up: it was significant. When she knew that:

$$x^2 - y^2 = (x+y)(x-y)$$

then she felt that she had grasped something, that she was liberated into an intoxicating air, rare and unconditioned. And she was very glad as she wrote her French exercise:

'J'ai donné le pain à mon petit frère.'

In all these things there was the sound of a bugle to her heart, exhilarating, summoning her to perfect places.

The third of these influences on Ursula was religion. The special character of Brangwen Christianity was its appeal to the absolute, the insistence on the otherness of God. It is as though the intimacy of their family relationships needed to be balanced by the remoteness of the Almighty. They – and most of all Ursula – had no patience with a familiar, domestic piety. 'They wanted the sense of the eternal and immortal, not a list of rules for everyday conduct. . . . It was the vulgar mind which would allow nothing extra-human, nothing beyond itself to exist. . . . But Ursula was all for the absolute. . . . To her Jesus was another world. He was not of this world.' The centre of their religious life was Christmas, and to a lesser degree, like a diminishing echo, Sunday. At Christmas they felt the reality of the absolute, and its closeness and power. 'Everywhere was a sense of mystery and rousedness. Everyone was preparing for something.' Then they felt the ecstasy, even if, as traditional religion declined, 'it was faint and inadequate. The cycle of creation still wheeled in the Church year. After Christmas, the ecstasy slowly sank and changed. Sunday followed Sunday, trailing a fine movement, a finely developed transformation over the heart of the family.' It is this great tradition, the richness and spirituality of which the novel superbly reconstructs, that dignifies and enlarges the lives of the children. Its more than temporal rhythms relax the tension of lives too frantically engrossed with the immediate. Its impersonal harmony incorporates into itself the stresses and muddle of the merely personal life.

So the children lived the year of christianity, the epic of the soul of mankind. Year by year the inner, unknown drama went on in them, their hearts were born and came to fullness, suffered on the cross, gave up the ghost, and rose again to unnumbered days, untired, having at least this rhythm of eternity in a ragged, inconsequential life.

The Child in the Poetry of Walter de la Mare

Walter de la Mare does not belong with Mark Twain, Henry James or D. H. Lawrence. He was a minor poet. This is not quite the platitude it ought to be. Naturally one discounts the amiable plaudits uttered at his death which seek to inflate his importance as a poet. But a proper emphasis is blurred by more specious attempts to set him up as a major prose writer. His prose works, of which the *Memoirs of a Midget* (a significant title) is the most interesting, offer us only in a diffuse way the characteristic qualities present in concentration in his poetry. They are the evidence of no different powers and testify to no new development or any essential change of interests. The death of a minor poet is an occasion for reflecting how hard, in our brutal times, is the part of the true minor talent. Circumstances like ours, so inimical to the development of artistic capacity, require even from the major writer dedication, originality, force and stamina. If we leave Lawrence aside as a great natural genius of surpassing powers, who must have been a great writer in this or any age, we can hardly estimate the immensity of effort exacted from the major modern writer by the conditions of our time. We cannot guess what it must have cost Eliot to have re-established his connexion with an older tradition or Yeats to have created a whole new idiom. These circumstances are peculiarly severe on the minor poet who may like de la Mare have the devotion and the integrity but not the great creative span. The minor writer desperately needs the support of a thriving tradition. Given the stability of a background and the solidity of a ground underfoot, given the soil and air, he may go on to nourish his own gifts with some prospect of success. But when de la Mare began writing in the early nineteen hundreds – his first books were published in 1906 and 1912 – there was available nothing but the residue of a decayed Romanticism, the bent of which was towards a cloistered and decorative poetry, not only remote from anything like 'a criticism of life' but even far from life itself. How then did he, with no more than a modicum of the creative power of the major

writer and with a markedly less positive sensibility than a writer
like Edward Thomas, succeed, as he did succeed, in achieving out
of the clichés of Romanticism a distinctively personal tone and a
recognizably individual vision?

The answer seems to be that what I have called the bent of
Romanticism accorded well with a bias of the poet's nature which
was set against the lucid and waking world and towards a
universe of dream and enchantment, where the most vivid life is
a period of drowsy consciousness between sleep and sleep.

> Very old are we men;
>   Our dreams are tales
> Told in dim Eden
>   By Eve's nightingales;
> We wake and whisper awhile,
>   But, the day gone by,
> Silence and sleep like fields
>   Of amaranth lie.

Validity is given to this minor Keatsian mood, a certain definition
and authenticity are communicated to it, by the poet's successful
identification with the consciousness of the child, since this is an
order of feeling which has a sanction in the life of the child. I say
identification with the consciousness of the child. But really it is
one sort of child, the sensitive, introspective child, lonely and a
bit odd, contemplative and shy. One can picture him, the chief
persona of de la Mare's poems, stalky and pale, with thin bones
and fine hair, inclined to lassitude, occasionally shaken with the
tremors of curious fears, inhabiting with a subdued happiness a
private world and resenting the intrusion of bumbling and uncomprehending adults. It is this child, 'perplexed and still' like
the Traveller in *The Listeners*, as he faces a massive and indifferent universe whose experience is the substance of de la Mare's
poetry. It is the combination of a child's feeling, the experience
of immaturity, with a sophisticated and highly literary language,
the vocabulary of maturity, which gives to de la Mare's poetry its
low-toned but unmistakable individuality. Look for example at
the conclusion of a well-known poem *The Ghost*:

> A face peered. All the grey night
>   In chaos of vacancy shone;
> Nought but vast sorrow was there –
>   The sweet cheat gone.

Here the 'chaos of vacancy', a Donne-like phrase, is no more than the shrouded landscape of a disappointed child, uninflected by hope, obscure, grey and dispirited, and the 'vast sorrow' is only the total misery of a thwarted child. The association of simple feeling and complex utterance governs not only the choice of words but also the form of the syntax. The unadorned statement, 'A face peered', a simple sentence of subject and verb, precedes a more elaborate and inverted statement, which is itself followed by the more intricate 'Nought but vast sorrow was there' with its inset qualification, and then by the compressed and elided structure of 'The sweet cheat gone'. In a sense the whole stanza is a 'sweet cheat'. It offers an insidious and lulling magic. But it is a '*sweet* cheat'. What it gives it gives with elegance and control. It is magic, but magic refined into ritual, and like ritual and unlike magic it is symbolic of an actuality of experience, of a certain state of being.

The actuality, the state of being to which the best poems of de la Mare correspond, is the mind of the young child, say between five and nine. It is this short space of life that the poet explores with address and realizes inwardly and subtly, and it is this particular kind of awareness which he adopts as a means – not of examining – that is for de la Mare too ratiocinative a word – hardly of looking at – but rather of glancing obliquely at his own experience. As I shall point out, it is a method attended by its own dangers. In this miniature cosmos size or the lack of it is very important. The child himself is small; the de la Mare child like the bird in his poem *A Robin* is:

> Changeling and solitary,
> Secret and sharp and small.

The things he cares for are diminutive – notice the many poems of de la Mare devoted to tiny subjects, *The Bottle, The Spark, The Robin, The Snowdrop, The Snowflake, The Owl, The Moth, The*

Linnet, Jenny Wren ('A tiny, inch-long, eager, ardent, Feathered mouse'). Beyond a certain point of size, indeed, things cease to engage the child's attention and recede into a vague and neutral background. The first stanza of *The Scribe* illustrates this concern with the tiny and the sharply detailed.

> What lovely things
>   Thy hand hath made:
> The smooth-plumed bird
>   In its emerald shade,
> The seed of the grass,
>   The speck of stone
> Which the wayfaring ant
>   Stirs – and hastes on!

The beginning of *The Bottle* shows the recession from the small particular thing to the vague and inscrutable

> Of green and hexagonal glass,
>   With sharp, fluted sides –
> Vaguely transparent these walls,
>   Wherein motionless hides
> A simple so potent it can
>   To oblivion lull. . . .

A sharp figure on a vague ground is a classical description of perception; but in the perception of the young child the figure is uncannily sharp, the ground mistily vague. And since the child must have a strong bond of interested attachment towards what is to hold his attention, the ground can never be merely vague or just neutral. For the child a merely neutral universe becomes actively indifferent and so oppressive and even terrifying.

> Start not! – 'twas but some wild thing's cry,
>   No wailing ghost you heard.
> Yet ghosts there are, remote and chill,
>   Waiting the moon's phantasmal fire. . . .[1]

Even time, which we think of as a colourless medium for events, utterly neutral and impersonal, has for the child a hint of menace, a sort of personal vindictiveness. It consumes itself away when he is happy and drags itself out when he is wretched.

> Time, heedless of the past,
> No loving-kindness knows;
> Chill unto mortal lip
> Still Lethe flows.[2]

In a world where the known is little, the familiar comfortingly small, and where the indifferent and the alien are immense and hostile, the young child is powerfully influenced to retreat into his own small, lit space, and especially into the comfort of the day-dream which suspends the rough operations of an intimidating reality.

> Isled in the midnight air,
> Musked with the dark's faint bloom,
> Out into glooming and secret haunts
> The flame cries, 'Come!'[3]

Here again is a quality which fits smoothly the poet's daylight-shunning temperament. It is clear that this could be a dangerous and retrogressive habit. It is one thing to recreate this childish tendency with delicacy and conviction, as the poet often does. It is another for the adult to take it over as a permanent device for evading the disagreeable. There is no doubt that in many poems de la Mare makes no bones about which of the two, the sleeping or the waking consciousness, he prefers.

> Two words they have – a globe forgot,
> Wheeling from dark to light;
> And all the enchanted realm of dream
> That burgeons out of night.[4]

Poetry of this sort is no more than an inducement to a self-indulgent reverie, an opiate for the active intelligence and all the more insidious for the skill with which the invitation is offered. Here are the beginnings of two poems which exhibit this betrayal of the adult mind.

> Softly along the road of evening
> In a twilight dim with rose....[5]

And again:

After the songless rose of evening,
  Night quiet, dark, still,
In nodding cavalcade advancing
  Starred the deep hill:
You, in the valley standing,
  In your quiet wonder took
All that glamour, peace, and mystery
  In one grave look.[6]

More effective are those poems in which the poet preserves sufficient of his own identity to allow him to hold the object some distance away, if only at arm's length. Then we are aware of the poet not only as participant but also as observer. It is a curious thing that what in most poets is a sign of failure – the reader's impression that the poet is writing *about* his experience, describing it instead of presenting it – is for de la Mare a condition of success. The reason is the nature of the experience the poet addresses himself to, which, with no gap left between him and it, with a too complete identification of the two, is liable to betray him into an indolent and self-deceiving fantasy. (On the other hand, when de la Mare stepped out of the guise of the articulate child and wrote as an adult of purely adult themes, he could be guilty of the lurid and garish *In the Dock* or the prim whimsy of *Mercutio*.)

But when he wrote with, or from, the awareness of the sensitive child and yet kept in reserve a measure of adult detachment, de la Mare composed many poems remarkable for fineness of discernment and remarkable also, within his chosen range, for virtuosity of theme. In these poems the language is sparer, the movement nimbler, the curve of the dreamy line more delicately modulated. *Martha* is a good example of the poet in his double role of participant and observer: he is both one of the spellbound audience and also the casually interested adult passing by. The enchantment and the dream are here the legitimate issue of the situation.

And her beauty far away
  Would fade, as her voice ran on,
Till hazel and summer sun
  And all were gone:

177

All fordone and forgot;
    And like clouds in the height of the sky,
Our hearts stood still in the hush
    Of an age gone by.

He had an unusal gift for evoking the stillness and the hush in which the children are suspended as in an element in this poem. D. H. Lawrence spoke of 'Walter de la Mare's perfect appreciation of life at still moments'. *The Sleeper* beautifully suggests how a child realizes the intense and positive quality of silence as Ann comes into the house to find her mother asleep in a chair.

Yet slumber lay so deep
Even her hands upon her lap
    Seemed saturate with sleep.
And as Ann peeped, a cloudlike dread
    Stole over her, and then,
On stealthy, mouselike feet she trod
    And tiptoed out again.

In *Myself,* another poem which evokes the quality of silence, he shows a different facet of his apprehension of the child mind. The poem figures with astonishing finesse one of those disturbing 'metaphysical' gropings of the young child. In *Myself* it is the child's strange capacity to be aware of himself, and simultaneously aware of himself as another, an *alter ego*.

Along the lonely paths,
    A little child like me
With face, with hands, like mine
    Plays ever silently. . . .

After the birds are flown
    From singing in the trees,
When all is grey, all silent,
    Voices, and winds, and bees;

And I am there alone:
    Forlornly, silently,
Plays in the evening garden
    Myself with me.

In this poem we note a subdued melancholy, a tone appropriate to the child's feeling of affectionate, and almost detached, pity for himself. The same combination of pity and 'metaphysical' speculation occurs in the famous *Fare Well*, except that now the pity is more prominent, but the speculation is there working to brace and control the feeling. The first lines might have been composed as de la Mare's version of the child's question, What is it like, what will it be like when I'm not there? –

> When I lie where shades of darkness
> Shall no more assail my eyes,
> Nor the rain make lamentation
>   When the wind sighs;
> How will fare the world whose wonder
> Was the very proof of me?

But what after all dignifies this poetry which some would want to dismiss as a poetry of the nursery? It seems to be this, that beneath the murmur of childish voices we hear a more ancient and wiser tongue, the language of myth and fairytale, dream and symbol. And why do we feel that these poems have a touch of universal truth? It is because under de la Mare's falling and lapsing rhythms we are aware of another rhythm, a faint and profound harmony, the rhythm of a regress to the womb, the sound of the timid soul in flight back to its origins. Walter de la Mare made his poetry out of what may be a radical failing but is certainly a permanent fact of human life.

CHAPTER 8

THE NOTION OF CHARACTER IN EDUCATION AND LITERATURE, AND W. B. YEATS

I

CHARACTER is a brisk, abrupt word, an executive word, so precise in sound that we may be misled into accepting it as equally definitive in meaning. It suggests a decisive, stable structure, consistent and strongly set, whereas reflection shows its meaning to be remarkably evasive. Like an oiled wrestler, it will not be held down. Simple awareness of self gives no final answer. '*Qu'est-ce que le moy?*' asks Pascal, and elsewhere he comments: '*L'homme ne sait à quel rang se mettre. Il est visiblement égaré, et tombe de son vrai lieu sans le pouvoir retrouver. Il le cherche partout avec inquiétude et sans succès dan des ténèbres impénétrables*'. It is possible that character is a word the meaning of which is immediately apprehended, which is indefinable just because we know at once what it is, and there may well be some justification for this view. Perhaps character which we are accustomed to offer as the ultimate source of action should remain unexamined, a primary datum which it is unprofitable to scrutinize and impossible to explain. If, nevertheless, we attempt to enumerate some of the chief notes involved in this very dense term, we do find prominent among them the notion referred to, character as the source of action and, in particular, of habitual action; another is character as individuality, the incommunicable self; and another is character as the person directed towards moral ends. Indeed, the habitual, moral self probably composes a large part of our ordinary understanding of character. But the defect of such a view, arising from an insistence on what is formed and static in character, is a failure sufficiently to take into account its potential and dynamic nature. Character is determined and finally cast only at the point of death; throughout life it has within it the power of turning, changing, deciding for the new. Certainly conditions limit character, which submits to boundaries and both assumes and persists with a certain shape, but it has, at a deeper and more significant place, impulses and movements towards the indeterminate and the unformed. Character is being, but it is also becoming.

There is a use of the term character which both illustrates the notion of character pointed at here and introduces at once its connexion with literature, namely, character in the theatre, character as *dramatis persona*. From Aristotle to Bradley, character has provided critics with a direct entrance into the central problems of drama and, in the memory of audiences throughout centuries, the history of drama, a chaos of conflicting styles, of different languages and antipathetic epochs, has arranged itself as a constellation of characters, an immense *dramatis personae*. It is true that some critics have overemphasized the importance of character in drama, forgetting that drama, being more comprehensive than character, includes also action, language, rhythm, imagery, tone, tempo and convention, and that all these are engaged in a system of complicated relations, which make sometimes one, sometimes another, dominant in contributing to the total effect. These critics have thought, in particular, of action as existing chiefly for the expression of character and implicitly of the dramatist as above all else a 'subtle-souled psychologist'. But the more rational view is that which holds that it is the plot, the whole of the action, which is primary, and that character is but one of the modes of its expression, a mode which is not fixed or static and never finally formulated, for it obeys both the demands of the whole and the necessities of the local situation. Such a theory of character in drama certainly reduces the dominance given it by the great Romantic critics, just as it loosens and reforms a dramatic criticism that has become a character-ridden technique, but it by no means causes the idea of character in drama to powder away into insignificance. On the contrary, it might with justice be maintained that the post-Bradley approach enriches our notion of character or at least that it compels us to attend to an essential but neglected truth about character, its fluidity and mobility, its irregular and turbulent vitality. And indeed this view of character would be appropriate to that category of art, the drama, and to its most intense and concentrated form, tragic drama, which is more than any other distinguished by life and energy, which is most remote from the elegiac, the contemplative and the reminiscent and closest to the actual, the present, the immediate transactions of life.

In the distillation of contemporary educational theory a larger and larger part is being taken not just by the findings of sociology and social psychology, but by their ruling assumption and by the attitudes provoked by them, a process which has gone with an intensifying insistence on the influential power of the group setting and the cultural pattern, and a prompt disposition to accept without much critical examination what may be called the Arapesh-Mundugumor hypothesis. One is led, in this situation, to wonder whether the dramatic view of character might not well be transposed as a corrective and counterweight from the understanding of character in literature to that of character in education. The prevalent phrase 'social engineering' with its equivalence of inert material and living persons, the main potentiality of whom is an aptness to be worked upon in the interests of a deified abstraction like the group, urges upon us the need for a more active and powerful theory of character; not, it should be stated, with a propagandist's futile effort to impugn what is valid, but with the purpose of preserving another essential dimension so that our theory may keep some relevance in the face of the actual complexity of the facts. An active and powerful theory of character may be observed, or rather experienced, embodied and in operation in drama and supremely in tragic drama. It asserts the primacy of the person against the group, an assertion which is urgently required at a time when the development of character is seen as a process of conforming and adjusting (the overtones of the mechanistic metaphor are suggestive) to an external system of group forces. But what stands out as a common mark of major dramatic characters – as the common quality of their various powerful individualities – is that their development, far from being a matter of closer and closer approximation to group norms, discloses an increasing hostility to the values of the worlds they inhabit. The distance between the tragic character and his universe is lengthened, not shortened, the tension between them becomes more not less acute, the original opposition quickens to a violence of rejection. Who could imagine an acquiescing Lear or a conforming Antigone? And these characters are not sports or aberrations; they are the symbols of a richer humanity, and we respond to them as we do because of our conviction that they perform an essential human office, the preservation of man's strangeness and his solitariness, his status as an alien.

If this is so, then surely the implied aim of much educational theory and practice, which is to fit man more easily into his situation, to muffle the sense of strangeness in the universe, ignores a permanent fact of human nature, the fact that man ultimately is not at home in the world, that he is a person, but a displaced person. Unlike the bird and the beast, to which the world offers the smooth caress of an environment whole and total as the womb, man, when not narcoticized by ignorance and brutality, must flinch at the inhospitableness of his world. The universe of man is at all times impregnated with the scent of anxiety; every man is an 'age of anxiety'. Does it not appear, therefore, that the aim enunciated for education, in particular by many social psychologists, namely, the achievement of an integrated personality, derives less from an appreciation of balance and wholeness and more from a fear of anxiety which is taken as an infallible symptom of neurotic distress, on a par with fever and pain, instead of what it may be, a condition of developed psychic life, and that in fact the ideal of character advanced here is really that of the monolithic personality which, homogeneous, eupeptic and untouched by any division or tension, deals in a competent, managerial way with its environment? Common experience denies the existence, and imagination recoils from the possibility, of a human being as such an hygienic, biological abstraction. Certainly it receives no support from tragic drama, where the essential relation is that of conflict, and where the relations of conflict between the person and the environment and between person and person are evidence of a more radical conflict within the protagonist himself.

This kind of inward conflict in drama occurs only when a civilization has advanced to a comparatively high degree of self-consciousness. It exists, if at all, in primitive drama as a promise of possible growth, and the development of drama can be seen as a process in which merely latent conflict sharpens into more definite existence, and then recedes from the bluntly external into a subtler, inner world. Moreover, by a form of literary recapitulation the growth of the individual major dramatist rehearses the general evolution, moving through a similar accentuation of conflict and towards a comparable recession from the outer world. It is, paradoxically, when the artist's experience of the private world of conflict has deepened, that his control of the public world gains in firmness and deftness; the grasp of the one leads not to evasion but to penetration of the other, to finer accuracy and sharper cutting power. The source of energy is at the centre, at the hub of the wheel. Lear's madness may be supposed to be one of the purest expressions of human conflict at its most agonizing, but his intolerable pain permits, and perhaps even provokes, intermittently, acute recognition and sure judgement of public issues, of corrupted justice, tainted authority, arrogant wealth.

It can be argued, then, that an education which is directed emphatically at the environment, a pragmatic and relativistic education which ignores or denies the fundamental stress in man's nature and regards as morbid its emotional concomitant, anxiety, will fall short even of its own purpose. It is the Dostoevskian mind which first and most fully comprehends that utterly 'objective' activity, the dynamics of revolutionary power, the Lawrentian feeling for 'the flow and recoil of sympathy' which can be the ground for an implacably exact diagnosis of contemporary malady. If the emotional correlative for the run of mankind of the tragic hero's 'dense and driven passion' is anxiety, its moral correlative is guilt. In the eyes of the psychologists, anxiety is suspect; in those of the sociologists guilt is condemned. The intentions of both appear to be bent, at least as they are reflected in educational thought, on the effort to dissolve the concept of guilt. What began with the aim of correcting disproportion has concluded by dispersing the substance of guilt (of dispersing it, that is, intellectually, for modern man exhibits the curious dichotomy of one groaning in the toils of a guilt the existence of which he rejects). Guilt, it is held, is irrational, and its irrationality, which can be inferred from the psycho-analytic account of the infantile origins of human behaviour and attitudes, is taken to be endorsed by the sociologists' reduction of morals to folkways or patterns of social learning.

There are two comments to be made on this view. In the first place, it is another example of the immoderately reductive habit of modern thinking which in its obsessive attachment to origins betrays an incapacity for certain kinds of immediate experience and a relative neglect of ends. In the second, the term irrational can be predicted of guilt only on an unduly narrow understanding of rational, one which assumes that the rational is to be equated with what satisfies the mathematical intelligence, a valid, but abstract and rigidly delimited category, emptied for its own purposes of all the concrete vivacity and the iridescent particularity found in life and in literature. Only if intelligence is restricted to *l'esprit de géometrie* and its area of exercise contracted to that crystalline sphere in which pure harmonies, already implicit in their premises, unfold according to the strictest logic, free of any alloy or alien essence, can guilt be accepted as irrational. The poetic intelligence, on the other hand, is not limited to the ratiocinative, and the world it works in has a thicker texture: here the organ of thought engages the widest reaches of personality, even its most divergent powers, so that in both the instrument and the act of poetic thinking there is productive discordance and fruitful controversy, while its object is the most varied and discrete experience, the chaos of actuality. In such a world the end is never a strict elaboration of the beginning nor the poetry merely a release of the implication of the intention; there is always the possibility of the operation of 'that force of poetry, that force which calls new powers into being, which embodies sentiment and animates matter'. In drama, as in life, given the appropriate circumstances, it is not the presence but the absence of guilt which is irrational, a form of moral imbecility, and although the fact of guilt may be foreseen and accounted for, its quality, the lacerating intensity of inward strife, is the creation of the person and the moment, and cannot be predicted. If literature is not just a marginal decoration of life but, as we must believe, both an accurate expression and a keen illumination of it, this is the kind of revelation about life which we may expect to discover in it and, it should be insisted, this is the kind of insight into life necessary for the educator. The disposition most valuable in education is closer, that is, to the poetic than to the mathematical intelligence. What is most required in the educator is intimacy of union, directness of contact with the deepest human experiences; and the temptation to which he is most exposed is the conceptual mediation of them, their blurring in a mist of theory. And the truth about conflict and guilt, a truth which is sustained by the greatest literature, is that they belong to this primary category and are not secondary inferences from the behaviour of society or derivations from a system of abstract assumptions. The correct direction is not from the collective to the individual or the concept to the fact, but the opposite.

If conflict, anxiety and guilt are intransigently part of the human predicament, then educational theory, though it may attempt to ignore, cannot contrive to circumvent them. The mood in which educational ends are formulated therefore, should be temperate rather than intoxicated; and although everyone will recognize the extravagance of Karl Popper's dictum, that the most education can hope to do is to do no harm, the modesty of its hope for education is not more absurd than the pretension of those for whom education, an amalgam of psychology, sociology and mental hygiene, is the successor of religion and philosophy, the creator of values and the guarantor of humanism. Those who set no limits to the powers of education can have neither a poetic nor immediate intuition nor a metaphysical or speculative vision of the nature of man. They can possess neither of the two appropriate criteria, the most particular and the most general. The educationists whose doctrine of man is neither tightly controlled by the particularity and immediacy of literature (which they reject because they regard it as saturated with subjectivity and assign impatiently to the limited category of the merely aesthetic), nor effectively directed by a philosophic vision of excellence (discarded through pragmatic hostility to the highest metaphysical generality), nevertheless employ, in place of standards, a functional paradigm of man, an operational ideal like an engineer's blueprint. But what is in engineering a declared, is in education a smuggled assumption, that the true and practical ends of education can be stated with absolute precision since of the material to be adjusted to the plan (character, human nature) one can have the kind of certainty possessed by the engineer in relation to precise forces and measured masses. The comprehension of the engineer is able to exhaust what is to be known of his material just because of its uniformity and homogeneity, because of the definition and regularity of its limits, qualities which can in no way be attributed to the material of the educator, the intricacy of character, the complex, intangible and evasive self. Just as the reality of conflict makes suspect the ideal of the homogeneous personality, so the evanescence of self renders derisory the possibility of a science of education which shall be total, inclusive and certain. Character cannot be reduced to the causes which have brought it about, nor broken down into the elements which constitute it, nor resolved into a series of factors, forces or vectors. It could be treated like this only on the supposition that categories might be applied which leave nothing in it inexplicable or unaccounted for. But this supposition is false, for what happens in the application of mathematical or statistical categories is not that character is imprisoned but that it evanesces. The discrepancy between the measure and the measured remains. The complexity of character is not the complexity of an association of elements or a combination of parts, all of the same order, in a closed system, which is susceptible to analysis by scientific intelligence; it is the complexity attendant on a plurality of orders. One is not, in saying this, making any Pyrrhonic assertion about character, but only insisting that it is not to be grasped by inappropriate instruments. Just as in drama it is the fuller, more resonant poetic intelligence that can create character, so in education it is a less formal intelligence than the scientific that can comprehend, sympathize with and promote the life of character.

Any serious theory of education has to give an account of the life of character; at least it must offer a provisional answer to Pascal's question. A main European tradition, which still flows through however clogged a channel into English education, has taken that life to be in essence a conflict, a rigorous and unending effort to impose a higher discipline. For Plato it is reason which must curb the violence of the passions, for Aquinas grace which is to master the turbulence of concupiscence, for Freud (who shows in this his true European temper) it is 'reality' which is to control the riot of libido. Plato and Aquinas quite explicitly take the battle to be one which has objective and universal implications; and even Freud, for whom it seems much more an enclosed and private quarrel, extends its operation, through the medium of myth, into the public and impersonal world. All alike maintain an unending conflict and a continuing tension and, as the ground of this, a fundamental duality in man. '*Cette duplicité de l'homme,*' says Pascal, '*est si visible qu'il y en a qui pensent que nous avions deux âmes. Un sujet simple leur paroissoit incapable de telles et si soudaines variétés d'une présomption démesurée à un horrible abattement de cœur.*' Nevertheless, with the Romantics it was the sense of duality that faded, the sense of simplicity that was strengthened. The life of character was no longer so emphatically read in the language of inward conflict and discipline; it was seen as the eliciting of an immanent form which had become accidentally tainted through contact with other things, civilization or common life or artificial feeling. By Rousseau and Wordsworth it was understood as a regress to, by Froebel as a progress towards, an uncorrupted perfection, by the first as a recovery, by the second as a revelation. The conflict that remained was decidedly of a more external sort, its area not within but beyond the borders of personality, its form the antagonism of the integrated artist for his unenlightened world, its symbolic figures a deracinated Byron and a revolutionary Shelley.

Romanticism, in so much as it simplified the idea of the nature of man, is a stage on the way to the American or Pragmatic view of life and education. It did, however, conserve that part of the European tradition which insisted on the autonomy and spontaneity of the individual and the inwardness of the educational process; what it rejected was the dualistic structure of character and its cosmic setting. With Pragmatism not only is conflict obliterated and implication with the universe cancelled (that is the melody reduced to *naïveté* and the orchestration abandoned), but even the secret and evasive reality of the individual is abolished in favour of a tougher, more obvious and more public reality, the community. The conductor is handed over to the orchestra. 'Earlier psychology,' writes Dewey, 'regarded mind as a purely individual affair in direct and naked contact with an external world. The tendency at present is to conceive individual mind as a function of social life, requiring continual stimulus from social agencies and finding its nutriment in social supplies.' If mind is a social function, it is not surprising that art, science and ethics should be given social motives, nor that the index of the worth of a motive should be the measure in which it has succeeded in society, and in contemporary society. Thus tradition is bowed out with individuality, and the life of character becomes a closer and closer approximation to the stereotype of the community at any given moment.

And this ideal is probably the gravest single difficulty that American education has to contend with. Romanticism, although it quickened the life of the imagination, nevertheless coarsened the concept of the nature of man, and Pragmatism, the stunted issue of Romanticism and nineteenth-century science, although it has greatly enlivened the method of education, making it active and exciting, has in turn vulgarized the notion of character. The imperative need of modern education is to maintain the vivacity of its means and to provide as their support a different, subtler and more mature concept of character; communication must be opened between positive knowledge and rooted wisdom, between Columbia and Byzantium.

'Byzantium' calls up the name of that modern writer who is gifted more abundantly than others with what educational thought most lacks: a quality of imagination which can make the immense, swooping leap, in appearance so irrelevant, in reality so pointed, and particularly in the situation described, represented by the movement between the end of the first and the beginning of the second of these stanzas:

(1)

> I walk through the long schoolroom questioning;
> A kind old nun in a long white hood replies;
> The children learn to cipher and to sing,
> To study reading-books and histories,
> To cut and sew, be neat in everything
> In the best modern way – the children's eyes
> In momentary wonder stare upon
> A sixty-year-old smiling public man.

(2)

> I dream of a Ledaen body, bent
> Above a sinking fire. . . .

The art of Yeats took its rise in a peripheral, even a parochial society, and in its progress it preserved the tang and flavour of that society, a verve and honesty of local accent; but it succeeded in arriving at a central, an authentically European vision of man. The poet managed so 'to purify the dialect of the tribe' as to turn it into a language apt to express an experience of man that was active and contemporary certainly, but also traditional and most deeply civilized: through the clarity and brilliance of the Irish idiom sound deeper and more ancient tones, the inflection of Dante, the resonance of Augustine, the voice of Plato:

> I, proclaiming that there is
> Among birds or beasts or men
> One that is perfect or at peace,
> Danced on Cruachan's windy plain,

Upon Cro-Patrick sang aloud;
Al that could run or leap or swim
Whether in wood, water or cloud,
Acclaiming, proclaiming, declaiming Him.

The quick of that experience may be indicated by the phrase, the dramatic organization of character. It hardly needs to be added that it is not to be found in Yeats's drama, which is singularly undramatic; it is present as an element, the ordering element, in the base of experience of self and others which is the source and impulse of that elaborate superstructure of myth, intuition, symbol and absurdity – 'the system'. And it is present as a reverberation, adding depth and dignity, to some of his finest verse. For Yeats personal life is in essence a duality (the Vision of Michael Robartes is a double vision), and the relation between the two poles is one of conflict. The life of character is not an interior monologue, but 'a dialogue between self and soul', the tension between mask and will, the opposition of man and daimon, the debate of *hic* and *ille*. Conflict is often expressed by Yeats in terms which, although idiosyncratic in utterance, seem for all that to be a version of traditional oppositions: the opposition of 'sensual music' and the 'monuments of unageing intellect', of 'the dying animal' and 'the artifice of eternity', of 'Isaiah's coal' and 'original sin', of 'Homer' and 'Von Hügel'. This is, of course, evidence of the European ancestry of his language, but it would be misleading to take these antitheses as meaning that for Yeats the radical conflict is, as these examples may suggest, the opposition within the character of part against part, of particular power against particular power. Conflict for Yeats is not a partial domestic brawl but a total 'tragic war'. It is the whole of character under one *persona* tensed against the whole of character under another *persona*. And these *personae* or masks are neither disguises, nor aspirations, nor partial representations, but true expressions, charged with the full energy of the complete person.

By the help of an image
I call to my own opposite, summon all
That I have handled least, least looked upon . . .
I call to the mysterious one who yet

> Shall walk the wet sands by the edge of the stream
> And look most like me, being indeed my double,
> And prove of all imaginable things
> The most unlike, being my anti-self,
> And, standing by these characters, disclose
> All that I seek.

It is the total deployment of forces on each side which makes the conflict intense and enduring, the long-drawn-out genesis of the firmness and vitality of character that Yeats loved and celebrated in those

> With beauty like a tightened bow, a kind
> That is not natural in an age like this,
> Being high and solitary and most stern;

and in those who

> may consume
> The entire combustible world in one small room
> As though damp straw.

It is, then, the inwardness, the deeply embedded situs of the conflict, which makes it at once so potently active (the 'tragic war' that is the origin of art which, Yeats emphasizes, is not 'the common dream' but 'a vision of reality'), and in addition the source of wisdom that can judge the cult of action, Pragmatism, as a mere lapse into unintelligibility, 'the struggle of the fly in the marmalade'. To a degree that the Columbian or Pragmatist attitude could not admit, the Byzantine sees character as self-creating, as distinguished from the passive product of external influences, not with the easy, flowing creativity of Romanticism, for which there are no obstacles to the soul's effusion, not 'with spontaneous joy and natural content', but with the more difficult, more intense creativity of the poet exerting himself against an elaborate stanza, and driven by 'the fascination of what's difficult'.

> Myself must I remake
> Till I am Timon and Lear
> Or that William Blake
> Who beat upon the wall
> Till Truth obeyed his call.

From this point of view, character consists in man's long, hard effort to remake himself, out of the actual and the potential, the present and the aspiration, the world of 'is' and the world of 'ought', but fundamentally from within himself, and primarily by himself. It consists in the tension and conflict between mask and mask, between self and anti-self, in the struggle to be born transformed.

> He, too, has resigned his part
> In the casual comedy;
> He, too, has been changed in his turn,
> Transformed utterly:
> A terrible beauty is born.

Complexity as a quality attaches not only to the structure of character but also to its context. Different as the schools of Columbia and Byzantium are in their account of character – on the one side a blind alley, on the other a labyrinth of being – they are even more opposed in their explanations of its setting; and the basis of their difference is, necessarily, their varied views on what is real. That is real for Pragmatism, which is here and now, the substantial and the measurable; it admits only the power of the present and the authority of the actual, both of which appear to be weightier in the community than in the individual. Pragmatism inhabits a statistical universe, and its terms of reference recognize none but actuarial problems. There is, however, another, a more ancient and a more complex attitude, for which what is real includes more than the brutality of fact, transcends 'this pragmatical, preposterous pig of a world, its farrow that so solid seem', for which knowledge is also, as Santayana said, 'recognition of something absent', and in which character is set in a context, more fluid, more embracing and more mysterious. This is the universe of poetry. It is a world of which the dialectic climbs to no necessary, reconciling synthesis – the vulgarity of optimism – but can fracture at any time into final disaster; and proper to it, therefore, is the tragic view of life.

This book is written in the belief that the tragic view of life corresponds with firmer general accuracy and more exact particular delicacy to things as they are, and that the persuasion of literature of which it is the most profound, the most enduring and the most convinced intuition, in this only confirms the compulsion of private experience. The life of the child and the adult is attended by stress and distress; the data of their experience combine to communicate, intimately and directly, touching upon the exposed nerve, tapping out on the tympanum, messages conveying the tragic pattern of existence. The immediacy of experience compels assent to this conclusion. Liability to error arises with the need for the conceptual organization of experience, when the truth of percept can be overlaid by the falsity of concept. Not of course that conceptual organization is not in itself a part of experience nor that reflection is not in a sense as immediate as intuition, but its more abstract nature, it organizing functions, its more conscious attitude, its tendency towards stability and order both tempt and require the mind to repose on assumptions which are necessarily other than one's own. The rhythms of experience are interpreted according to a metric of assumptions, and distortion occurs when the mind succumbs to the lure of a specious coherence at the expense of actual complexity, when fullness is sacrificed to neatness. Although, as Plato argues in the *Meno*, it is impossible for the teacher to fabricate experience whether of value, knowledge or feeling, for the pupil, it is impossible for him not to affect the pupil's intellectual organization of it, and all the more powerfully by example, attitude and presupposition, when there is no deliberate intention of doing so. The pupil will accept the translation of his experience offered by the teacher, who is invested with some of the parent's authority and the expert's prestige. Today, almost without fail, the translation will be phrased in the language of Columbia, and if so, it is decidedly a case of *traduttore, traditore*. But the frame of reference should bear to the body of experience a relation of intrinsic fidelity, and we have the evidence of literature for asserting that between the most valuable experience of the finest minds and the tragic outlook there is such a correspondence. And we must go on, if we believe in the community of character and the validity of literature, in the unity of man and the power of literature to make available for our possession some part of reality, to the further assertion that a like correspondence exists between the deepest experience of every man and the tragic outlook.

Tension and conflict, anxiety and guilt, the dramatic form of character, and character set in a tragic universe – to accept these is to acknowledge what in our day so many influences conspire to stain, the peculiar dignity of man. Involved in this acknowledgement are a recognition of the difficulty and complexity of man's situation, and a rejection of the comforting illusion, pervasive and corrupting in education, that a greater accumulation of positive information, a more thorough psychology, a more exhaustive sociology, a fuller mastery of teaching method, will disperse the painful and the incomprehensible in man's predicament and finally pluck out the heart of the mystery. The theory of modern education requires to be braced with the austerity of thought that knows its real strength and the asceticism of attitude that admits its proper limits, which are the qualities of a mature study.

> Through all the lying days of my youth
> I swayed my leaves and flowers in the sun;
> Now I may wither into the truth.

CHAPTER 9

THE WRITER AS TEACHER: THE EDUCATIONAL IDEAS OF D. H. LAWRENCE

I

LAWRENCE was an artist who felt with a racking intensity the wounded nature of man in contemporary society. It was an injury, in Lawrence's view, which was a wound of negation, a terrible vacancy. An essential part of a healthy human nature had been allowed to sink beneath the level of accessibility, and was no longer operative in the modern consciousness. It was a constant endeavour of Lawrence to recover the lost element, and since he was a diagnostician of extraordinary skill, it was a constant endeavour also to define its character and conditions. This double intention makes Lawrence a writer peculiarly rich in suggestiveness for the educator. On the one hand, his work is sustained by 'a perceptive wisdom about ends', and about ends as they need to be seen by the injured modern mind; on the other, his work is made urgent by a moving concern for correction, and made relevant by an unusual power to envisage, in our baffling and tangled circumstances, a route towards spiritual health. To realize, to define, to correct – these are the purposes of Lawrence, as they are the goals of the teacher. Lawrence indeed exemplified, perhaps more brilliantly than any other modern writer, the role of the writer as teacher.

I must at once anticipate the objection that in saying this I am absurdly confining the scope and limiting the purposes of a major literary artist, that I am substituting a moralistic for a creative intention and replacing a dramatic with a didactic aim. But the objection itself rests on an unduly narrow conception of teacher, and certainly on a very inadequate conception of good or ideal teacher. For him instruction – the didactic – is strictly subordinate to a larger purpose which is in intimate sympathy with the undertaking of a literary artist, namely, the tactful and intelligible communication of life, and of the life of feeling and of value as well as of reason. Furthermore, it will be agreed, the novel has developed in such a way as to make the title – The Writer as Teacher – much more apt to the nature of the novel than it might have been once, when even the best novels were taken to be just cultivated entertainment. In saying this, I am referring to more than an increase in the technical devices at the novelist's command, to such things as the focusing consciousness or the interior monologue. The novel in the hands of Melville, Conrad, James and Lawrence has become a species of poetry, perhaps the form in which the poetic imagination now expresses itself most naturally, fully and powerfully. And the kind of poetry to which the novel has assimilated itself is not the poetry of concentrated lyrical intensity, but the long poem, the organ of traditional wisdom and sensibility, the kind of which *The Divine Comedy* is the greatest example, and of which *The Prelude* is the last unquestioned example, and of which *The Waste Land* is the nearest modern example.

The transmutation of its form means an astonishing extension of the universe of the novel. The object of the novel is to be, according to Lawrence, no less than 'the whole man alive' – that is both the object to which the novel attends and the object, the audience, to which it is addressed.

The novel [Lawrence says] is the one bright book of life. Books are not life. They are only tremulations on the ether. But the novel as a tremulation can make the whole man alive tremble. Which is more than poetry, philosophy, science or any other book-tremulation can do. . . . Plato makes the perfect ideal being tremble in me. But that's only a bit of me. Perfection is only a bit in the strange make-up of man alive. The Sermon on the Mount makes the selfless spirit of me quiver. But that too is only a bit of me. The Ten Commandments set the old Adam shivering in me, warning me that I am a thief and a murderer, unless I watch it. But even the old Adam is only a bit of me. I very much like all these bits of me to be set trembling with life and the wisdom of life. But I do ask that the whole of me shall tremble in its wholeness some time or other. . . . (Novels) in their wholeness affect the whole man alive, which is the man himself beyond any part of him. They set the whole tree trembling with a new access of life, they do not just stimulate growth in one direction.[1]

Because he is concerned to add to the life of the complete person, the novelist, like the teacher, is also – or rather is simultaneously – concerned in a fundamental way with moral issues. 'Right and wrong is an instinct,' says Lawrence, 'but an instinct of the whole consciousness in a man, bodily, mental, spiritual at once. And only in a novel are *all* things given full play, or at least they may be given full play when we realize that life itself, and not inert safety, is the reason for living.'[2] For what, if we think about it, asks Lawrence, 'does our life consist in ? It consists *in* this achieving of a pure relationship between ourselves and the living universe about us . . . an infinity of pure relations, big and little . . . and morality is that delicate, for ever trembling and changing *balance* between me and my circumambient universe, which precedes and accompanies a true relatedness.' It is the business of art

to reveal the relation between man and his circumambient universe, at the living moment. As mankind is always struggling in the toils of old relationships art is always ahead of the 'times', which themselves are always far in the rear of the living moment. . . . Now here we see the beauty of the great value of the novel. . . . The novel is the highest example of subtle interrelatedness that man has discovered. . . . The novel is a perfect medium for revealing to us the changing rainbow of our living relationships.[3]

Clearly the novel so conceived is very different from, more complex, more important than, the novel conventionally understood. The names given by Lawrence in the passage quoted above – Plato and the Sermon on the Mount – help to define the difference. The great theme of the Lawrentian novelist is the discrepancy between what man is, actually, concretely, in his tissues, nerves, feelings and beliefs, and what man ought to be. This is in a radical way a philosophic theme, involving a metaphysical conception and an ethical intention, an idea of being and a doctrine of amendment. It is all the more necessary for the novel to offer itself as a centre for such permanent human concerns since the main trend of current philosophic opinion has decided that such questions are unreal, an astounding finding to the unphilosophic person leading his difficult ordinary life, in which the one sure thing is that he will be confronted with searching, upsetting questions of this kind every day and at every turn. To supply in fiction what philosophy disregards, to rescue the novel from sentimentality and philosophy from the deadest, abstracted unreality – this was an essential undertaking of the novelist in Lawrence's eyes. 'It seems to me it was the greatest pity in the world, when philosophy and fiction got split. They used to be one, right from the days of myth. Then they went and parted, like a nagging married couple, with Aristotle and Thomas Aquinas and that beastly Kant. So the novel went sloppy, and philosophy went abstract-dry. The two should come together again – in the novel.'[4] And of course the novel must pursue this end without doing damage to its own integrity. Lawrence is not recommending the writing of illustrated theses or marginally illuminated propaganda. The novel has to help us develop 'an instinct for life', not 'a theory of right and wrong'. 'The novel has a future. It's got to have the courage to tackle new propositions without using abstractions; it's got to present us with new, really new feelings, a whole line of new emotion, which will get us out of the emotional rut.'[5] What makes a novel 'serious', therefore, is an apprehension of reality as deep as this, its organization about a moral impulse and its translation into the terms of art. It is the novel so understood which 'can help us to live, as nothing else can; no didactic Scripture, anyhow'. It is of the novel so understood that Lawrence is a master.

A novelist who took his art so seriously, whose intentions were so radical and whose powers were equal to his intentions, had to be more than a fanatical advocate of a mindless cult of blood and sex, more than the apostle of the irrational and the immediate. There are, of course, spheres of human action, in orthodox religion and science for example, where Lawrence's opinions were eccentric or even, as Aldous Huxley said, absurd, and where we should not be disposed to seek for guidance from him. These failures of discernment and appreciation are perhaps inevitable in a talent so positive and original as Lawrence's. But Lawrence's occasional diatribes of incomprehension were not part of a general polemic against consciousness. He was never, what he is often accused of being, an opponent of consciousness. How could he be when his works brilliantly exemplify the most subtle and complex kinds of awareness? What Lawrence was opposed to was not consciousness but 'the irritable, cerebral consciousness we're afflicted with',[6] a consciousness unfed by, even blocked from, the deep springs of spontaneous life. 'I believe in the living extending consciousness of man. I believe the consciousness of man has now to embrace the emotions and passions of sex, and the deep effects of human physical contact. This is the glimmering edge of our awareness and our field of understanding, in the endless business of knowing ourselves.'[7] The living consciousness exhibits a flowing continuity between what 'it thrills to' and 'intellectual appreciation'; in the modern mind the one has been almost totally obliterated by the other. Sex, the feeling for and in the origins of life, is only the most intense and immediate form of that organic force, 'the principle of the universe' that man should thrill to. But sex itself has become a mental reaction nowadays, and a hopelessly cerebral affair'.[8] And this was so, and increasingly so, both in literature and in life. 'Byron, Baudelaire, Wilde, Proust: they all did the same thing, or tried to, to kick off, or to intellectualize and so utterly falsify the phallic consciousness, which is the basic consciousness, and the thing we mean in the best sense by common sense.'[9]

Lawrence used the terms *intellectual* and *ideal* as synonyms for hopelessly cerebral and a merely mental reaction, for the disconnected, rootless, mechanized mind, just as he used *physical*, *naïve* and *innocent* for the mind freely in communication with the deep springs of being. But the idiom was never intended to cloak a plea for oblivion and blind instinctive action, and to think that it was is to be both uncomprehending of and unjust to him. 'One had to be intensely conscious,' he wrote, 'but not intellectual or ideal.'[10] Equally uncomprehending, equally unjust is the accusation that Lawrence morbidly encouraged sex. 'God forbid that I should be taken as urging loose sex activity,' he exclaimed. 'There is a brief time for sex, and a long time when it is out of place. But when it is out of place as an activity there still should be a large quiet space in the consciousness where it lives quiescent. Old people have a lovely, quiescent sort of sex, like apples, leaving the young quite free for *their* sort.'[11] Sex represented the creative as opposed to the readymade, the unmanipulated and the free as against the fabricated and the calculated, and his attitude to it was reverent and religious. It stood for life at its source and for consciousness at its roots, and it symbolized what the modern mind, a mechanism unacquainted with, or on the barest nodding acquaintance with life most desperately needed. 'One fights and fights for that living something that stirs way down in the blood, and creates consciousness. But the world won't have it. To the present human mind, everything is ready made, and since the sun cannot be new there can be nothing new under the sun. But to me, the sun, like the rest of the cosmos, is alive, and therefore not ready made at all.'[12] Lawrence was concerned to open to the modern consciousness the neglected springs of life which are the origins of a full consciousness, and in separation from which the mind is crippled and incomplete. His purpose was to put man religiously in touch with the natural life of the universe.

And I do think that man is related to the universe in some 'religious' way even prior to his relations to his fellow men. And I do think that the only way of true relationship between men is to meet in some common 'belief', but physical not mental. . . . There is a principle in the universe towards which man turns religiously – a life of the universe itself. And the hero is he who touches and transmits the life of the universe. . . .[13]

The severance of a religious connexion with the life of the universe produces increasingly disorder in man's psyche and disharmony in his surroundings. It soils what Lawrence in a striking phrase called 'the clarity of being'. 'I am weary of this world of ugly chaos, I am sick to death of struggling in a cauldron of foul feelings with no mind, no thought, no understanding, no clarity of being anywhere, only a stinking welter of sensations.'[14] Everywhere in our world, whether in the character of man or the place in which he lives, we see 'the clarity of being' clouded and 'true relatedness' distorted. In man's soul this means an unnatural emphasis on the egotistic will – 'Shove and be shoved' is the motto of our civilization – and a compulsion 'to strive and strain and force things' so that man has become incapable of growth and acquiescence in the flow of life. 'That fundamental pathetic faculty for receiving hidden waves that come from the depths of life'[15] has withered. Wordsworth's 'wise passiveness' has been replaced by an imbecility of action, and 'we toil in a circle of pure egotism'.[16]

Throughout Lawrence's analysis of his age the stress is on negation, the absence of true being, in man, in his society, in the very place he lives in. In this world the *bourgeois* and the proletariat are combined in a failure of the sense of pure being, of the instinct for life. But 'a thing isn't life just because somebody does it . . . it is just existence. . . . By life we mean something that gleams, that has fourth-dimensional quality.'[17] The proletariat –

these men, whom I love so much – *understand* mentally so horribly: only industrialism, only wages and money and machinery. . . . They are utterly unable to appreciate any pure ulterior truth: only this industrial-mechanical-wage idea. . . . The strange, dark, sensual life, so violent and hopeless at the bottom, combined with this horrible paucity and materialism of mental consciousness, makes *me* so sad. . . .[18]

As for the *bourgeois* –

The modern Englishman has a few borrowed ideas, simply doesn't know *what* to feel. . . . The intuitional faculty which alone relates us in direct awareness to physical things and substantial presences, is atrophied and dead, and we don't know *what* to feel – Oh tell us what! And this is true of all nations, the French and Italian as much as the English. Look at the new French suburbs! Go through the crockery and furniture department in the *Dame de France* or any big shop. The blood in the body stands still before such *crétin* ugliness. One has to decide that the modern *bourgeois* is a *crétin*.[19]

The incomplete modern person, whether worker or *bourgeois*, lives in a world of 'falsity, a stupendous assertion of non-being'.[20]

Like himself his society is organized about a negation. 'This present community consists, as far as it is a formed thing, in a myriad contrivances for preventing us from being let down by the meanness in ourselves and in our neighbours.'[21] It is a society in its extreme manifestations incapable of more than an external, inorganic union. 'It's very difficult to do anything with the English: they have so little "togetherness": like grains of sand that will only fuse if lightning hits them. . . .'[22] Such a group can hardly be said to be informed by life, only by 'extraneous, sporadic, meaningless sensationalism'.[23] Its formlessness of soul – 'this wretched conglomerated messing' – is reflected in the hideous disorder of its environment: 'But what a mess the French make of their places – perfect slums of villadom, appallingly without order or form or place. A ghastly slummy nowhereness.'[24]

Meanness of understanding, ugliness of *milieu*, the attitudes of the robot, these are the characteristics of an age suffering from an anaemia of the imagination, the organ most vividly and intimately concerned with life.

. . . the imagination is a kindled stake of consciousness in which intuitional awareness predominates . . . imagery is the body of our imaginative life, and our imagination is a great joy and fulfilment to us, for the imagination is a more powerful and more comprehensive flow of consciousness than our ordinary flow. In the flow of the imagination we know in full, mentally and physicall at once, in a greater, enkindled awareness. At the maximum of our imagination we are religious. And if we deny our imagination and have no imaginative life we are poor worms who have never lived.[25]

The consequence of a life lived or gone through with a starved imagination is boredom, 'the great and fatal fruit of our civilization'. Man is bored because he experiences nothing and he experiences nothing because the wonder has gone out of him.

When all comes to all, the most precious element in life is wonder. Love is a great emotion and power is power. But both love and power are based on wonder. Love without wonder is a sensational affair, and power without wonder is mere force and compulsion. The one universal element in consciousness which is fundamental to life is wonder . . . which we may call the religious element inherent in all life: The sense of wonder. That is our sixth sense. And it is the natural religious sense. Somebody says that mystery is nothing, because mystery is something you don't know, and what you don't know is nothing to you. But there is more than one way of knowing. Even the real scientist works in a sense of wonder. The pity is when he comes out of his laboratory he puts aside his wonder along with his apparatus, and tries to make it all didactic. Science in its true condition of wonder is as religious as any religion.[26]

It is characteristic of the versatility of Lawrence's genius to be able to bring an issue into a more distinct clarity by construing it under a variety of forms. His thought progressed by means of manifold observations taken from many points of view. He would circle and swoop, frequently and from different quarters of the air. The loss or corruption of man's true condition of wonder is made sharper for us, more explicable and more poignant, by a further distinction which Lawrence draws in his brilliant essay on Galsworthy between the individual and the social being. There he asks why it is that we feel a repulsion from the Forsytes which we never feel for Sairy Gamp or Jane Austen's characters or even Meredith's Egoist. The answer he gives is that we feel they have lost caste as human beings in the same category as ourselves. Galsworthy's characters exemplify the fatal change of today, 'the collapse from the psychology of the free human individual into the psychology of the social being'. In the true human individual there is a 'core of innocence and *naïveté* which defies all analysis, and which you cannot bargain with, you can only deal with it in good faith from your own innocence or *naïveté*.' That is not to say that the free individual is all of a piece; he is also prudent, calculating or mercenary. 'He is Mr Worldly Wiseman also to his own degree.' But material assurance isn't his controlling principle, the central theme of his being, as it is with the social man.

It seems to me that when the human being becomes too much divided between his subjective and objective consciousness, at last something splits in him and he becomes a social being. When he becomes too much aware of objective reality, and of his own isolation in the face of a universe of objective reality, the core of his identity splits, his nucleus collapses, his innocence or his *naïveté* perishes, and he becomes only a subjective-objective reality, a divided thing hinged together but not strictly individual.[27]

Social beings keep up convention, but they cannot carry on a tradition. 'There is a tremendous difference between the two. To carry on a tradition you must add something to the tradition. But to keep up a convention needs only the monotonous persistence of a parasite, the endless endurance of the craven, those who fear life because they are not alive, and who cannot die because they cannot live – the social beings.'[28]

In conditions not only fatal to human dignity and the harmony of the soul but even dangerous to its very structure, to 'the inward order that should be preserved inviolable in the soul', in conditions like these, no mere palliatives, no superficial rearrangements could prove a remedy adequate to the disorder. Only a revolution can save us. And Lawrence is clear as to the kind of revolution we require: not a revolution for work or money, and least of all for the dead materialism of Marxist socialism, but a revolution to give life itself a chance.[29]

What is involved in revolution for the sake of life may perhaps be indicated by referring to a passage in the writings of George Santayana, a writer in so many ways different from Lawrence, and yet sharing with him a disinterested love and an unaffected reverence for life. The passage occurs when Santayana is writing of Protestantism, and we may remember how much a Protestant Lawrence was, how conscious of and grateful for his Congregationalist upbringing and discipline. Santayana discriminates between 'that antecedent integrity which is at the bottom of every living thing and at its core' and 'that ulterior integrity, that sanctity which might be attained at the summit of experience through renunciation and speculative dominion'. The fruit of the former is, he says, 'vitality', and of the latter, 'the spiritual life'.[30] Lawrence's great gift was an unparalleled sense for 'the antecedent integrity' of many forms of existence, of vegetation and animals and above all of man, together with an intimate apprehension both full and subtle of the characteristic 'vitality' in each. The great discovery which Lawrence's gift unfolded, and the moral legacy of his art, was that unless 'antecedent integrity', the primary core of innocence and *naïveté*, were sound and free, had room and scope, then 'ulterior integrity', the life of reason and the spirit, could only be thwarted and starved, impure and malformed.

It is only from his core of innocence and *naïveté* that the human being is ultimately a responsible and dependable being. Break this human core of *naïveté* . . . and you get either a violent reaction or as is usual nowadays a merely rational creature whose core of spontaneous life is death. . . . It is one of the terrible qualities of the reason that it has no life of its own, and unless continually kept nourished or modified by the naïve life in man or woman, it becomes a purely parasitic and destructive force.[31]

A revolution for the sake of life, therefore, meant for Lawrence a corrected system of priorities which gave a firmer recognition to the primary and fundamental source of human vitality. It meant a juster estimate of all that restless activity for the sake of possession, pleasure or prestige which our world ordinarily understands by living. It meant a descent into self and a reforming of the broken connexion with the root of being, with the essential spring of every form of human life (of 'life' in Lawrence's sense, not just 'existence') from the simplicities of good sense to the most austere discipline of rational thought, from the elements of conduct to the heights of spirituality. This is not a revolution which we can organize collectively or bring into operation by an act of the will because we decide it is necessary. We cannot bully life.

I know [Lawrence wrote] there has to be a return to the older vision of life. But not for the sake of unison. And not from the *will*. It needs some welling up of religious sources that have been shut down in us: a great *yielding* rather than an act of the will: a yielding to the darker, older unknown, and a reconciliation. Nothing bossy. Yet the natural mystery of power.[32]

To invite a revolution in favour of life, to encourage a return to an older vision of life: this was a primary intention in the hierarchy of purposes controlling Lawrence's art. Lawrence was not content to analyse with fidelity and to render with power; he had also to strive to correct. The obligation he felt to truth Lawrence observed in the accuracy of his diagnosis of the individual malady, the social infection; the obligation to his art he honoured in his brilliant figuring of men in such conditions; he had also an obligation to that 'finer morality' which, as he said, the 'true artist *always* substitutes for a grosser';[33] and it was because he acknowledged the claims of *this* morality that he was a teacher. He summarized his educative intentions vividly in these words: 'How to prevent suburbia spreading over Eden (too late! it's done!), how to prevent Eden running to a great wild wilderness ... 'How to regain the naïve or innocent soul ... and at the same time keep the cognitive mode for defences and adjustment and "work" – *voilà*!'[34] These purposes and especially the most central of them – how to regain the naïve or innocent soul – must surely be the concern not just of the novelist as teacher but of every teacher. There could be no theory of education responsive to the deep necessities of the age which neglected it, no practice of education with a genuine feeling for the texture of the period which disregarded it. Or so at least Lawrence thought.

Both desire and impulse tend to fall into mechanical automatism: to fall from spontaneous reality into dead or material reality. All our education should be a guard against this fall ... the fall from spontaneous, single, pure being, into what we call materialism or automatism or mechanism of the self. All education must tend against this fall; and all our efforts in all our life must be to preserve the soul free and spontaneous.[35]

No one would want to claim absolute originality for Lawrence either on account of his responsiveness to 'single, pure being' or because of the clarity with which he understood that the recovery of the 'innocent soul' must be an essential undertaking in education. We must suppose that a like apprehension energized the sounder thought of Rousseau and sustained the more genuine art of Tolstoy. But Lawrence never committed what he called 'the

Tolstoian fallacy of repudiating the educated world and exalting the peasant'.[36] Neither the noble savage nor the peasant nor the American Indian, merely by being what he was, seemed to Lawrence to incorporate this sort of insight into his ordinary perception as a fact of nature. Lawrence understood that the real savage, given the chance, would embrace automatism, mechanism and materialism with haste and pleasure; he knew that the true peasant as an individual was no better than the *bourgeois* or aristocrat, and in the mass was probably worse, meaner and more cruel, the most greedily selfish and brutal of all. Rousseau and Tolstoy, that is, put their faith in abstractions, turning a genuine perception into a mechanical law, but Lawrence believed only in an idea quick with living actuality, in 'the concrete universal'. 'If only we look for God let us look for him in the bush where he sings.'[37] What Lawrence appealed to was precise and personal, indeed, unique. It was the 'sincere and vital emotion' of his own nature, a nature rich in resource, subtle and exact in feeling, strong and lucid in intelligence. There is no better account of his gifts than that given in a remarkable passage where Lawrence sets out the qualities of the literary critic. A critic who 'must be able to *feel* the impact of a work of art in all its complexity and its force' must be 'a man of force and complexity himself'. 'A man with a paltry impudent nature will never write anything but paltry impudent criticism.' More than this, he must be a man of good faith. 'He must have the courage to admit what he feels. . . . A critic must be emotionally alive in every fibre, intellectually capable and skilful in essential logic, and then morally very honest.'[38]

In what ways, then, can education tend against this fall from pure being, how can it help man to recover his 'peculiar nuclear innocence'? Lawrence, himself a man 'emotionally alive in every fibre, intellectually capable and skilful in essential logic, and then morally very honest', gave this answer – by helping him to achieve a true relatedness to the living universe about him. 'This is how I "save my soul" by accomplishing a pure relationship between me and another person, me and other people, me and a nation, me and a race of men, me and the animals, me and the trees or flowers, me and the earth, me and the skies and sun and stars, me and the moon: an infinity of pure relations, big and little. . . .'[39] 'There is nothing to do but to maintain a true relationship to the things we move with or amongst or against.'[40] And in what does a true relationship consist? Not in attitudes held by one towards another, whether they be of superiority, inferiority or even of equality. Equality indeed is doubly deceptive, being both morally commendable and politically fashionable.

Where each thing is unique, there can be no comparison made: one man is neither equal nor unequal to another man. When I stand in the presence of another man, and I am my own pure self, am I aware of the presence of an equal, or of an inferior, or of a superior? I am not. When I stand with another man who is himself, and when I am truly myself, then I am only aware of a Presence, and of the strange reality of Otherness. There is me, there is another being. That is the first part of the reality. There is no comparing or estimating. There is only this strange recognition of *present otherness*.[41]

To have access to this 'first part of reality' requires a certain ease and freedom of the inner life, a certain insouciance of the self, unlikely to be present in those too consciously engaged in playing – or playing up to – a role assigned by convention or dictated by some personal inadequacy. Then attention which should play unobstructed on the object is deflected to the person attending, as when grit in an eye distracts from the observed to the observer, bringing more consciousness of function and less efficiency of operation. But that ease and freedom of the self, Lawrence reminds us, before it is a freedom from convention or a freedom from neurosis is first of all a moral condition. 'It is first freedom from myself, from the lie of myself, from the lie of my all-importance even to myself.' And this productive modesty again is the quality only of one who has reached a certain point of awareness and discernment, 'who has come to the limits of himself and become aware of something beyond him',[42] who realizes 'that we are not self-contained or self-accomplished. At every moment we derive from the unknown.'[43]

In cultivating exactness, relevance and purity in relations – a true relatedness – we sacrifice nothing of the flavour of individuality. For it is precisely the richness of our relations which constitutes our individuality. The isolated individual – history is full of examples and every human life in some phase testifies to the truth – goes numb, hardens and petrifies. Individuality does not consist in the set of characteristics contained within a particular skin. Its impulse is connexion, its growth the elaboration of connexion, its quality the refinement of that.

The fact remains [says Lawrence] that when you cut off a man and isolate him in his own pure and wonderful individuality, you haven't got the man at all. You've only got the dreary fag-end of him. . . . We have our very individuality in relationship. Let us swallow this important and prickly fact. Apart from our connexions with other people, we are barely individuals; we amount, all of us, to next to nothing. It is in the living touch between us and other people, other lives, other phenomena that we move and have our being. Strip us of our human contacts and of contact with the living earth, and we are almost bladders of emptiness.[44]

The means by which we inaugurate, sustain and modify relationships is feeling. Not emotion, Lawrence is careful to warn us, not emotion, not a blind, instinctive drive, or 'a helpless unconscious predilection', but feeling. And the marks of feeling are direction, and a certain degree of precision, of propriety and of intelligibility. On this last Lawrence is especially insistent. For there is no natural antagonism, in his view, set between feeling and thought. 'Men *can* only feel the feelings they know how to feel. The feelings they don't know how to feel they don't feel. This is true of all men, and all women and all children. It is true children do have lots of unrecognized feelings. But an unrecognized feeling, if it forces itself into any recognition, is only recognized as "nervousness" or "irritability".'[45] And it is just here in our feelings, our trembling organ of communication and mutuality, by which we weave 'the two ends of darkness together with visible being and presence', that we are so desperately, so tragically uneducated, thick, crude, uncivilized.

Come now, in what are we educated? In politics, in geography, in history, in machinery, in soft drinks and in hard, in social economy

and social extravagance: ugh! a frightful universality of knowing.
. . . (But) we know nothing, or next to nothing about ourselves. After
hundreds of years we have learned how to wash our faces and bob
our hair, and this is about all we *have* learned, *individually*. Collectively, of course, as a species we have combed the round earth with a
tooth-comb, and pulled down the stars almost within grasp. And then
what? Here sit I, a two-legged individual with a risky temper, knowing all about – take a pinch of salt – Tierra del Fuego and relativity
and the composition of celluloid, the appearance of the anthrax
bacillus and solar eclipses and the latest fashions in shoes; and it don't
do me *no* good! as the charlady said of near beer. It doesn't leave me
feeling no less lonesome inside! as the old Englishwoman said, long
ago, of tea without rum. We are hopelessly uneducated in ourselves. . . . We have no language for the feelings, because our feelings
do not exist for us. . . . Educated! We are not even *born*, as far as our
feelings are concerned.[46]

How then are we to educate our feelings, which in their un-
faked state are the true voice of our real identity. How are we to
learn a language for our feelings, instead of that rag-bag of clichés
which is their customary expression? Well, 'not by laying down
laws, or commandments, or axioms and postulates'. Honesty is
the first requirement; to be utterly honest with ourselves is the
beginning. Never to gloss or varnish according to the social code,
which renders us, finally, spurious in our inmost selves, able only
to summon up at roughly appropriate moments, not feelings at
all, but 'clues to clichés'. And then by 'listening'. 'Listening' is a
word which, in Lawrence as in Wordsworth, bears a great weight
of meaning. It includes training an ear attentive to our feelings, a
mind capable of understanding them, a will ready to accept them.
It includes patience in attending, acuteness in recognizing,
generosity in admitting. It enfolds within itself references to the
faculties which make possible the fruit of real feeling, a complete
imaginative experience. 'What we want is *complete* imaginative
experience which goes through the whole soul and body':[47] 'the
whole consciousness of men working together in unison and oneness: instinct, intuition, mind, intellect all used into one complete consciousness, and grasping what we may call a complete
truth, or a complete vision, a complete revelation. . . . And the

same applies to the genuine appreciation of a work of art, or the *grasp* of a scientific law, as to the production of the same.'[48] A comprehending honesty of feeling is the condition of such complete experience in every department of life. But to arrive at such virtue we need help from outside ourselves; our solitary resources are insufficient, and particularly in our broken and divided world. The best help we could have would be to exist in the context of a living tradition, in the remnant of which Lawrence himself grew up, as he acknowledges in his tribute to the Congregationalist worship and discipline that penetrated through and through his childhood. Such an influence, unsentimental, dignified, vital, exerts a profound effect on the consciousness and is the natural education of deep and genuine feeling.

And where are we, living in a society in which neither social nor religious tradition is able to play this powerfully educative part, where are we to discover this essential aid? We are to look for it, says Lawrence, in the tradition of literature, in 'the poems which after all give the ultimate shape to this life' and especially in 'the great novels', 'the highest example of subtle inter-relatedness that man has discovered'. Here we may learn a living language for our feelings, and not just the vocabulary but the syntax, not just the names, the elements, but these related in subtle and coherent patterns. And because they are subtle and coherent these patterns of thought and feeling in the novel are the remedy for what most ails us: routine thought-forms and conventional feeling-patterns. 'We are starved to death, fed on the eternal sodom-apples of thought-form.'[49] 'This is our true bondage. This is the agony of our human existence, that we can only feel things in conventional feeling-patterns. Because when these feeling-patterns become inadequate, when they will no longer body forth the workings of the yeasty soul, then we are in torture. It is like a deaf-mute trying to speak. Something is inadequate in the expression-apparatus, and we hear strange howlings. So are we now howling inarticulate, because what is yeastily working in us has no voice and no language.'[50] The language of literature can make our dumbness articulate, and release us from servitude to set forms of thought, and established modes of feeling, from the routine of the repetition of the cliché. Literature is so necessary to us because 'our consciousness is pot-bound. Our ideas, our emotions, our experience are all pot-bound.'[51] And the essential quality of literature is that 'it makes a new effort of attention, and "discovers" a new world within the known world'.[52] Literature embodies in itself and provokes in us a free and open consciousness. It is the full, articulate intelligence, the impassioned mind, neither driven by the force of unenlightened emotion, nor dry and abstract and subject to the tyranny of the syllogism. It is the product of, it includes and it encourages 'the whole imagination . . . that form of complete consciousness in which predominates the intuitive awareness of forms, images, the physical awareness'.[53] It gives a complete vision of man, of a sort which in our circumstances offers the main hope of health, for modern man is damaged in his primary organs of perception themselves. His injured psyche is only able to see in a restricted and mechanical way. Civilized man has formed during the whole course of civilization 'the habit of seeing just as the photographic camera sees. . . . He sees what the Kodak has taught him to see. . . . As vision developed towards the Kodak, man's idea of himself developed towards the snapshot. . . . Each of us has a complete Kodak idea of himself. . . .'[54] In literature we have not a snapshot but the total man. And we find him only if we go in to literature as literature. 'If we can hear – we can look in the real novels and there listen in. Not listen to the didactic statements of the author, but to the loud, calling cries of the characters, as they wander in the dark woods of their destiny.'[55]

2

We have no need to make uncertain inferences about the application of Lawrence's beliefs to education. He has given us an explicit expression of his views in his remarkable treatise, *Education of the People*, posthumously published in *Phoenix*, and as we would expect, a characteristic combination of the clearest insight, mischievous wit, eccentricity and good sense. Lawrence, it will be remembered, was a trained teacher in the technical, professional sense, certainly the first, probably the only great genius to have undergone this vocational discipline, and he had a deep sense of the fundamental importance of education, 'that higher form of being' as he called it in *The Rainbow*. He understood that education depends upon a metaphysic and that it incorporates a morality and a faith. 'It is useless to think that we can get along without a conception of what man is, and without a belief in ourselves, and without the morality to support this belief.' He saw that education, an improved state of being, must have a nature which is in sympathetic correspondence with the nature of man, and the nature of man is of such a sort that it takes its rise from, continually corrects itself by reference to, and finally comes to rest in, principle.

> We cannot act without moral bias. Still more we are influenced by our conception of the nature of man. We believe that being men and women, we are therefore such and such and such. . . . Lastly, though we express it or not, we believe that life has some great goal, of happiness and peace and harmony, and all our judgements are biased by this belief. . . . Such is man: a creature of beliefs and of foregone conclusions. As a matter of fact we should never put one foot before the other, save for the foregone conclusion that we shall find the earth beneath the outstretched foot.[56]

It is decisively, therefore, on the note of principle that Lawrence conducts his arguments throughout, and it is directly for a defect of principle that he criticizes our modern system of education. It is true that we cannot act but by faith and principle. 'We must have an ideal.' But, says Lawrence, making the point of every reflective educator since Socrates, it is the inveterate tendency of ideals to lose their actuality. Their virtue is drained of its validity. They lose their spring and fold into tired, repetitive forms, or, in Lawrentian language, we habitually find that they have 'dropped from the Tree of Life'.

The worn ideal, the tired abstraction which in Lawrence's view controls and distorts our education, is the idea of equality. To us, brought up in a Christian and liberal ethos, or at least in a society where what passes for value is derived from Christian and liberal sources, this opinion of Lawrence may seem disturbing, and even shocking. The excellence of equality is perhaps the most unquestionable of our 'foregone conclusions', and the criticism most often levelled at our education is that it fails sufficiently quickly and sufficiently thoroughly to bring about equality. But perhaps our distress is excessive. We have to remember that the common characteristics of the patterns of belief constructed by the greatest modern writers is that they all, whatever their differences, involve rejection of, or if this is too positive, indifference to, the prevailing system of assumptions and attitudes. They have all chosen solutions which are hard, unpopular and out of sympathy with the present state or foreseeable development of the current ethos. The point has been made by Lionel Trilling in *The Liberal Imagination*:

And if we were those writers who by the general consent of the most serious criticism are to be thought of as the monumental figures of our time, we see that to these writers the liberal ideology has been at least a matter of indifference. . . . All have their own love of justice and the good life but in not one of them does it take the form of the ideas and emotions which liberal democracy has declared respectable.

And Lawrence's rejection of equality as a necessary aim of education is a case in point. It is also in place to notice that in our materialist society equality means not the absence of status but the raising of status to such an ultimate importance that everyone must possess it, and possess it in the same way. But for Lawrence status was a subordinate and contingent part of life, which deserved to be given only a minor and inconsiderable part of attention.

But when Lawrence maintains that we have shaped education according to 'a faulty idea of equality and the perfectibility of man', he is not arguing the superiority of inequality. He is not recommending an education designed to produce inequality. He is insisting not so much on the wrongness of such categories as their irrelevance in determining the relations between man and man. His opinion on this issue is so important to an understanding of his thought and so liable to be misjudged that I must give it at length:

215

Men are palpably unequal in *every* sense except the mathematical sense. Every man counts one and this is the root of all equality: here, in a pure intellectual abstraction.

The moment you come to compare them, men are unequal, and their inequalities are infinite. But supposing you *don't* compare them. Supposing, when you meet a man, you have the pure decency not to compare him either with yourself or with anything else. Supposing you can meet a man with this same singleness of heart. What then? Is the man your equal, your inferior, your superior? He can't be if there is no comparison. If there is no comparison, he is the incomparable. He is the incomparable. He is single. He is himself. When I am single-hearted, I don't compare myself with my neighbour. He is immediate to me, I to him. He is not my *equal*, because this presumes comparison. He is incomparably himself, I am incomparably myself. We behold each other in our pristine and simple being. And this is the first, the finest, the perfect way of human intercourse. . . .

The moment I begin to pay direct mental attention to my neighbour, however; the moment I begin to scrutinize him and attempt to set myself over against him, the element of comparison enters. Immediately, I am aware of the inequalities between us. But even so, it is inequalities and not inequality. There is *never* either any equality or any inequality between me and my neighbour. Each of us is himself, and as such is single, alone in the universe and not to be compared. Only in our parts are we comparable. And our parts are vastly unequal.

The use of equality as an educational aim means the intrusion of social and political considerations into the educational world. It also means a debasement of standards, for it turns our attention from where it should be fixed on to quite irrelevant ends. 'We want,' Lawrence says, 'quality of life, not quantity. We don't want swarms and swarms of people in back streets. We want distinct individuals, and these are incompatible with swarms and masses. A small, choice population, not a horde of hopeless units.' Equality makes us want precisely what Lawrence says we should not want. It disturbs a proper hierarchy of purposes. It also involves the supposition that all are theoretically capable of intellectual culture. This is a very dangerous assumption which generates in a large number a profound contempt for education and for all educated people.

Drag a lad who has no capacity for true learning or understanding through the processes of education, and what do you produce in him, in the end? . . . Go down in the hearts of the masses of the people and this is what you'll find: the cynical conviction that every educated man is unmanly, less manly than an uneducated man. Every little Jimmy Shepherd has dabbled his bit in pseudo-science and in the arts; he has seen a test-tube and he has handled plasticine and a camel's hair brush and he knows that $a+a+b=2a+b$. What is there for him to know? Nothing.

If 'equality' will not serve as a directing educational principle, on what, in Lawrence's view, can we construct an educational system? Lawrence's answer is this:

Here then is the new ideal for society: not that all men are equal but that each man is himself. . . . Particularly this is the ideal for a new system of education. Every man shall be himself, shall have every opportunity to come to his own intrinsic fullness of being. . . . We must have an ideal. So let our ideal be living, spontaneous individuality in every man and woman. Which living, spontaneous individuality, being the hardest thing of all to come at, will need most careful rearing. Educators will take a grave responsibility upon themselves. They will be the priests of life, deep in the wisdom of life.

At first glance and to unsympathetic eyes this might seem a romantic effusion in favour of a facile and undisciplined egotism. But of course it is nothing of the sort. A generalization in Lawrence, as in Wordsworth, is never a mere label attached to a variety of partly similar experiences. It is always most firmly grounded in the particular, the fruit – the organic metaphor irresistibly suggests itself – of deep and living roots. And this particular affirmation is made with full advertence to the objections that might be urged against it. Lawrence *knew* that when he spoke of 'intrinsic fullness of being' and 'living spontaneous individuality' he was not advocating an extreme and disorderly individualism.

Which doesn't mean anarchy and disorder. On the contrary, it means the most delicately and inscrutably established order, delicate, intricate, complicate as the stars in heaven, when seen in their strange groups and goings. Neither does it mean what is nowadays called individualism. The so-called individualism is no more than a cheap egotism, every self-conscious little ego assuming unbounded rights to display his self-consciousness. We mean none of this. We mean, in the first place, the recognition of the exquisite arresting *manifoldness* of being, multiplicity, plurality, as the stars are plural in their starry singularity.

Lawrence was concerned with what lay beneath the surface of individuality, with *being* rather than personality, something more objective and impersonal, at once unique and universal.

We are apt in the modern world to believe that an aggregation of many is in some way more real and more important than one alone. Lawrence is quick to expose so gross a fallacy. For him nothing could be more real than the person, 'in its purity of singleness and perfect solitary integrity'.

Vitally, intensively, one human being is always more than six collective human beings. Because, in the collectivity, what is gained in bulk or number is lost in intrinsic being. The *quick* of any collective group is some consciousness they have in common. But the quick of the individual is the integral soul, for ever indescribable and unstateable. . . Being-in-common means the summing-up of one element held in common by many individuals. But this one common element, however many times multiplied, is never more than one mere part in any individual, and therefore much *less* than any individual.

It is towards this then, 'the perfected singleness of the individual being', that we are to educate our children and ourselves. For Lawrence 'to educate' entailed the strictest restraint of self on the part of parent and teacher. But it implied no release from responsibility, no encouragement to easy self-expression, nothing passive and acquiescent. It meant indeed a dedicated, active and continuing sacrifice. 'We've got to educate our children. Which means, we've got to decide for them: day after day, year after year, we've got to go on deciding for our children . . . to guide the steps of their young fates seriously and reverently.' These decisions have to be taken not only by the individual parent and teacher but they are also the responsibility of the community. And that means that we must have a system of education.

Lawrence had no patience with those who would trace every defect to the existing system. The system is only the organization of our intentions past and present, and the first stride in modifying the system is to change ourselves; but many who want the first are unwilling to undertake the second. Organization and system are inevitable for they are the direct expression of the organic differentiation present even in the least speck of rudimentary life. 'There must be a system: there *must* be classes of men: there *must* be differentiation: either that, or amorphous nothingness.' Our choice is not between system and no system, but between one like ours established for the purposes of material production, and therefore a mechanism, a social machine, and an organic system of human life capable of producing 'the real blossoms of life and being'. And since we do not want revolutions and cataclysms, let our reformation begin at once with a new system of education, 'a forming of new buds upon the tree, under the old harsh foliage'.

Lawrence does not shirk the obligation to give a precise and detailed description of such a sensible system of education. All education, he insists, should be conducted by the State; the children should all start together in a common school to give us 'a common human basis, a common radical understanding'. A child should begin his schooling at the age of seven – five is too soon – and learn reading, writing and arithmetic as the only necessary mental subjects. Three hours a day is sufficient; another might be devoted to physical and domestic training. At the age of twelve, a division should be made. Teachers, inspectors and parents will carefully decide what children shall be educated further. These will be sent to secondary schools, where the curriculum will be extended to include Latin or French, and some true science. These secondary scholars will remain at school till the age of sixteen. Those not judged capable of benefiting from the secondary schools will at the age of twelve have their academic instruction reduced to two hours a day, while three hours a day will be given to physical and domestic training. This is to continue for three years, and at sixteen they will enter on their regular labour. On the completion of their fourteenth year these pupils will be apprenticed half-time to some trade to which they are thought fitting by a consensus of parents, teachers and pupils themselves. For two years they will spend the morning at their own trade, and some two hours in the afternoon in physical and domestic training and in reading. The secondary scholars from twelve to fourteen will do four hours a day of academic study, one hour a day in the workshops, and one hour of physical training. On the completion of the fourteenth year, those whose mental education is apparently complete will be drafted into an apprenticeship. The remaining scholars at the age of sixteen will be drafted into colleges, where those of a scientific bent will receive scientific training, those with an inclination for the liberal arts a corresponding training, and those with gifts in the pure arts or in the technical arts an artistic training. An hour every day is to be spent on some craft and another hour on physical training. Every man must be practised in a craft at which he is finally expert, whatever profession he is destined for. These scholars will remain in their colleges till the age of twenty, when they will enter on their years of final training as doctors, lawyers, priests, and so on.

An important, perhaps the most important part of this very Platonic scheme of education is the right judging of the scholars. A primary aim is to recognize the true nature of each child and to give each its natural chance. Children, who are not sufficiently conscious, cannot choose for themselves. 'A choice is made, even if nobody makes it.' To avoid what happens today, when 'the bungle of circumstances decrees the fate of almost every child' and makes 'most men hate their destinies, circumstantial and false as they are', the decisions will be taken by teachers, masters, inspectors and parents together. The child will be consulted, but the last decision will rest with the headmaster and the inspector. It may be argued, Lawrence admits, that this arrangement puts too much power into the hands of schoolmasters and inspectors. 'But better there than in the hands of factory-owners and trades-unions!'

And what is it that has to be decided? Not merely the child's capacity, not just his aptitude for this or that.

The whole business of educators will be to estimate not the particular faculty of the child for some particular job; not at all: nor even a specific intellectual capacity: the whole business will be to estimate the profound life-quality, the very nature of the child, that which makes him ultimately what he is. . . . Technical capacity is all the time subsidiary.

And therefore what is to be looked for in education, and above all in headmasters, is 'living understanding – not intellectual understanding. Intellectual understanding belongs to the technical activities. But vital understanding belongs to masters of life.' The system he wants, Lawrence insists, is primarily religious, and only secondarily practical. It is to be established upon the living religious faculty in men, and conducted in its key places by religious men who recognize that the mind with all its great powers 'is only the servant of the inscrutable, unfathomable soul'.

Beliefs religious in Lawrence's sense are at least the same as beliefs religious in a more formal sense in strongly disapproving of our current materialist system, and not least on the grounds of inconsistency. The brutal confidence of a thoroughgoing materialism would hardly be a better breeding-ground for vulgarity, and certainly less efficient in producing cynicism, than ours in which we stand for idealism but live by materialism. And materialism for Lawrence means plainly the love of money and keeping up appearances. 'Our system of education tacitly grants that nothing but money matters, but puts up a little parasol of human ideals under which human divinity can foolishly masquerade for a few hours during school-life, and on Sundays.' Our love of money is born of a fear of penury absurd in a country like ours where, as Lawrence points out, no one is going to starve. There can be no cure for our obsession with money, our abject terror of poverty, except in an education which quickens the human virtues of courage and insouciance.

Courage and independence are two virtues which Lawrence wants home and school to make it their first business to foster. (They were, incidentally, virtues which Lawrence admirably exemplified in his own life.) His repeated advice *Leave the child alone* is an injunction to parent and teacher to respect the natural form of the child's being so that ultimately the man's destiny shall be shaped according to it, 'not as now, where children are rammed down into ready-made destinies, like so much canned fish!' It is not a plea for self-expression in children – 'this foolery', as Lawrence calls it, which 'means, presumably, incipient Tanagra figurines and Donatello plaques, incipient Iliads and Macbeths and Odes to the Nightingale: a world of infant prodigies'. Like Coleridge, and unlike Wordsworth, Lawrence had no false awe of childhood.

Instead of worshipping the child and seeing in it a divine emission which time will stale, we ought to realize that there is a new little clue to a human being, laid soft and vulnerable on the face of the earth. Here is our responsibility, to see that this unformed thing shall come to its own final form and fullness, both physical and mental. Which is a long and difficult business.

If the parent is to respect the integrity of the child, the child also must be taught to respect quality in living, and for him that must begin with grace and economy of movement. 'Let children be taught the pride of clear, clean movement. If it only be putting a cup on the table, or a book on the shelf, let it be a fine pure motion, not a slovenly shove. . . . When there is no pain of effort there is a wretched, drossy degeneration.' An alert and poised control of his bodily movements will awaken in a child a fine sense of responsibility and self-dependence, something essential to his human development, and particularly valuable in an age when, as Lawrence says, 'life is a sort of sliding-scale of shifted responsibility'. In this intimate conviction of responsibility is the beginning of all true education, and parent and teacher must do everything possible to strengthen and sustain it. 'Self-dependence is independence', Lawrence reminds us. To be unnecessarily dependent on others in the details of day-to-day living is a constriction of liberty, a cramping of the possibility of growth. Whatever the child can do, therefore, let him do for himself; let him wash and dress himself, clean his shoes, brush and fold his clothes, fetch and carry for himself, mend and patch and as soon as

possible make for himself. And let him do things for the joy of
doing them, not for alien motives projected upon him by moraliz-
ing adults.

If I wash the dishes I learn a quick, light touch of china and earthen-
ware, the feel of it, the weight and roll and poise of it, the peculiar
hotness, the quickness or slowness of its surfaces. I am at the middle
of an infinite complexity of motions and adjustments and quick,
apprehensive contacts. Nimble faculties hover and play along my
nerves, the primal consciousness is alert in me . . . not self-consciously,
however, not watching my own reactions. If I wash dishes, I wash
them to get them clean. Nothing else.

These words convey Lawrence's final educational principle.
We may call it the principle of separation or the exclusion of
irrelevant modes of consciousness. We should keep the physical
out of the mental, the mental out of the physical, and preserve
the moral for genuine moral situations. He gives example after
example to enforce his belief that we should keep apart activities
that are incompatible, not incompatible in the same individual
but incompatible with each other. If we are teaching arithmetic,
let it be pure and theoretic, a pure mental act, everything
abstracted and not adulterated with 'objects'. Mindwork should
not be handwork. If we are learning to solder a kettle, the theory
is told in a dozen words. 'But it is not a question of applying a
theory. It is a question of knowing, by direct physical contact,
your kettle-substance, your kettle-curves, your solder, your
soldering-iron, your fire, your resin, and all the fusing, slipping
interaction of these.' And again let us keep the mind, the idea,
out of games and physical culture: a caution very appropriate for
the contemporary school and university, in which we see daily
growing stronger a decadent mystique of athletics. 'A man sweating and grunting to get his muscles up is one of the maddest and
most comical sights. . . . The physique is all right in itself. But to
have your physique in your head, like having sex in the head, is
unspeakably repulsive . . . to have one's own physical self prank-
ing and bulging under one's own mental direction is a good old
perversion.' We must not muddle and transfuse the two distinct
modes of consciousness. 'If our consciousness is dual, and active

in duality; if our human activity is of two incompatible sorts, why try to make a mushy oneness of it. . . . What connexion is necessary will be effected spontaneously.'

What, we may ask in conclusion, is the most intense and lasting impression we take away from Lawrence's writings, on education as on anything else? It is that he was an artist with an extraordinarily undeceived and exact sense for 'truth in being', a man with a superlative sense of reality. It is this, ultimately, which gives strength to his art and point and meaning to his educational advice. In a letter written in 1917 he has a remarkable comment on an old Viennese lady.

The world doesn't matter; you have died sufficiently to know that the world doesn't matter, ultimately. Ultimately, only the other world of pure being matters. One has to be strong enough to have the just sense of values. One sees it in the old sometimes. Old Madame Stepinak was here yesterday. I find in her a beauty infinitely lovelier than the beauty of the young women I know. She has lived and suffered, and taken her place in the realities. Now, neither riches nor rank nor violence matter to her, she *knows* what life consists in, and she never fails in her knowledge.[57]

For Lawrence too, we are sure, 'only the other world of pure being matters'. Of him, too, we feel that he has taken his place in the realities, that he knows what life consists in and that he never fails in that knowledge.

CHAPTER 10

THEORY OF LANGUAGE AND PRACTICE IN EDUCATION, AND T. S. ELIOT

LANGUAGE is the one indispensable means of education, both in the stricter sense of formal education, in which stress falls on the communicative function of language, and in the looser sense of incidental education, in which the expressive function of language is emphasized. No matter how practical or empirical an education may be, language must serve as the agency by which the teacher is related to the taught, and each to the subject of instruction; no matter how individual an education, how independent of the fluid and intricate relations constantly forming and wavering among the members of a group and expressed in the modulations of speech, language must act as the fine tool of analysis, the instrument of intellectual construction, and the medium, plastic and responsive, of emotional expression. Language is the means by which the setting of the human being is immensely enlarged and the context of his action made immeasurably more complex. Through language the biological individual becomes the historic person. The sentence-patterns we use, the idioms, the words and the images, and the categories of thinking, feeling and valuing which they imply, come to us ripened by time, and both enriched by the insight, imagination and aspiration of many generations, and distorted by their errors, evasions and fatigues. Through language we receive not just the education provided by our teachers and by our own lives, but also that offered by history, and through language we make our own unique mark on history, and leave a trace, minute but ineffaceable, on the impersonality of time.

The quality of an education depends most on the quality of the teacher, and the quality of the teacher is best indicated by his use of language. The logical sense, the paraphraseable content of what the teacher says, is, as Richards's analysis of meaning in poetry bears out, but a part of what is conveyed by his words, and to none more certainly than to the innocent, implacable mind of the child: it is but a part, that is, if we accept what is fundamental to the argument, that the use of language in poetry is in essence not other than, but only an intensification and concentration of the use of language in ordinary life. The difference between the language of poetry and the language of customary usage appears from the point of view of the result as a difference in kind, but from the point of view of structure it is no more than a difference of degree. The language of poetry is indeed a selection of the language of ordinary men, its rhythm depends for its energy on the buoyancy of the spoken tongue and for its subtlety on the dispersed and broken movements of the living voice, the lustre of its imagery is of the same order as the dim figures of ordinary expression, its organization is much more a generally human one than a specifically poetic or inspired one. The point is made by Collingwood[1] when he writes: 'Similar formal patterns are always emerging in the structure of prose only to be lost again; they emerge because without them language would be wholly non-poetical and would therefore cease to be language; they are lost again because form is here subordinate to matter, and the poetry inherent in language is therefore shattered into an infinity of inchoate poems.' Poetry, which is an unusually heightened form of the language of men, deceives us if we are persuaded that it is the language of gods. When Richards[2] claims, therefore, that meaning in poetry embraces, in addition to its content of sense, *feeling*, 'some special direction, bias or accentuation of interest towards it, some personal flavour or colouring of feeling', *tone*, 'an attitude to the listener, an awareness of this relation', and *intention*, 'the aim conscious or unconscious, the effect he is endeavouring to promote', his claim must be allowed to be valid for ordinary language also, and with peculiar propriety for the language of the teacher. But the meaning of the teacher's language includes even more than sense, feeling, tone and intention. His closeness to his pupils, his deputed parenthood, his being under the necessity of employing spoken language over a wide range of discourse in a variety of situations, language given a richer resonance by intonation, gesture and expression, compel him to reveal or betray through innumerable particular evaluations his most sincere principles of value.

Given that language is of primary importance in education, how account for the indifference or hostility with which it is now regarded by so many teachers and theorists of education? One reply is to impute it to a movement of correction and redress, to a realization by modern teachers of the excessively verbal character of nineteenth-century education and to a conviction that education needs to be rescued from the anaemia of verbalism and made much more full-bloodedly virile and alive. The activist, pragmatic attitude which has been largely responsible for the genuinely more lively, more vigorous and natural bent of the daily commerce of education, the conduct of lessons in the classroom and of life in the school, bears some responsibility from its very emphasis on action for the diminution in status of language as an educative instrument since language is held to be an inferior or mistaken substitute for action. But to take the pragmatic influence as the sole or even the weightiest cause is to fall into the error of supposing that educational change is always or mainly the result of educational thought or practice. Education as a discipline of mediation is always open to the sway of ideas, to an interpretation, or application, or misapprehension, if not of the best, at least of the most dominant or vocal philosophic tendencies of the time. Education provides irrefutable if rather delayed evidence of the power of speculative thought to produce practical effects, and the ruling attitudes in education are more often than not a function of the thought of philosophers only remotely interested in its problems. The present attitude to language is a case in point.

The theory of language most influential today is a theory of the incapacity of language. The elements of the situation are commonly seen to assume a pattern of this sort. On the one hand there is the subject, the interpreting power, intelligence, on the other the object, the material of interpretation, reality, and between them stands the means of interpretation, language, maimed in its origins and radically inadequate for its purpose, and by reason of its coarseness and clumsiness incapable of any but blurred and inaccurate kinds of transmission, of the merest gestures at meaning. Even, and some may say particularly, developed uses of language suffer from an unavoidable openness of texture, an inability to put down on the object a mesh of sufficiently fine a gauge, and in consequence they can convey at best but obscure and shrouded hints, and at worst gross and violent distortions of the fact. On this view the ideal condition of language is one of utter transparency, the action condition one of relative opaqueness. The several proponents of the view ground it on widely divergent premises, but the descriptions they give of language, the epithets they apply to it, suggest with massive unanimity membership of a single party. For Bergson[3] language is a 'veil' between the act and the object of intuition, 'the cleverly woven curtain of our conventional ego', and he goes on, 'the word with well-defined outlines, the rough and ready word, which stores up the stable, common and consequently impersonal element in the impression of mankind, overwhelms or at least covers over the delicate and fugitive impressions of our individual consciousness'. According to Whitehead,[4] 'deficiencies of language stand inexorably in the way of a fundamental statement of the nature of things'. 'The philosopher', says Russell,[5] 'is faced with the difficult task of using language to undo the false beliefs that it suggests', as for example, 'a definiteness, discreteness and quasi-permanence in objects which Physics seems to show that they do not possess'. And, he complains,[6] 'although the dictionary or the encyclopaedia gives what may be called the official or socially sanctioned meaning of a word, no two people who use the same word have just the same thought in their minds'. On this remark a critic[7] comments, 'It is to be supposed from this statement of Russell's that a word is like an ill-fitting garment for the thought which it clothes, since it is used to clothe so many different thoughts.' Wittgenstein[8] takes up the same burden: 'language disguises the thought, so that from the external form of the clothes one cannot infer the form of the thought, because the external form of the clothes is constructed with quite another object than to let the form of the body be recognized'. The images in these comments – veil, closely woven curtain, covers over, stands in the way of, ill-fitting garment, disguises, clothes – which have an almost compulsive quality of uniformity, enforce the community of attitude, and both state and insinuate that language which we are accustomed to consider as above all a mode of access and illumination is more correctly thought of as obstructive and occulting. The measures these authors recommend follow smoothly on the positions they advocate. Bergson advises stillness and silence; language must be transcended before the proper, intuitive activity of man can begin, and his mystical abdication is echoed with curious fidelity in Wittgenstein's peroration.[9] 'My propositions are elucidating in this sense: he who understands them finally recognizes them as senseless, when he has climbed out through them, on them, over them. . . . He must surmount these propositions; then he sees the world rightly. Whereof one cannot speak, thereof one must be silent.' Whitehead[10] thinks that the traditional categories of language must be shattered and redesigned 'in the same way that, in a physical science, pre-existing appliances are redesigned'. Russell,[11] more ambitious perhaps, undertakes to construct an ideal language, purged of the stubborn absurdities and deceptions of ordinary language 'with its ambiguities and abominable syntax', such a tongue as might have been framed 'by scientific trained observers for purposes of philosophy and logic'.[12]

Granted what has been said about the openness of education to general ideas, it might still be argued that the contemporary denigration of language is exclusively a matter of philosophic interest, that criticisms like those quoted are made by philosophers for their own purposes of language as a philosophic instrument. But unless we are persuaded that philosophy is an activity without influence upon or relation to the concerns of ordinary life, which is surely inadmissible on the evidence of both history and common sense, then we must believe that the devaluation of language applies as much to ordinary language as to philosophic discourse, and that it is as likely to produce a sceptical and contemptuous attitude towards language in the street as in the study, in the classroom as in the lecture hall. As indeed it has. No other educational terms throb with so peculiar a vibration of detestation as verbal and verbalism, and the alarm and distrust they evoke have more in common with the *odium theologicum* of a positivist ethos than with a rational reaction from Victorian chalk and talk. (We are, after all, in the second half of the twentieth century.) Controversy over language is the current version of a brawl about universals, and it is invested with the same fume of intellectual malice.

Scepticism as to the value of language gains as much in iconoclastic shock effect from its modernity as from its unanimity, from its decisive character of reflecting the way things are set as from its being the one flag under which the differences of so many philosophers are reconciled. It is important to realize, therefore, if one is not to be overwhelmed by its impetus, that the movement is a solidly established orthodoxy and that it has an ancestry respectable not only in point of eminence but also of duration. We are confronted here not with one of those sudden, revolutionary and final insights which cause a geological shift in opinion, but rather with the contemporary expression of an ancient tradition. Its genealogy, the inter-relations of its distinguished families, Greek sophists, later scholastics, Renaissance logicians, eighteenth-century epistemologists, has been drawn up by Urban,[13] who notes the common inherited lineament, 'nominalism in one form or another and the distrust of language which inevitably follows'. If in order not to be swept away by fashion it is important to be aware how remote are the origins of this view, and how embedded the attitude it begets, it is equally important, in order not to be overborne by authority, to understand that there is a different tradition, as old and as strong, although at the moment less effectively insistent. 'The history of European culture', Urban[14] writes, 'is accordingly the story of two great opposing evaluations of the *Word*.' In this country, for example, alongside and opposed to the line of spokesmen for the low evaluation, Hobbes, Locke, Bentham, James Mill and Horne Took, runs the line of the representatives of the high evaluation, the Cambridge Platonists, the third Earl of Shaftesbury, Blake, Coleridge and Matthew Arnold. Over against 'the growth of philosophic radicalism', 'the theory of fictions' and the hardening of conviction on what Berkeley calls 'the embarrass and delusion of words', there is the development of certainty about the creative power of language, 'the theory of an active principle implying indeterminacy'[15] and confidence in the word. 'The philosophy of as if' is balanced by 'the philosophy of symbolic forms'. What is remarkable and idiosyncratic in the present interpreters of the low evaluation is the extreme and rigorous thoroughness with which original suspicion of poetic and literary language is generalized to cover all language. The most of Hobbes's abhorrence was reserved for 'the decaying sense of imagination', for literary language and especially for 'metaphors, tropes and other rhetorical figures', but he acknowledged at the same time 'the light of the human mind is perspicuous words' if they are 'first snuffed and purged from ambiguity'. Locke, although he repeatedly stressed 'the imperfection that is naturally in language, and the obscurity and confusion that is so hard to be avoided in the use of words', nevertheless thought 'with this imperfection they may serve for civil . . . but not philosophic use'. And he recognized the possibility with language cleansed of simile and metaphor of arriving 'at the inside and reality of the thing'. The modern positivist appears, however, unwilling to grant validity to any language, however plain and unmetaphorical, except the scientific, and certain ideal and as yet unformulated languages like Russell's. Only the minority of statements which approximate to the scientific mode can state truths or falsehoods. The rest blur and dissolve into a mist of nonsense.

Many influences, distant and at hand, have joined to bring about the present puritanic suspicion of language, but among recent influences three may be singled out as exercising a particular weight of authority: the belief that language is an 'invalid surrogate' for experience, an annihilating ideal of scientific accuracy, and the neglect of the distinction between the genesis and the structure of language.

The belief that language is 'an invalid surrogate' for experience assumes, according to Urban,[16]

the dualism of experience and expression – that immediate experience and its expression in language are two wholly different things which may so to speak tragically diverge . . . that we first have knowledge by simple acquaintance and then knowledge by description. The latter involving as it does language may do violence to this experience . . . and the only way to pure experience is by stripping off language and its symbolism.

It is impossible, it is held, for language faithfully to trace the sinuous and intricate subtlety of experience, and in its effort to do so language only freezes and falsifies the deliquescence of experience into immobile and abstract shapes. Language is a kind of treachery. There can be no relation of fidelity between the symbolism of language, fixed, common, formal, and the dynamic process of private experimental events. But the discreteness of experience and expression is a philosophic fiction of a most unconvincing sort. Experience completely free of expression, lacking even latent reference to language, is experience utterly uninformed by meaning, and it is not only unknown but inconceivable as human experience. We may think of it as experience appropriate to the star and the stone, as mineral experience, the character of which it is to be an invasion of a passive subject, to be successive and sustained only by being built into a physical configuration. Human experience, on the contrary, is apprehended by an active subject, is to some degree simultaneous and sustained by a more than physical unity. Its activity, simultaneity and unity are made possible by powers of abstracting and symbolizing, by forces of distillation, of which the primary and fullest manifestation is language. This is not to assert with Croce the identity of intuition and expression, nor with Müller the identity of thought and language, and it is more than to insist with the psychologists on their intimate and necessary connexion. It is to affirm first that by language the light of intelligibility is let into experience that would otherwise remain no more than a 'cloud of unknowing', and further that the intelligible is the source of the responsible, and that the double power in the phrase of Henry James, 'to be finely aware and richly responsible' is the proper attribute of the fully human. The route to humanity is the way of language. By the operation of language on the original endowment of man is secured, as Coleridge said in the *Biographia*

Literaria, 'in due time the information of a second nature' and the conversion of the brutal to the human, a transformation which the life of every child rehearses familiarly and continuously about us, and which is realized with compressed dramatic force in the life of Helen Keller. To censure the imprecision of particular communications is one thing, to be convinced of a natural incapacity in language to do justice to a theoretical experience is quite another. It is infected in itself since it springs from a deep confusion. It is dangerous in its consequences in education. It renders suspect language itself, which Coleridge also thought was 'a means already prepared for us by nature and society, of teaching the young mind to think well and wisely, by the same unremembered process and with the same never forgotten results, as those by which it is taught to speak and converse', and at the same time it neglects 'those advantages which language alone, at least which language with incomparably greater ease and certainty than any other means, presents to the instructor of impressing modes of intellectual energy'.

If the first more philosophic influence contrasts the impurity of language with the purity of an assumed experience, the second more scientific influence insists on the inaccuracy of the report made by language on experience. Language for it is the rhetorical commemoration of experience, its 'gross effigy and simulacrum'. a cartoon of reality, and the roughness of its approximation is compared to the precision of the reports of science. This criticism is impelled by an ideal, an annihilating ideal, of scientific accuracy. It is derived from the activity of scientific symbols, in which symbol and referent fit so exactly that the finest of Indian papers could not be inserted between. It is an annihilating ideal because to the degree that language approaches it, language ceases to be itself.

It has sometimes been maintained [writes Collingwood[17]] that all language consists of sounds taken at pleasure to serve as marks for certain thoughts or things,[18] which would amount to saying that it consists of technical terms. But since a technical term implies a definition, it is impossible that all words should be technical terms, for if they were we could never understand their definitions. The business of language is to express or explain: if language cannot explain itself nothing else can explain it; and a technical term, in so far as it calls for explanation, is to that extent not language but something else which resembles language in being significant, but differs from it in not being expressive or self-explanatory. . . . The technical vocabulary of science is thus neither a language nor a special part of language but a symbolism like that of mathematics. . . . But language proper does not presuppose technical terms for in poetry where language is most perfectly and purely itself no technical terms are either used or presupposed, any more than in the primitive speech of childhood or the ordinary speech of conversation. Thus the technical element in scientific language is an element foreign to the essence of language as such.

Words are not formulae. Scientific symbols are engaged exclusively in pointing beyond themselves, they neither require nor reward involvement, they are thoroughly bleached of everything but reference. Words as symbols, on the other hand, always contain more than reference; what they point to is also in part embodied in and enacted by them, and they compel in consequence some degree of involvement. The symbols of science invite our assent, those of language our consent. It is clear, then, that scientific symbols have a firmness and objectivity of meaning beyond the scope of language, but it would be incongruous, therefore, to condemn language for failing to enjoy a kind of perfection alien to it and absurd to recommend that it aspire towards such perfection. But these or similar aims are undoubtedly among the motives of those who in schools make a cult of impersonal or scientific prose. Their effect is evident in the questions in the crucial scholarship paper which require children of eleven to describe objects like a hammer, a satchel, a glass of water, a needle, a pair of scissors: which is to ask them, as C. S. Lewis[19] said, to achieve 'an eccentric *tour de force*', language being 'the worst tool in the world for communicating knowledge of complex three-dimensional shapes'. For older children the objectivity of scientific prose, in the manner of Darwin or T. H. Huxley, is contrasted with the uncertainty of coloured or subjective writing. It is claimed that turbid and misleading feeling has been quite rinsed out of it, and there remains a cool translucent medium, an amber of neutrality, with nothing to detract from the pure auto-nomy of the object. What is ignored or denied is that the best writing in this mode is the product of sophisticated literary skill, and moreover – and more importantly – that such writing is informed with a rare and intense 'predominant passion', the secular correlative of Spinoza's intellectual love of God, a con-centrated and devoted submission to the radiance of a certain order of reality. It is hardly necessary to add that it would be surprising to find this feeling common among the young. And without it the ideal of scientific accuracy encourages descriptive writing which is no more than a patient aggregation of un-organized particulars, where, as Coleridge[20] wrote, 'all is so dutchified by the most minute touches that the reader naturally asks why words and not painting are used'.

The third influence, the failure to observe the distinction be-tween the genesis and structure of language, the disposition to accept solutions to problems of origin as answers to problems of system, has, in Cassirer's[21] view, invalidated much of the treat-ment of this subject.

For many centuries the systematic question was overshadowed by the genetic. It was thought to be a foregone conclusion that the genetic question once solved, all the other problems would readily follow suit. From a general epistemological point of view, however, this was a gratuitous assumption. The theory of knowledge has taught us that we must always draw a sharp line of demarcation between genetic and systematic problems. Confusion of these two types is misleading and perilous.

How misleading may be estimated when we consider that ex-planation of language exclusively in terms of origins, as uninter-rupted development from gesture to speech, or from interjection to communication, or from mimicry to metaphor, leave unex-plained precisely that problem, the discontinuity, the leap from one to the other, which most requires explanation; how perilous may be judged when we reflect that accounts of language relying solely on physical and historical causality are driven to disregard the inmost quality of language, that with which we are familiar in its purest and most powerful form in poetry, but with which we are also acquainted in every kind of human speech, its activity, energy, creativity. It is what we taste in the flavour of colloquial salt, what we encounter in the verve and variety of dialect, what disconcerts us in the novel collocations of the child's phrase as it surprises us in the unexpected revealing word of the major writer. It is the potency of the word. Because of it we delight to speak and are grateful to be spoken to. It is the power which belongs to human language in the most dissimilar contexts, whether to the idioms expressing the depraved attitudes of urban alleys or to utterances like:

> In the juvescence of the year
> Came Christ the tiger.

If what is is no more than an elaboration of what was, and if language is no more than a complication of instinctive impulses, then there is no place for what is always present to us, the abrupt eloquence of man. (And we must add, if language is but a highly conditioned and subtly inflected babbling and in no way related to man's freedom, then indeed the phrase, 'a creature of circumstance', is a true and serious description of man filtered of every tincture of the sadness or irony which makes it ordinarily significant or tolerable.) The creativity of language, it should be stressed, is not to be opposed to the objective and referential and equated with the subjective and exclamatory. It bursts out of the solipsistic circle and explodes into the communal world. The act of creation is consummated in communication. At all times the originating energy of language has been felt to be most present in the life of metaphor: to be most present because metaphor enshrines no unique quality of language but only concentrates what is a general characteristic of language as of thought, its analogical structure. Metaphor in relation to plain language does not stand as sole centre of light to 'vacant, interstellar spaces', but rather, in the idiom of the Gestalt School, as figure to ground, between the two of which multiply incessant and intricate relations of influence and reciprocity. Metaphor, like every vehicle of meaning, incorporates, as Richards[22] has shown, the contribution of a context, a fact which goes to confirm the belief that a general creative power flows through all language. It is just the quickening, creative force of language that the Positivists' distribution of language into sharply independent categories succeeds in obscuring. Their classification of language, according to a criterion of the behaviour of propositions, into a series of uses – devices for communicating facts, for calculation, for expressing and inciting feeling, for persuading and commanding and for ritualistic incantation – is one in which, to adapt a comment of Gabriel Marcel, the being of language is submerged in its functions. There remains a plurality in which the separate extinguishes the singular and structural in language. The bleak and illiberal attitudes which such an approach to language promotes are nowhere more impoverished than in education. In the school the Positivist analysis has arrived in the guise of a blunt distinction between the referential and the emotive, where the term referential is contracted to contain only what is quantitative, statistical and demonstrable, and the term emotive is expanded to embrace whatever is not. Thus tracts of being and realms of experience are displayed as beneath the dignity of serious attention or derided as exotic, personal indulgence. To many bred in this habit the universe of value is a condition of tortured nerves, the world of imagination a product of hallucination.

But the view recommended here would claim for language adequacy to experience since without language there would be no human experience. Where language appears to be inadequate it is not through any radical incapacity to express a theoretically perfect experience but because the experience itself as a whole is threadbare. And further it would say that the datum in language is creativity, the effect meaning. Language is words organized into a system of expressive symbols, the function of which is to quicken the unformed into significance. It belongs to the structure of language to create, to its method to symbolize, to its result to signify. But, it may be objected, the assertion that a generative force flows through all language obliterates the category of the authentically creative and reduces Plato and Shakespeare to an insipid equality with Tom, Dick and Harry. This objection fails to discriminate between the given in language and the gift of language. The given in language, creativity, symbolism, significance, is always the same; the gift of language, like every human power, is unimaginably variable. There is a single structure and an infinite variety of degrees of organization, from person to person and moment to moment. To describe the stable in the given is not to deny the variousness of the gift. Indeed, it is to attribute to the gift a rational instead of a magical content. An aridly rationalist account of poetic power, being so dumbfoundingly irrelevant, ironically enough confirms its status as mystery. But if all language is creative, the highest reaches of the gift are a matter of relative refinement and coherence of organization of the given.

Again, a question may be raised as to the justification for claiming that all language creates meaning. A creative source, it may be argued, should flow into a novel result, and language, if creative, should well into novel meaning. And many disposed to allow that Plato's language created a new world of philosophic meaning and Shakespeare's a new world of poetic meaning could not agree to make at a lower pitch a similar admission of ordinary language. But it is hard to see why not. The language of Plato and Shakespeare created worlds of meaning of the most elaborate complexity and the utmost coherence. But these worlds are not other than those created by ordinary language. They are only finer. They are not structurally different. They are only more complete. Their superiority lies not in their uniqueness but in the degree of their qualification. And to exempt them from community with ordinary language, to confer uniqueness on them, is not to preserve their value but in the last resort to render it irrational. We may think of the relation of ordinary language to Plato's and Shakespeare's as a movement from meaning confined, snarled in its context and disturbed by externals to meaning untrammelled, in possession of itself, lucidly ordered; but never wholly confined and never finally untrammelled. Or we may think of it as a procession from private, constrained and exclusive meaning to open, autonomous and inclusive meaning; but never completely the first, or utterly the second.

The contemporary author whose works, and supremely the *Four Quartets*, compose the subtlest commentary on and the most powerful example of language as the construction of meaning, or in Harding's[23] term 'the creation of concepts', is Eliot; and Eliot writes, in words that may be taken to include not only the poems that gave occasion to them but every human speech:

> And so each venture
> Is a new beginning, a raid on the inarticulate

and again:

> . . . every attempt
> Is a wholly new start, and a different kind of failure.[24]

Novelty belongs to the undertaking of language, originality to the idea of meaning. The conventional is not a total absence of novelty, the orthodox a mere vacancy of originality. Nor should it be forgotten, as it so lamentably often is in education, that the orthodox may be a triumph of originality for a particular person, the conventional may be alive with novelty at a particular moment. The old, one insists, shares a single structure with the new. And even considered as a result achieved, as an effect wrought out, the most recognizably creative, the most authentically new language, is only a higher kind of success as compared with the old and familiar; or what is the same thing, 'a different kind of failure'.

A concern to uphold an inherent creative force in language should not be read as an anxiety to encourage a facile, effusive fluency, nor should a case for the *vis poetica* in language be construed as an argument against clarity, organization and reflection. Part of the effort to construct meaning is an unremitting contest, involving the use of compulsion against the recalcitrance of meaning and resistance to the pull of the anonymous and the inarticulate. 'The intolerable wrestle with words and meanings'[25] – not, it should be remarked, of meanings with words, not, as Whitehead[26] said, 'the struggle of novel thought with the obtuseness of language' – this 'intolerable wrestle with words and meanings' requires virtues of character, energy, stamina, a braced will, together with qualities of critical intelligence, tact, discrimination, decision guided by standards of value. The great poet is both Romantic and Augustan, the human being is both creative and critical; or rather his creation is critically exercised. 'The critical activity,' writes Eliot,[27] 'finds its highest, its true fulfilment in a kind of union with creation in the labour of the artist.' And, as has been observed before, judgements of this order apply, with due difference but equal validity, to the ordinary discourse of men.

A theory of language exerts an effective if oblique and diffused influence on practice in education. It is deep down, however, that its influence is direct and strong, at the roots, among the motives of practice where the ripest achievements are prepared and the most profound disasters begin. Suppose, then, a wider acceptance and a firmer credence for the view advocated here. What realignment of purposes could we hope for? What redistribution of stress could we expect to ensue? It seems that there would be a threefold shift, in the status of language in education, in the manner of its teaching, and in consequence in the attitude to experience itself. First, the intimacy of language and meaning being recognized –

> . . . our concern was speech and speech impelled us
> To purify the dialect of the tribe
> And urge the mind to aftersight and foresight.[28]

– its supremely civilizing power would be acclaimed. A place and importance closer to Coleridge's estimation of it would be accorded to language. It would not be considered, as in the nineteenth century, a neat and sufficient substitute for action, nor, as in the twentieth century, an untidy and insufficient one, but it would be seen as the completion and refinement of action, as that by and in which mere action assumes the character of human experience. Again, a strengthened conviction in the creative energy of language must increase active awareness of the source of creation, the person. And this more vivid realization means a new direction in the teaching of language. The study of the different uses of language – and these must be studied to stretch the scope of experience, to enlarge the possibility of maturity, 'a recognition implicit in the expression of any experience, of other kinds of experience which are possible'[29] – this study will take into account not just the manifold and impersonal in the medium but much more the unity and life of the personal. It will be, that is, not a study of a variety of detached, objective functions but an effort to enter dramatically into the experience of a variety of persons: not the expository use of language, therefore, but the expositor's, not the scientific but the scientist's, not the critical but the critic's, not the poetic but the poet's.

But a Coleridgean concept of language, if the view proposed may be so dignified, would do more than modify our notion of the place of language in education, more than alter our practice in teaching: it would reconstitute our attitude to experience itself. And it would do so by rescuing it from *total* servitude to the dominance of the past. Modern man, besides his other performances, uneasily straddles this curious contrariety: as anti-traditionalist he disowns the past, as positivist he is enslaved by experience that is always past. Where there can be no beginning, there can be nothing but conclusion. Where nothing is original, everything is servile. But a theory of creativity does not admit an absolute enforcement of the past, a refusal which gives point to the present without denying the force of the past. It allows man to relish and be nourished by the past, and also enables him to confess

> Last season's fruit is eaten
> And the fullfed beast shall kick the empty pail.
> For last year's words belong to last year's language
> And next year's words await another voice.[30]

That educational theory is in thrall to the past – one does not speak of educational machinery and its frequent redesigning – is clear to the philosopher. For Whitehead[31] the most prominent characteristic of our political philosophy and our educational theory is 'their overwhelming emphasis on past experience'.

How much we deceive ourselves in submitting to the despotism of completed experience the poet declares:

> There is, it seems to us,
> At best, only a limited value
> In the knowledge derived from experience.
> The knowledge imposes a pattern, and falsifies,
> For the pattern is new in every moment
> And every moment is a new and shocking
> Valuation of all we have been.[32]

It is the *limitation* of the value of experience that the teacher must acknowledge. It is the possibility of the 'new and shocking' that he must not shut out. He must be apt to provoke, prompt to encourage, quick to pursue the startling and the unrehearsed. He must have the insight to discern and the patience to accept the power of the impromptu to transform the pattern of experience. With this awareness and this character, the teacher will not be among those who collaborate with the quotidian in strangling the creative, or those who conspire with what is smothering what is to be. He will belong with those who, as Yeats said, 'are continually making and un-making mankind'.

NOTES

CHAPTER I

1. *Inquiring Spirit*, ed. K. Coburn, p. 68.
2. Suttie, I. D., *The Origins of Love and Hate* (London 1935), p. 15.
3. Eliot, T. S., *Selected Essays*, pp. 317–20.
4. To Davy, 25 July 1800.
5. To Godwin, 22 September 1800.
6. To Sotheby, 27 September 1802.
7. *The Friend*.
8. Biog. Lit., XXII.
9. *Inquiring Spirit*, ed. K. Coburn, p. 204.
10. *Lectures on Shakespeare*, XI.
11. To Poole, 9 October 1797.
12. *The Friend*.
13. VIIth Lecture: 'New System of Education'.
14. *The Friend*.
15. ibid.
16. *Aids to Reflection*.
17. *Table Talk*, 21 July 1830.
18. *Lectures on Shakespeare*, XI.
19. Biog. Lit., XVIII.
20. *Coleridge on Logic and Learning*, ed. A. D. Snyder, p. 105.
21. ibid., p. 127.
22. *The Philosophical Lectures of S. T. Coleridge*, ed. K. Coburn, p. 115.
23. *Coleridge on Logic and Learning*, ed. A. D. Snyder, pp. 126–7.
24. ibid., pp. 132–3.

CHAPTER 2

1. To S. T. Coleridge, 19 April 1808.
2. To E. H. Handley, 4 October 1830.
3. To Sir George Beaumont, 17 October 1805.
4. *The Prelude*, ed. E. de Selincourt 1926: edition of 1805, II, 280–87. All verse quotations are from this edition of *The Prelude*.
5. II, 244–50.
6. II, 259–73.
7. II, 265–6.
8. II, 263–4.
9. II, 324–5.
10. I, 422–4.
11. I, 162–4.
12. II, 250–54.
13. Whitehead, A. N., *Adventures of Ideas*, pp. 209–10.
14. *The Prelude*, II, 208–15.
15. XI, 258–68.
16. I, 312–13.
17. I, 391–4.
18. I, 482–6.
19. XI, 269–73.
20. I, 313–16.
21. I, 318–24.
22. I, 466–73.
23. I, 305–306.
24. I, 348–50.
25. I, 418–20.

26. I, 497–501.
27. *Journals of Dorothy Wordsworth*, ed. E. de Selincourt, Vol. I, p. 83.
28. *The Prelude*, II, 420–28.
29. To W. S. Landor, 21 January, 1824.
30. To Catherine Clarkson, December 1814.
31. *The Notebooks of Henry James*, ed. Matthiesson and Murdock, p. 145.
32. To Catherine Clarkson, December 1814.
33. To Allan Cunningham, 23 November 1823.
34. To S. T. Coleridge, 22 May 1815.
35. Preface to *What Maisie Knew*.

36. *The Prelude*, VIII, 624–9.
37. II, 431–3.
38. II, 221–4.
39. III, 156–67.
40. To W. R. Hamilton, 24 September 1827.
41. *The Prelude*, II, 299–303.
42. II, 308–12.
43. To W. R. Hamilton, 23 December 1829.
44. To John Wilson, June 1802.
45. To H. J. Rose, 11 December 1828.
46. Cf. *The Prelude*, VI, 113–34.
47. XIII, 169–70.
48. To S. T. Coleridge, 19 April 1808.
49. *The Prelude*, I, 351–5.

CHAPTER 3

1. *The Friend*, II, 4.
2. *Biog. Lit.*, XVIII.
3. *The Friend*, II, 7.
4. *Lit. Rem.*, I.
5. *Table Talk.*
6. *The Friend*, I, 3, footnote.
7. ibid., II, 6.
8. *Aids to Reflection*, Preface.
9. *The Friend*, II, 11.
10. *Biog. Lit.*, I.
11. ibid., XXII.
12. *Lectures upon Shakespeare:* Notes on Othello.
13. Cf. Willey, B., *Nineteenth Century Studies*, London, 1949, p. 30.
14. *The Friend*, II, 10.
15. *Aids to Reflection*, Introductory Aphorisms, 8.
16. *The Friend*, II, 11.

17. ibid., II, 9.
18. *The Friend*, I, 14.
19. ibid., II, 11.
20. *Aids to Reflection*, Preface.
21. ibid., Aphorisms of Spiritual Religion, 10.
22. *Biog. Lit.*, XXII.
23. *Aids to Reflection*, Preface.
24. ibid., Prudential Aphorisms, 1.
25. *Biog. Lit.*, I.
26. To Poole, 1797.
27. ibid., 1801.
28. *Aids to Reflection*, Introductory Aphorisms, 24.
29. *The Friend*, II, 4.
30. ibid, II, 4.
31. *Lit. Rem.*, II.
32. *The Friend*, II, 4.
33. ibid., First Landing Place, I.

CHAPTER 4

1. *Heinrich Heine.*
2. *Literary Influence of Academies.*
3. *Anima Poetae.*
4. *The Function of Criticism.*
5. *The Church and State.*
6. *The 'Great Books' and a Liberal Education, Commentary,* 1954.
7. *The Function of Criticism.*
8. *The Church and State.*
9. *Table Talk.*
10. *The Friend.*
11. *Education and the University.*
12. ibid.
13. *The Function of Criticism.*
14. *The Church and State.*
15. ibid.
16. To William Rowan Hamilton, 4 January 1838.
17. *The Function of Criticism.*
18. ibid.
19. *The 'Great Books' and a Liberal Education.*
20. *The Function of Criticism.*
21. *Scrutiny,* XVIII, No. 1.
22. ibid.
23. *Church and State.*
24. *Table Talk.*
25. *Church and State.*
26. ibid.
27. *Literary Influence of Academies.*
28. *Education and the University.*
29. ibid.
30. ibid.
31. ibid.
32. ibid.
33. ibid.
34. ibid.
35. ibid.
36. *Literary Influence of Academies.*

CHAPTER 5

1. *The Letters of John Keats,* ed. Maurice Buxton Forman (London, third edition, 1947), p. 305 (cited henceforth as *Letters*).
2. *Letters,* p. 155.
3. ibid., p. 93.
4. ibid., p. 108.
5. ibid., pp. 156-7.
6. ibid., p. 228.
7. ibid., pp. 227-8.
8. ibid., p. 72.
9. ibid., p. 104.
10. ibid., pp. 222-3.
11. ibid., p. 111.
12. ibid., p. 138.
13. ibid., p. 53.
14. ibid., p. 222.
15. ibid., p. 426.
16. ibid., p. 96.
17. Santayana, George, *The Life of Reason,* p. 212.
18. *Sleep and Poetry.*
19. *To my Brother George.*
20. *Sleep and Poetry.*
21. Santayana, George, *On the Elements of Poetry.*
22. Cf. *Letters,* p. 370.
23. *Letters,* p. 517.
24. ibid., p. 527.
25. ibid., p. 88.
26. ibid., p. 347.
27. ibid., p. 421.
28. ibid., p. 345.
29. ibid., p. 134.
30. ibid., p. 241.
31. ibid., p. 80.
32. ibid., p. 228.
33. ibid., p. 52.

34. *Letters*, p. 316.
35. ibid., p. 426.
36. ibid., p. 140.
37. ibid, p. 142.
38. ibid., p. 140.
39. ibid., p. 112.
40. ibid., p. 103.
41. ibid., p. 103.
42. ibid., p. 112.
43. ibid., p. 103.
44. ibid., p. 88.
45. ibid., p. 130.
46. ibid., p. 242.

47. *Letters*, p. 31.
48. ibid., p. 96.
49. ibid., p. 233.
50. ibid., p. 235.
51. ibid., p. 335.
52. ibid., pp. 315–16.
53. ibid., pp. 143–4.
54. ibid., pp. 335–7.
55. Leavis, F. R., *Revaluation* (London, 1936), p. 251.
56. ibid., p. 267.
57. *Hyperion*, Book III.
58. *Letters*, p. 67–68.

CHAPTER 6

1. *Letters of G. M. Hopkins to Robert Bridges*, ed. C. C. Abbott (London, 1935), p. 28.
2. *Further Letters of G. M. Hopkins*, ed. C. C. Abbott (London, 1938), p. 240.
3. *Selected Literary Criticism* (1955), ed. Anthony Beale, p. 290.
4. *The Correspondence of G. M. Hopkins and R. W. Dixon*, ed. C. C. Abbott (London, 1935), p. 133.
5. *Letters to Bridges*, p. 66.
6. ibid, p. 83.

7. *On Metaphysical Poetry*, in *Determinations* (Chatto & Windus, London, 1954).
8. *Letters to Bridges*, p. 216.
9. ibid., p. 225.
10. ibid., p. 218.
11. ibid., p. 89.
12. ibid., p. 160.
13. *Correspondence with R. W. Dixon*, p. 139.
14. ibid., p. 70.
15. *Letters to Bridges*, pp. 174–5.
16. ibid., p. 66.
17. *Correspondence with R. W. Dixon*, p. 7.
18. *Letters to Bridges*, p. 231.

CHAPTER 7

1. *The Tryst.*
2. *Clear Eyes.*
3. *The Moth.*

4. *Sleep.*
5. *Nod.*
6. *The Unchanging.*

CHAPTER 9

1. *Selected Literary Criticism* (1955), ed. Anthony Beale, p. 105 (cited henceforth as Beale).

2. Beale, p. 108.
3. ibid., pp. 109–13.
4. ibid., p. 117.

5. Beale, p. 118.
6. Letters of D. H. Lawrence, ed. A. Huxley, p. 710 (cited henceforth as Letters).
7. ibid, p. 761.
8. ibid., p. 713.
9. ibid., p. 716.
10. ibid., p. 672.
11. ibid., p. 773.
12. ibid., p. 635.
13. ibid., p. 688.
14. ibid., p. 404.
15. ibid., p. 232.
16. ibid., p. 356.
17. Beale, p. 111.
18. Letters, p. 300.
19. Beale, p. 61.
20. Letters, p. 344.
21. ibid., p. 220.
22. ibid., p. 697.
23. ibid., p. 404.
24. ibid., p. 766.
25. Beale, p. 62.
26. ibid., p. 8.
27. ibid, pp. 120–21.
28. ibid., p. 123.
29. Cf. Letters, p. 771.
30. Santayana, G., The Life of Reason, Vol. 3 (London 1905), pp. 115–18.
31. Phoenix, p. 245.
32. Letters, p. 605.
33. Phoenix, p. 525.
34. Letters, p. 688.
35. Phoenix, pp. 714–15.
36. ibid., p. 246.
37. ibid., p. 708.
38. Beale, pp. 118–19.
39. Phoenix, p. 528.
40. ibid., p. 525.
41. ibid., p. 715.
42. ibid. p. 185.
43. ibid., p. 695.
44. ibid., p. 190.
45. Beale, p. 258.
46. Phoenix, pp. 755–7.
47. Beale, p. 160.
48. Phoenix, p. 574.
49. Beale, p. 160.
50. ibid., p. 258.
51. Phoenix, p. 325.
52. ibid., p. 255.
53. ibid., p. 574.
54. ibid., p. 525.
55. ibid., p. 757.
56. Unless otherwise stated, all quotations in this section are from Education of the People, Phoenix, pp. 587–665.
57. Letters, p. 405.

CHAPTER 10

1. Collingwood, R. G., Philosophical Method (London, 1933), p. 201.
2. Richards, I. A., Practical Criticism (London, 1929), pp. 181–2.
3. Bergson, H., Time and Free Will (London, 1910), pp. 132–3.
4. Whitehead, A. N., Process and Reality (London, 1929), p. 6.
5. Russell, B., Human Knowledge: Its Scope and Limits (London, 1948), p. 76.
6. Russell, B., A History of Western Philosophy (London, 1945), pp. 50–51.
7. Ambrose, A., The Problem of Linguistic Inadequacy in Philosophical Analysis, ed. M. Black (New York, 1950), p. 32.
8. Wittgenstein, L., Tractatus Logicus Philosophicus (London, 1922), p. 63.
9. ibid., p. 189.

10. Whitehead, A. N., op. cit., p. 16.
11. Russell, B., *Philosophy of Bertrand Russell*, ed. Schilpp (Evanston, 1946), p. 694.
12. Russell, B., *The Analysis of Mind* (London, 1921), p. 193.
13. Urban, W., *Language and Reality* (London, 1939), p. 9.
14. ibid., p. 9.
15. Vivante, L., *English Poetry* (London, 1950), p. 322.
16. Urban, W., in *The Philosophy of A. N. Whitehead*, ed. Schilpp (Evanston, 1941), p. 309.
17. Collingwood, R., *Philosophical Method* (London, 1933), p. 203.
18. Cf. Hobbes, *Computation or Logic*, I, pp. 2, 4.
19. Lewis, C. S., *Times Educational Supplement*, 13 February 1953, p. 37.
20. Coleridge, S. T., *Coleridge's Literary Criticism*, ed. Mackail (London, 1908), p. 213.
21. Cassirer, E., *Essay on Man* (New Haven, 1944), p. 118.
22. Richards, I. A., *The Philosophy of Rhetoric* (London, 1936), pp. 93–4.
23. Harding, D. W., *Scrutiny*, Vol. XI, No. 3.
24. *East Coker*.
25. ibid.
26. Whitehead, A. N., *Adventures of Ideas* (Cambridge, 1933), p. 153.
27. Eliot, T. S., *Selected Essays* (London, 1934), p. 31.
28. *Little Gidding*.
29. Eliot, T. S., op. cit., p. 303.
30. *Little Gidding*.
31. Whitehead, A. N., op. cit., p. 117.
32. *East Coker*.

INDEX

Academy, 79
Aquinas, 188, 199
Aristotle, 181, 199
Arnold, M., and the Education of an *élite*, 67–83, 87, 111, 230
Augustine, St, 190
Austen, J., 204

Bacon, Lord, 50
Bailey, B., Keats's letter to, 116
Baty, J., 43
Baudelaire, C., 200
Bell, A., 16
Bentham, J., 230
Bergson, H., 228, 229
Berkeley, G., 231
Blake, W., 19, 230
Bradley, A. C., 181
Bridges, R., 124
Browning, R., 121, 128
Byron, Lord, 188, 200

Calendar of Modern Letters, 68, 70
Cambridge Platonists, 230
Cassirer, E., 235
Chaucer, G., 53
Cimarosa, D., 65
Clarkson, C., Wordsworth's letters to, 44, 45
Coburn, K., 28
Coleridge, D., 19–20
Coleridge, H., 19–20
Coleridge, S. T. C., and childhood, 13–30, 31, 46; and education, 52–66; and the education of an *élite*, 67–83, 88, 95, 105, 119, 134, 222, 230, 232, 233, 235, 240
Collingwood, R. G., 226, 233
Conrad, J., 197
Croce, B., 232

Dante, 190
Darwin, C., 234
De Gourmont, 85
De la Mare, W., 13, 136, 172–9
Dewey, J., 189
Dickens, C., 13, 14, 15, 31
Dilke, C., 90, 104
Dixon, Canon, Hopkins's letters to, 128, 132
Dostoevsky, F., 184
Dryden, J., 86
Dry Salvages, The, 143

Education, and childhood, 13–30; and the self, 17–18; and play, 19–20; and the intellect, 21; and the moral life, 21–2; and authority, 23–4; and imagination, 25–7; education and the growth of the mind, 31–51; the education of teachers, 52–66; the education of an *élite*, 67–83; the education of sensibility, 84–117; education and a sense of the particular, 118–33; the novel as a source of educational thought, 134–71; the child as a realist, 127–45; the 'neglected' child, 145–60; the too-loved child, 161–71; Walter de la Mare's poetry and the child, 172–9; education and the notion of character, 180–95; education and D. H. Lawrence; 196–224; education and the theory of language, 225–42.
Education of the People, 213–24.
Eliot, T. S., 15, 19, 65, 68, 142, 143, 172, 239–41
English School, The, 80–83

Fall of Hyperion, 90–92

MORE ABOUT PENGUINS
AND PEREGRINES

If you have enjoyed reading this book you may wish to know that *Penguin Book News* appears every month. It is an attractively illustrated magazine containing a complete list of books published by Penguins and still in print, together with details of the month's new books. A specimen copy will be sent free on request.

Penguin Book News is obtainable from most bookshops; but you may prefer to become a regular subscriber at 3s. for twelve issues. Just write to Dept EP, Penguin Books Ltd, Harmondsworth, Middlesex, enclosing a cheque or postal order, and you will be put on the mailing list.

Some other Peregrines are described on the following pages.

Note: *Penguin Book News* is not
available in the U.S.A., Canada or Australia.

another new Peregrine

SOME SHAKESPEAREAN THEMES *and*
AN APPROACH TO HAMLET
L. C. Knights

'Whereas in the older view Shakespeare was the god-like creator of a peopled world, projecting – it is true – his own spirit into the inhabitants, but remaining essentially the analyst of "their" passions, he is now felt as much more immediately engaged in the action he puts before us.'

Professor Knights demonstrates, in *Some Shakespearean Themes*, the poet's interest in the profoundest themes of human life. The public world, time and change, appearance and reality, the fear of death and the fear of life, the meanings of nature and of relationship – such themes are successively examined by him against the texts of historical plays and sonnets, with complete chapters on *Troilus and Cressida*, *King Lear*, *Macbeth*, *Antony and Cleopatra*, and *Coriolanus*.

His subsequent lectures on *Hamlet* can be taken as supplementary. The play is seen, in the context of *Othello*, *Julius Caesar*, and *Timon of Athens*, as not merely a study of corruption but an example of Shakespeare's concern with the relationship of the mind, the whole reflective personality, and the world with which it engages.